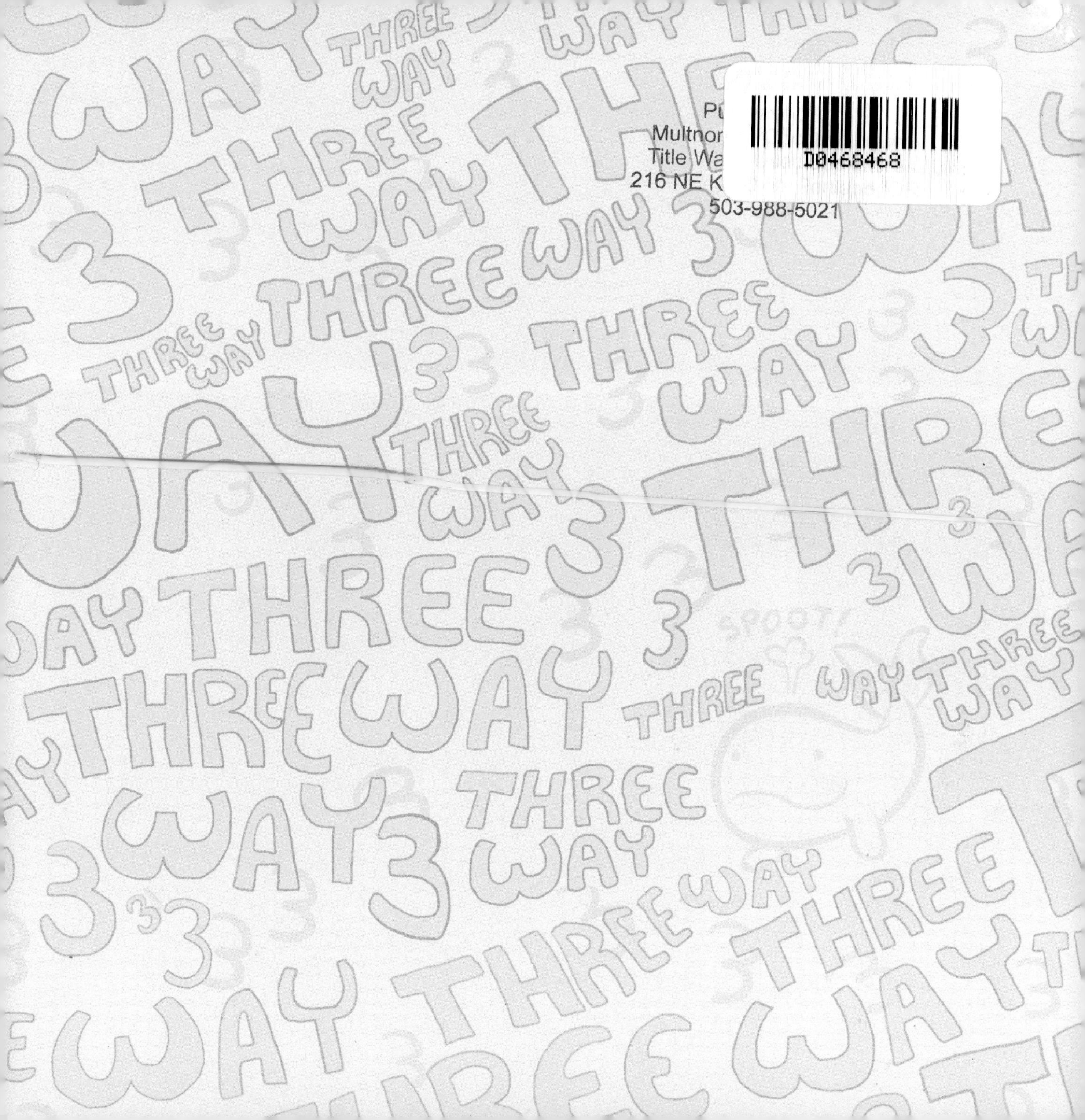
THREE WAY
3
SPOOT!

BUCKO™

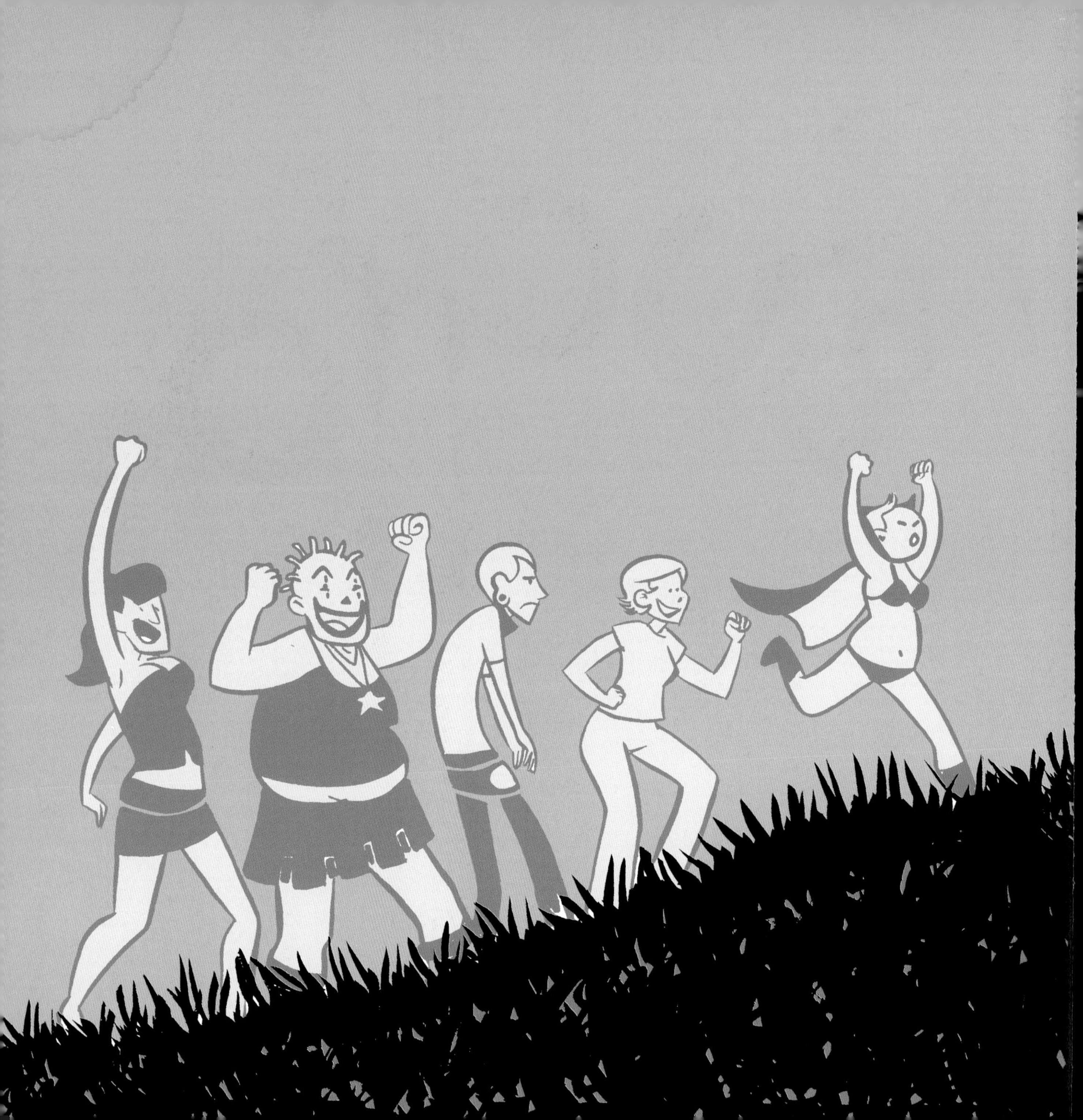

BUCKO ™

story by
JEFF PARKER * ERIKA MOEN
art by

DARK HORSE BOOKS

digital production
CHRISTIANNE GOUDREAU

design
ALLYSON HALLER

editor
BRENDAN WRIGHT

publisher
MIKE RICHARDSON

Published by Dark Horse Books
A division of Dark Horse Comics, Inc.
10956 SE Main Street
Milwaukie, Oregon 97222

DarkHorse.com

Library of Congress Cataloging-in-Publication Data

Parker, Jeff, 1966-
  Bucko / story by Jeff Parker ; art by Erika Moen. -- 1st ed.
    p. cm.
  ISBN 978-1-59582-973-3
  1. Graphic novels. I. Moen, Erika, 1983- II. Title.
  PN6727.P37B83 2012
  741.5'973--dc23
                            2012014986

First edition: September 2012

10 9 8 7 6 5 4 3 2 1
Printed at 1010 Printing International, Ltd., Guangdong Province, China

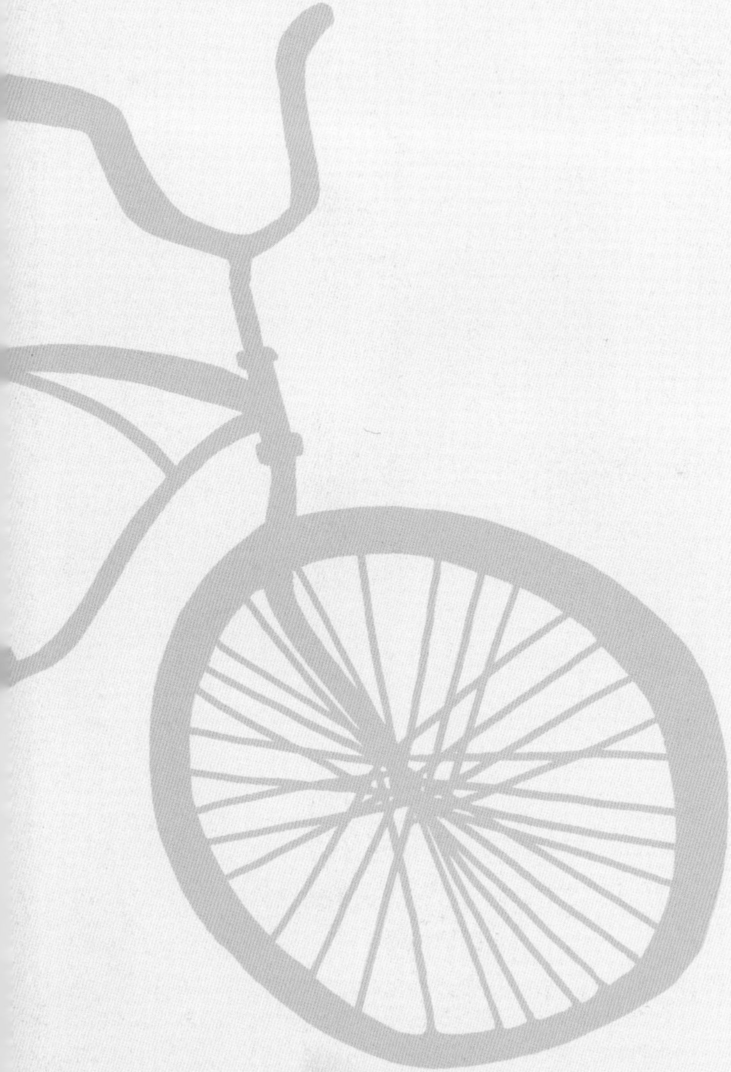

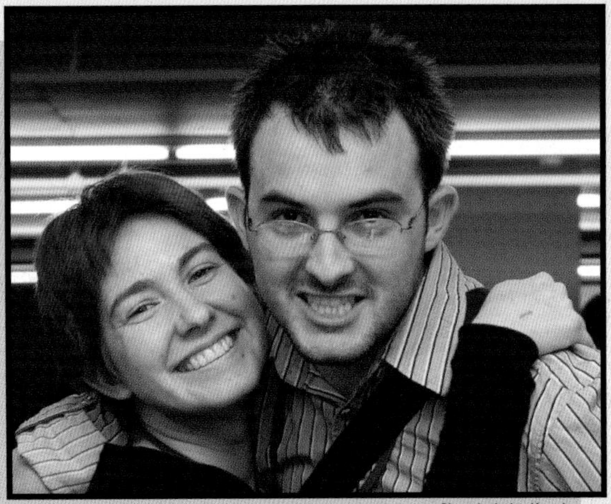

Photo by Joshin Yamaha

ERIKA:

To my wonderful husband, Matthew Nolan, who encourages and supports me through everything.

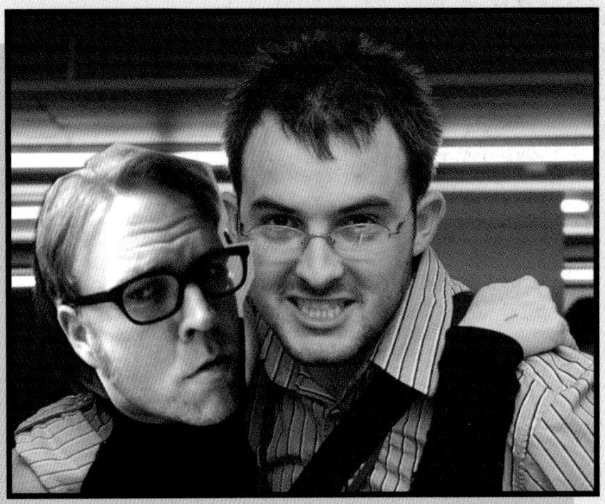

JEFF:

I would also like to dedicate this book to Matt.

FOREWORD

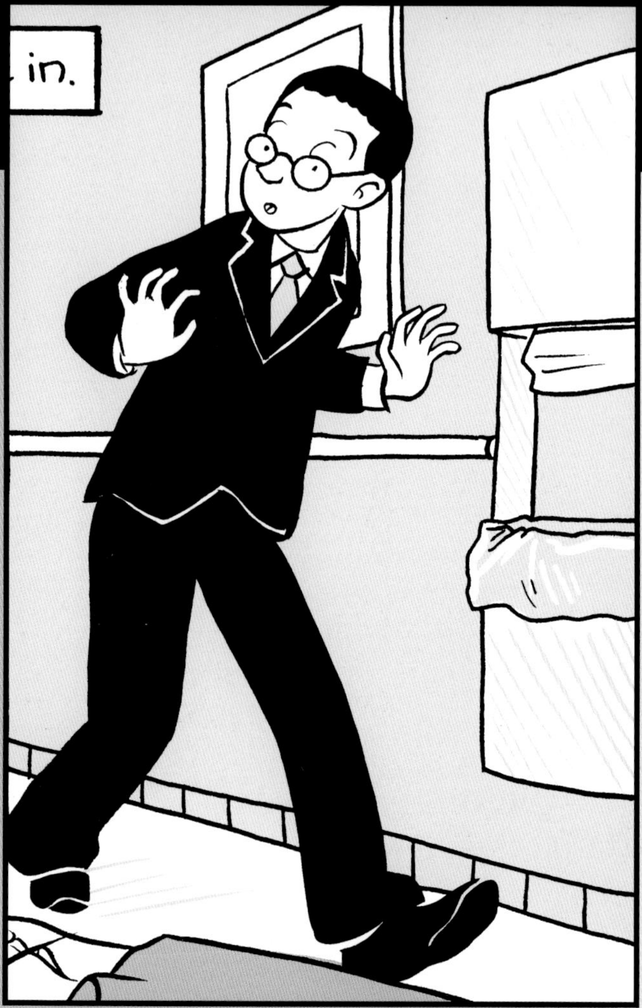
in.

It was once a popular belief that a pair of recording angels follow each of us, noting "the deeds of all individuals for future reward or punishment" and keeping "a general account between man and his maker," as the *Jewish Encyclopedia* phrases it. Sounds nice, but being Old Testament angels, I suspect they'd pay much closer attention to bad behavior than good. Or perhaps I'm just projecting, because that certainly describes my relationship with Jeff Parker and Erika Moen as they created *Bucko*.

I was there for much of the project's creation. Long before Erika joined Periscope Studio—the all-freelancer art studio in Portland, Oregon, of which we're all members—Jeff liked to drop weird questions in our laps. He knew they'd get us so hung up arguing that no one would get a goddamn bit of work done for the rest of the day. Our editors would hate us, our incomes would drop, and he'd just chuckle and put on headphones, knowing he'd trolled the room. One of these questions concerned a desperate need to take a dump when there's a corpse on the bathroom floor. It destroyed our productivity and had us arguing for weeks.

No one knows how Erika came to be a member of Periscope. She certainly never came out and asked anyone if she could join. She just sort of hung around until we figured she ought to at least pay us something for taking up space and ripping one heinous fart after another, polluting the room. The spark for their collaboration came when Erika mentioned in an interview that she might like to work with Parker someday. That passive approach is typical of Periscope. Why nut up and say something to your studiomate's face when you could tell some jackass podcaster about it instead? Erika in particular has an astonishing ability to avoid telling anyone anything directly, leaving her open to the worst interactions imaginable. Horrible people are drawn into Erika's orbit because they know she won't tell them to fuck off, rendering her one of Portland's most powerful shit magnets.

Fortunately, their comic is largely concerned with those sorts of people. *Bucko*'s Portland boasts a population that's self-absorbed, lazy, stupid, rude, manipulative, self-congratulatory, and flat-out creepy—just like the real Portland! Yeah, there's a lot of the delightful stuff here, too—the things that have the *New York Times* standing beneath Portland's bedroom window holding up a boom box—but none of that is as entertaining as the shots *Bucko* takes at clueless freaks and self-conscious weirdoes, the twin cancers that are killing our city.

Make no mistake; this is a harsh comic. Jeff Parker is whaling hard on the people he's writing about. But because he's using Erika Moen's likable, friendly drawings to do it, it all seems affectionate. And he knows that with Erika's much higher Internet profile, she'll take the flak for anything really offensive. This is another way that "passive approach" I mentioned before manifests itself: every time Parker writes something horrible, Erika loses Twitter followers.

Some might say they're heaping all this abuse out of love for their city. It's possible, but if so, you'd think they'd want to keep their portrait more balanced. Then again, I could have done the same with this intro. But who wants to read about Erika spending long hours at the drawing board, or Parker carefully honing six panels into a perfect gag? It happened, but it isn't interesting. Parker and Moen are Portland's recording angels, and if they give our virtues short shrift while harping on our faults, it just means that the final ledger is going to be one hell of an engaging read.

Steve Lieber
Portland, 2012

Steve Lieber is a founding member of Portland's Periscope Studio and an Eisner Award–winning artist who has worked with every major American comics publisher.

INTRODUCTION

Hi, I'm Jeff Parker, the writer of *Bucko*. From here on out, most of the text in black can be considered me speaking. Any text in blazing magenta should be heard in the voice of artist Erika Moen. Time travel with me about two years into the past and you can experience the moment *Bucko* the concept begins.

You're me, getting some water from the sink area at Periscope Studio, and heading back to your desk to write some superhero comics. On your right is Erika by her desk answering her cell phone: "Hey, what's up, Bucko?" This means that she looked at the incoming-calls readout, saw "Erik," and assumed her brother, who she at some

point tagged "Bucko" (presumably so she wouldn't feel like she was talking to herself), was calling. Yeah, real creative, Erika's parents, making their names off by one letter. Anyway, there's some confusion between Erika and the caller and she raises an eyebrow like a cartoon character and asks, "Are you fucking with me, Bucko?" Soon her needling expression of confusion turns to a more aghast one as she realizes this isn't her brother, but rather the art director of a job she's started work on.

The AD was understanding, but the phone call stuck in my head and is why, at the beginning of our webcomic, the real main character—Gyp—essentially renames her new friend Bucko like his name isn't quite good enough and she prefers something she can remember. Because she calls him that, everyone does—even he seems to forget his actual name at several points. Incidentally, since no one ever remembers it, his name is Rich—picked because when I needed a name just then I looked up and went with the first person I saw, cartoonist Rich Ellis.

Now you know most of what you need to about my process in writing this comic. I made extra effort (or no effort, depending on how you view it) to let outside life get in and build the world of *Bucko*. Particularly anything that orbited Erika herself, who explicitly stated to me, "I want to get away from doing autobio material; I want to create something that's pure fiction." In short, if you tell me you really don't want "X" in something, bank on me making it SUPER X, THE MOST X THING OF ALL TIME, PART X. But Erika, in keeping with the very zen nature of this feature's creation, went with it and completely embraced the process. As a result, I think we made something fresh that neither of us would have created alone.

Hey, Erika here! Oh man, I don't even know where to begin.

Wait! No, I do. Okay. Like you did with Parker a few paragraphs ago, we're going to go back in time about two years, when I'd just finished reading two graphic novels written by Parker: *Underground*, drawn by our fellow Periscope Studio member Steve Lieber, and *Mysterius the Unfathomable*, illustrated by Tom Fowler. They are both really good! Really, *really* good. And even though Parker and I are both in Periscope Studio together, I did not actually know him all that well back then (our desks were on opposite sides of the room). Well, an interviewer asked me who I'd like to work with someday and, as I mentioned, I'd just read these two phenomenal books, so I answered, "Jeff Parker!" not thinking that anything would come of it or that Parker would be sent an autoalert as soon as his name appeared anywhere online. Imagine my surprise when that interview went up a month or two

later (long enough for me to totally forget about it in the meantime) and Mr. Jeff Parker strolls over to me, all business, and demands, "So, you wanna do a comic with me, huh?"

My first thought was that he must be offended that I, an artist far less talented and professional than the ones he's accustomed to working with, would have the audacity to think I could represent his intelligent, funny, and accomplished writing with my dick-and-fart doodles. (Of course, that is not what he was thinking, because he is a really kind, enthusiastic guy who was excited at the prospect of teaming up, but, y'know, the worst possible interpretation of any exchange is where my mind always goes first.) I stammered out something like, "Oh! I, uh! Uh, yes! I mean, if that's okay . . . I . . . uh . . . I l-like your writing?" His arms folded, all serious, he looks me in the eye, says, "Okay then," and walks off.

And that is how *Bucko* got started. I signed on to draw a Parker story, he signed on to write an Erika story, and the result is a very unique meshing of our experiences and craft that could never have existed without each other.

Lemme just say that working with Parker has been one of the best things to ever happen to me in my decade-plus of making comics. Joining Periscope Studio was life changing, to be sure—my studiomates really opened my eyes and educated me about creating comics—but to actually work one on one with a seasoned veteran of both writing *and* drawing monthly titles for the biggest comics publishers was like going through Comics Boot Camp. In the year we worked together, Parker completely blew my mind with all the new insight he gave me into drawing and inking and laying out my pages and lettering and, goddamn it, pretty much every step that goes into making a page. He is a great instructor, and there's always gonna be a little bit of him in my artwork from now on.

So, yeah! This is the comic we made. I hope you like it.

ACT ONE

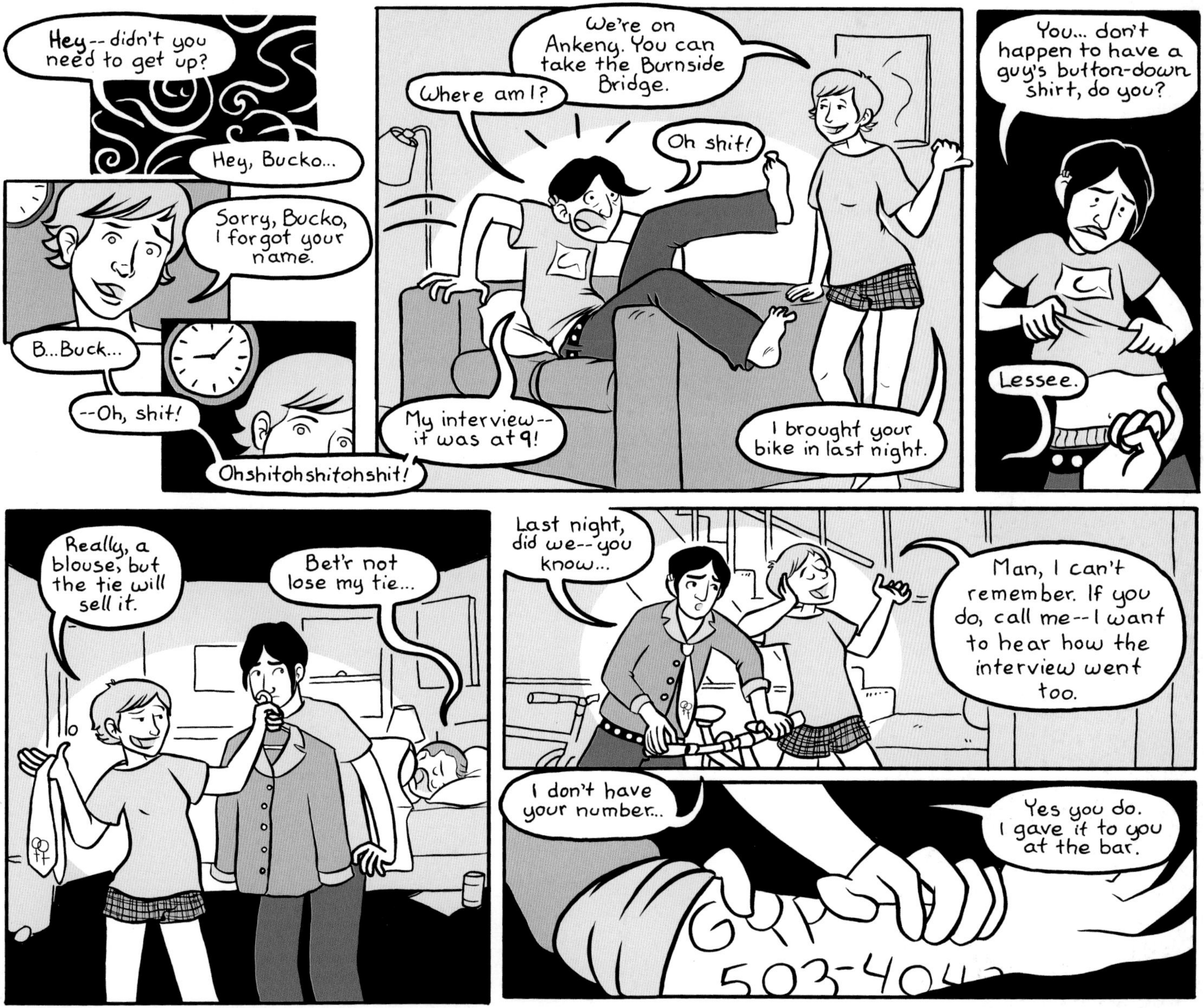
Hey-- didn't you need to get up?
Hey, Bucko...
Sorry, Bucko, I forgot your name.
B...Buck...
--Oh, shit!
Ohshitohshitohshit!
Where am I?
We're on Ankeny. You can take the Burnside Bridge.
Oh shit!
My interview-- it was at 9!
I brought your bike in last night.
You... don't happen to have a guy's button-down shirt, do you?
Lessee.
Really, a blouse, but the tie will sell it.
Bet'r not lose my tie...
Last night, did we-- you know...
Man, I can't remember. If you do, call me-- I want to hear how the interview went too.
I don't have your number...
Yes you do. I gave it to you at the bar.
503-404

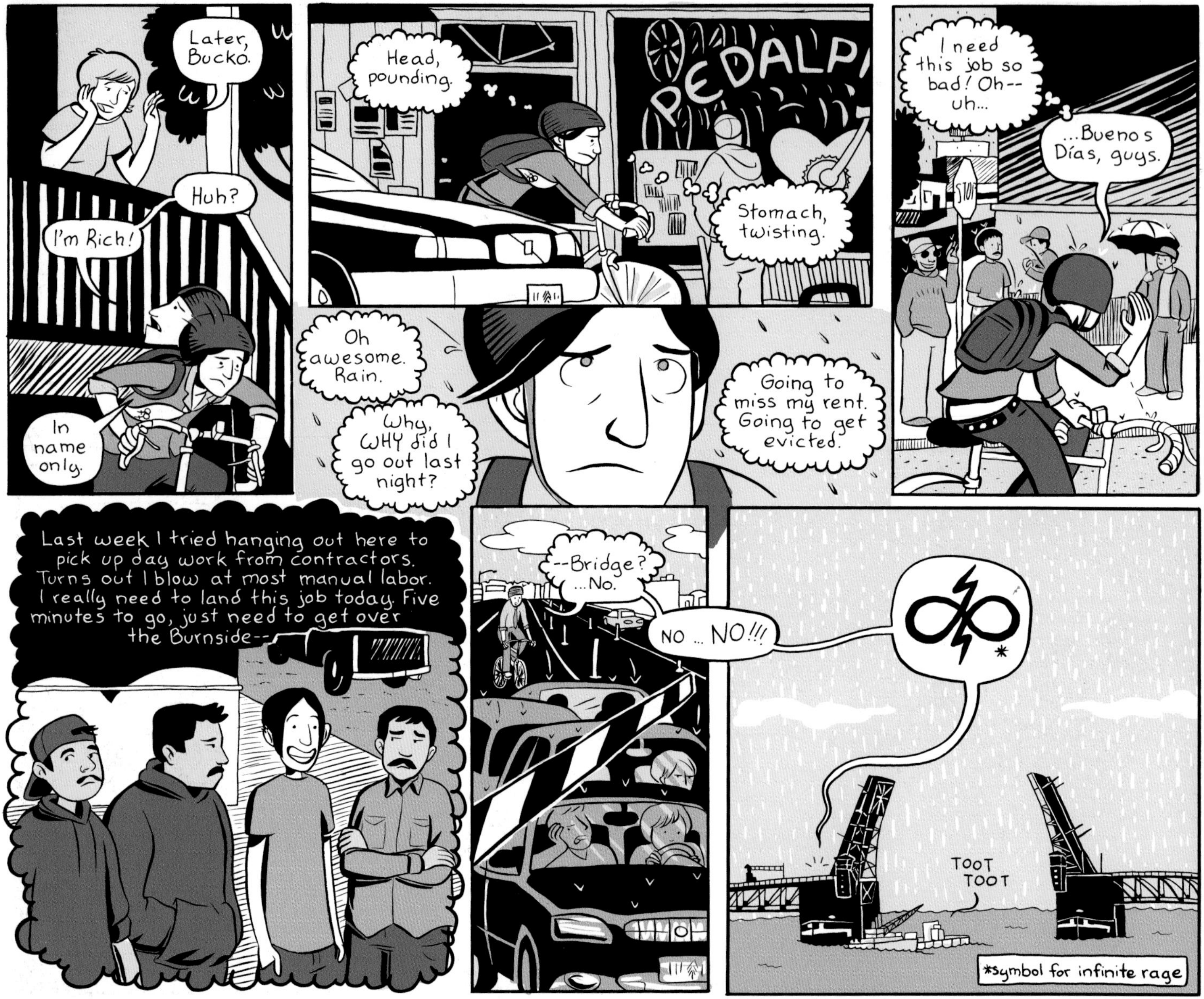
Later, Bucko.
Huh?
I'm Rich!
In name only.
Head, pounding.
PEDALP
Stomach, twisting.
I need this job so bad! Oh-- uh...
...Buenos Días, guys.
Oh awesome. Rain.
Why, WHY did I go out last night?
Going to miss my rent. Going to get evicted.
Last week I tried hanging out here to pick up day work from contractors. Turns out I blow at most manual labor. I really need to land this job today. Five minutes to go, just need to get over the Burnside--
--Bridge? ...No.
NO ... NO!!!
TOOT TOOT
*symbol for infinite rage

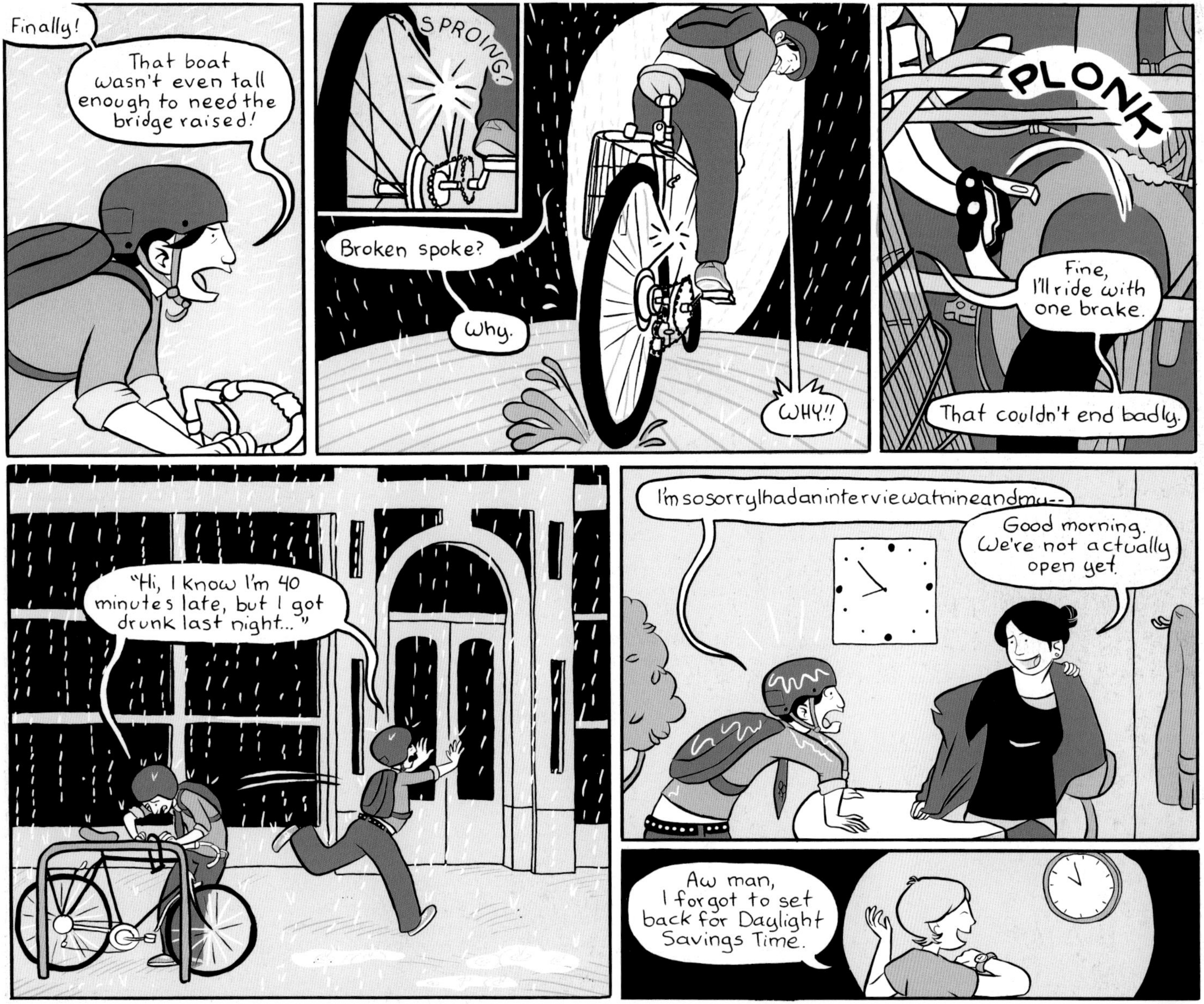
Finally!
That boat wasn't even tall enough to need the bridge raised!
SPROING!
Broken spoke?
Why.
WHY!!
PLONK
Fine, I'll ride with one brake.
That couldn't end badly.
"Hi, I know I'm 40 minutes late, but I got drunk last night..."
I'msosorryIhadaninterviewatnineandmy--
Good morning. We're not actually open yet.
Aw man, I forgot to set back for Daylight Savings Time.

Hello, Mr. Richardson.

You can call me Bu-- uh, Rich!

The interview finally begins.

That's an interesting shirt...

Oh, yeah... looks silky because... the rain...

Does she smell alcohol reeking from my pores?

She must.

I'm babbling. Saying every interview cliché ever spoken.

I once interned for Zeus Shoes.

I'm a self-starter.

I welcome criticism.

I don't mind working on my own time.

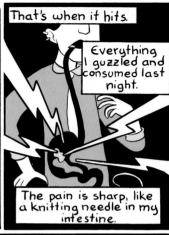

That's when it hits.

Everything I guzzled and consumed last night.

The pain is sharp, like a knitting needle in my intestine.

There is no waiting.

What is in me...

Must. Get. OUT.

--so the position calls for

Excuse me!

Is there... a restroom?

Down by the elevator, but if you can wait--

CAN'T.

The job is gone now. I know that.

You'll need a key.

I don't care.

Nothing matters but making it to the bathroom.

Nothing.

Ohplease oh pleaseohplease--

Just one more second-- three more seconds--

Will I make it!?!

Come on, come onnnnn...

klackakakakakakaklackakakakakakaklack

klackakakakakaklackakakakakaklakak

klackakakakakaklackakakakaka

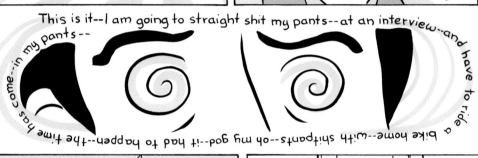

This is it--I am going to straight shit my pants--at an interview--and have to ride a bike home--with shitpants--oh my god--it had to happen--the time has come--in my pants--

CLICK

I'm!

Going to!

Make it.

So there I was. I'd made it into the bathroom just in time...

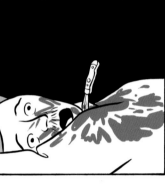

... and found that extremely dead guy. And as horrible and shocking as it was...

...it didn't change that I still really-really-really HAD TO GO.

After all, it wasn't going to change anything. He was still going to be dead whether I went or not, right?

click-clickk

Of course then that guy came in.

The one who called you.

Let's go back to the victim with the knife in his neck.

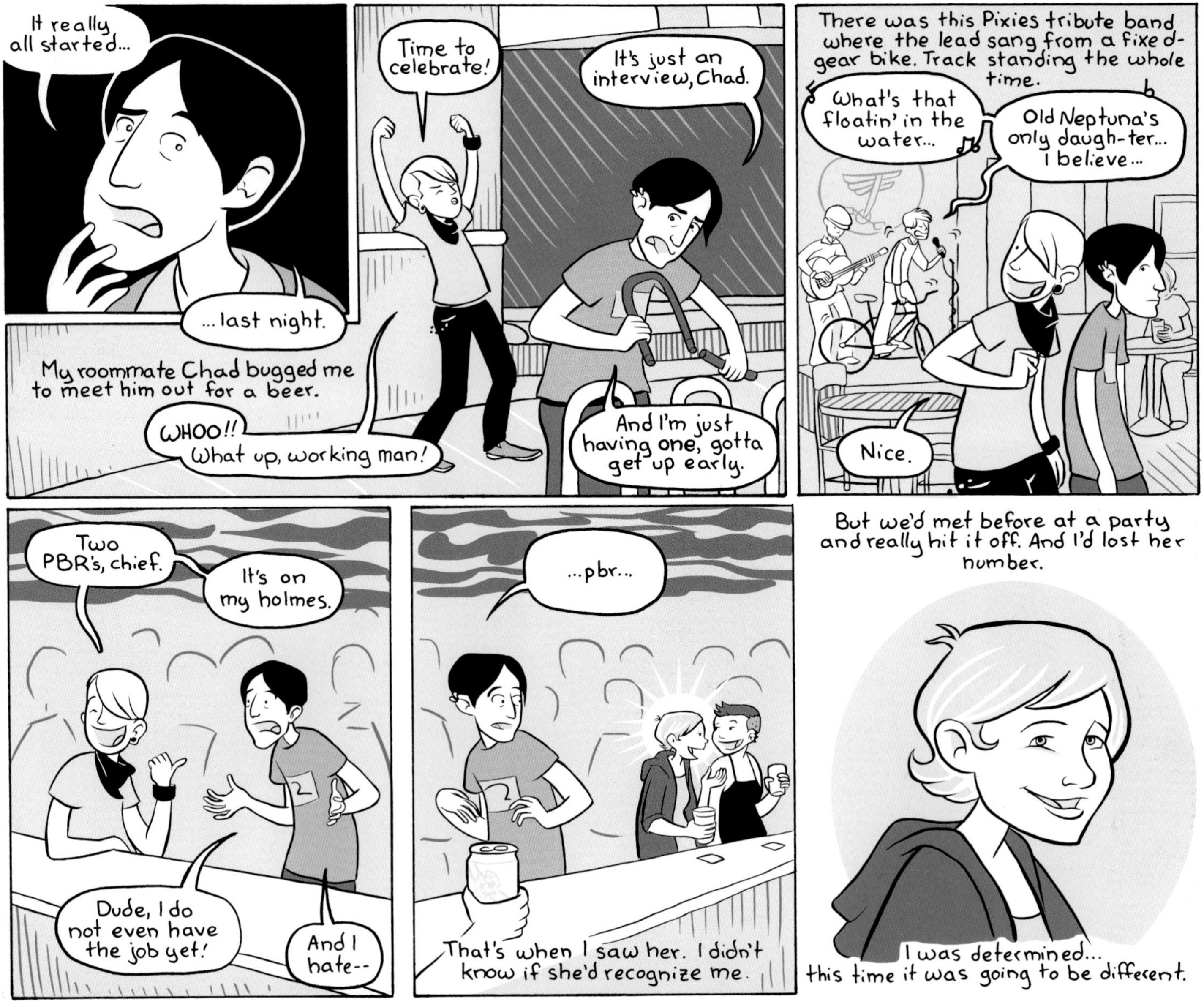

It really all started...
...last night.
My roommate Chad bugged me to meet him out for a beer.
WHOO!! What up, working man!
Time to celebrate!
It's just an interview, Chad.
And I'm just having one, gotta get up early.
There was this Pixies tribute band where the lead sang from a fixed-gear bike. Track standing the whole time.
What's that floatin' in the water...
Old Neptuna's only daugh-ter... I believe...
Nice.
Two PBR's, chief.
It's on my holmes.
Dude, I do not even have the job yet!
And I hate--
...pbr...
That's when I saw her. I didn't know if she'd recognize me.
But we'd met before at a party and really hit it off. And I'd lost her number.
I was determined... this time it was going to be different.

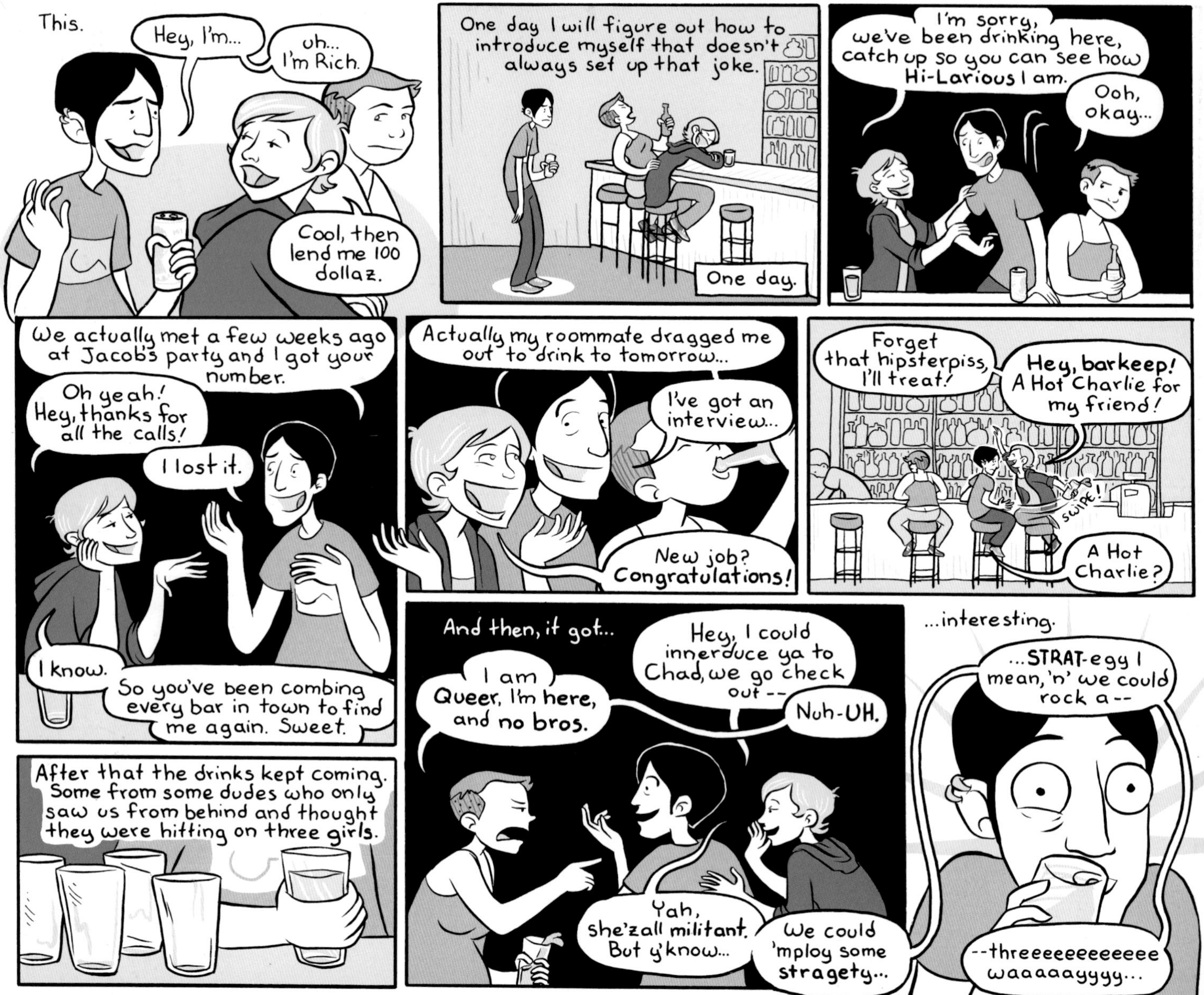

This.
Hey, I'm...
uh... I'm Rich.
Cool, then lend me 100 dollaz.
One day I will figure out how to introduce myself that doesn't always set up that joke.
One day.
I'm sorry, we've been drinking here, catch up so you can see how Hi-Larious I am.
Ooh, okay...
We actually met a few weeks ago at Jacob's party and I got your number.
Oh yeah! Hey, thanks for all the calls!
I lost it.
I know.
So you've been combing every bar in town to find me again. Sweet.
Actually my roommate dragged me out to drink to tomorrow...
I've got an interview...
New job? Congratulations!
Forget that hipsterpiss, I'll treat!
Hey, barkeep! A Hot Charlie for my friend!
SWIPE!
A Hot Charlie?
After that the drinks kept coming. Some from some dudes who only saw us from behind and thought they were hitting on three girls.
And then, it got...
I am Queer, I'm here, and no bros.
Hey, I could innerduce ya to Chad, we go check out --
Nuh-UH.
Yah, she'zall militant. But y'know...
We could 'mploy some stragety...
...interesting.
...STRAT-egy I mean, 'n' we could rock a --
--threeeeeeeeeeee waaaaayyyy...

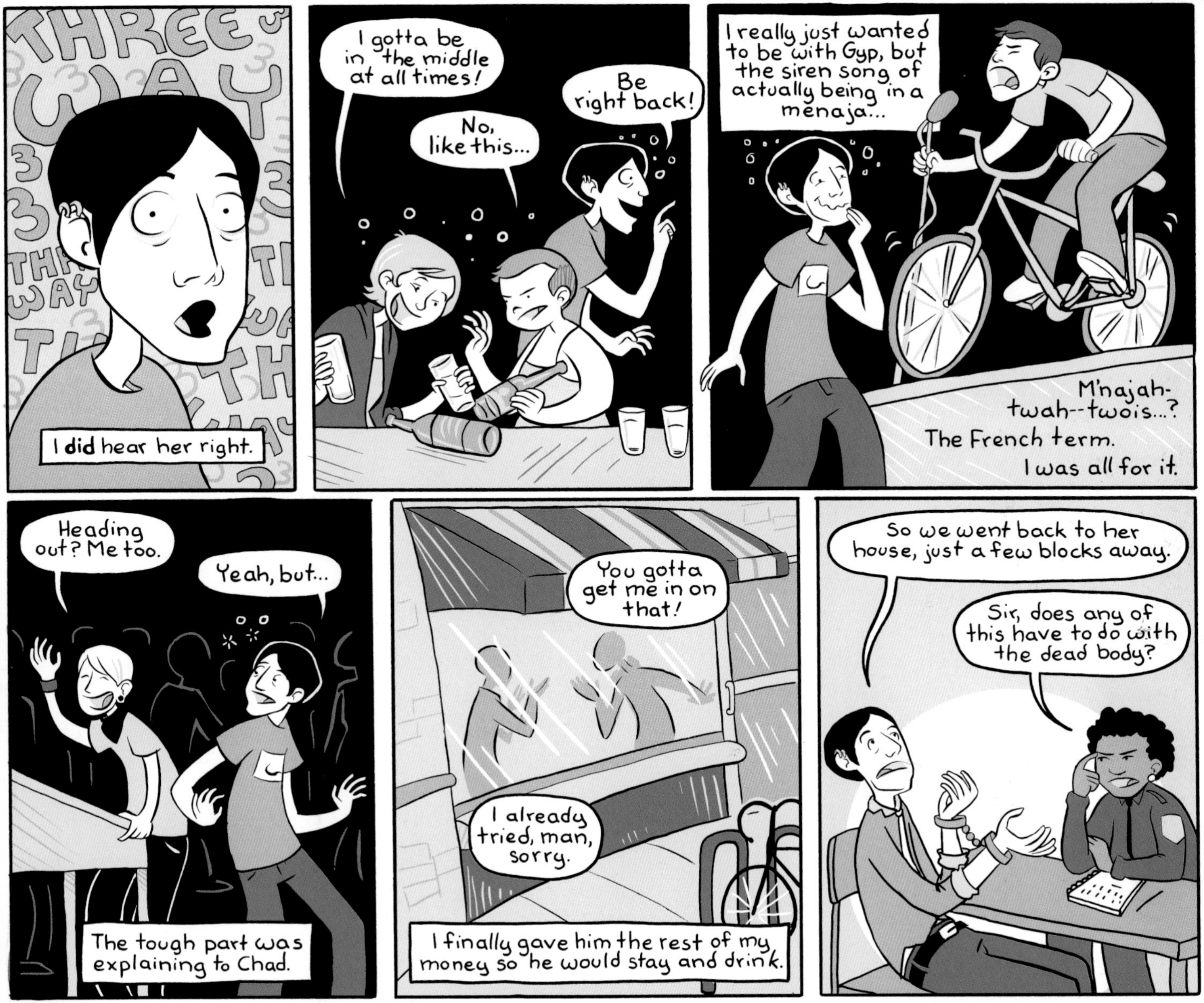

THREE WAY
I did hear her right.
I gotta be in the middle at all times!
No, like this...
Be right back!
I really just wanted to be with Gyp, but the siren song of actually being in a menaja...
M'najah-twah--twois...?
The French term.
I was all for it.
Heading out? Me too.
Yeah, but...
The tough part was explaining to Chad.
You gotta get me in on that!
I already tried, man, sorry.
I finally gave him the rest of my money so he would stay and drink.
So we went back to her house, just a few blocks away.
Sir, does any of this have to do with the dead body?

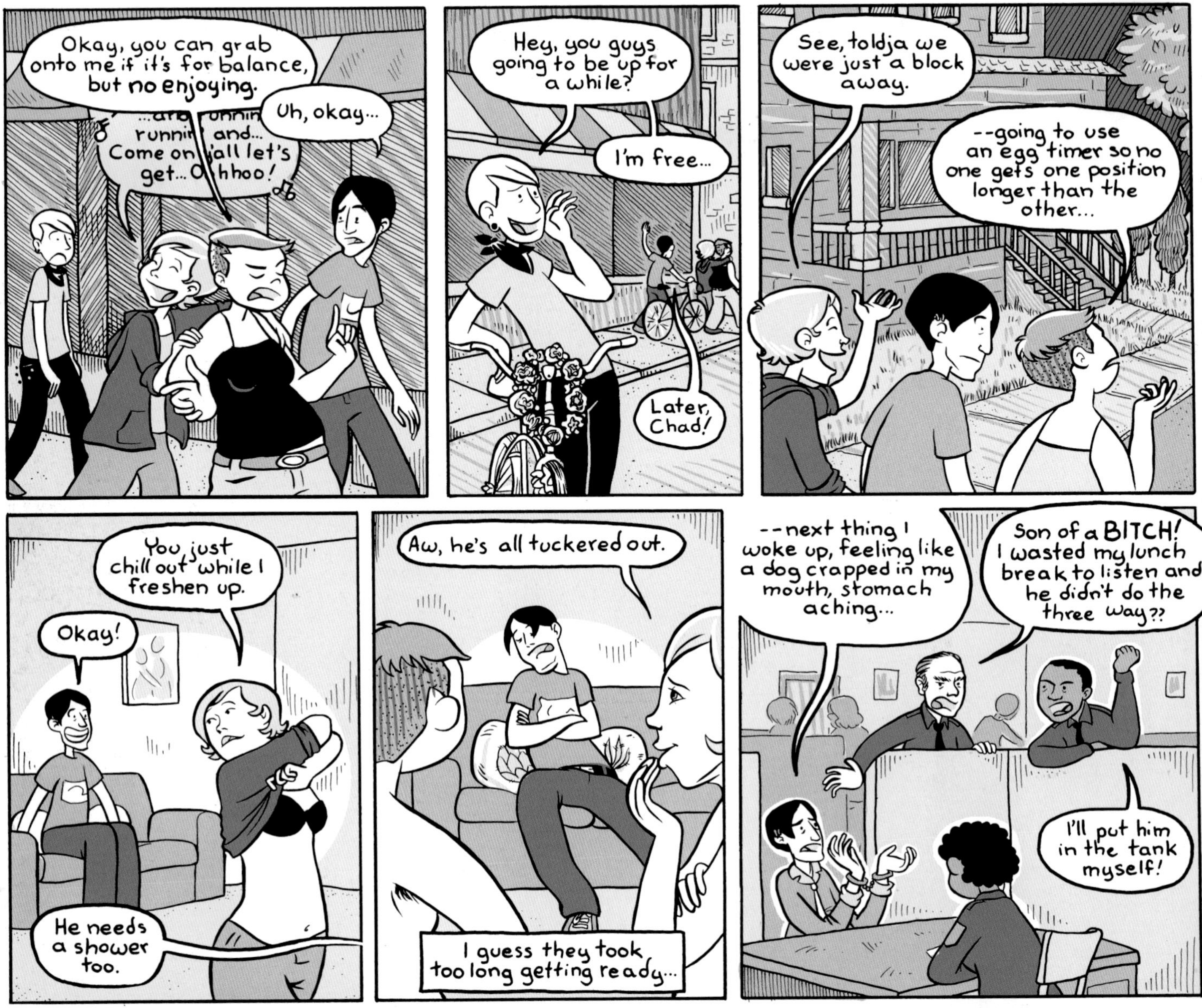
Okay, you can grab onto me if it's for balance, but no enjoying.
Uh, okay...
Hey, you guys going to be up for a while?
I'm free...
Later, Chad!
See, toldja we were just a block away.
--going to use an egg timer so no one gets one position longer than the other...
You just chill out while I freshen up.
Okay!
He needs a shower too.
Aw, he's all tuckered out.
I guess they took too long getting ready...
--next thing I woke up, feeling like a dog crapped in my mouth, stomach aching...
Son of a BITCH! I wasted my lunch break to listen and he didn't do the three way??
I'll put him in the tank myself!

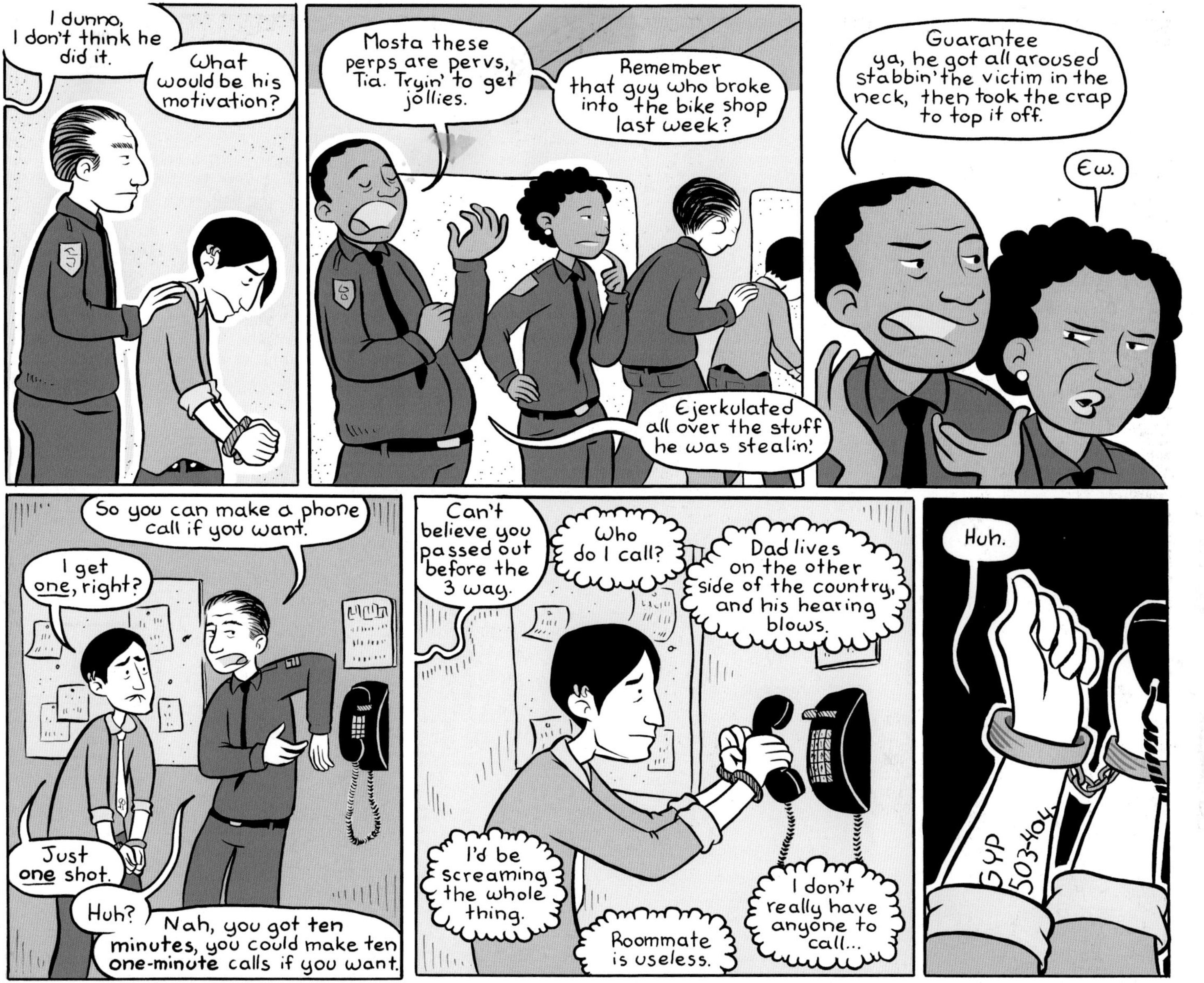
I dunno, I don't think he did it.
What would be his motivation?
Mosta these perps are pervs, Tia. Tryin' to get jollies.
Remember that guy who broke into the bike shop last week?
Ejerkulated all over the stuff he was stealin'.
Guarantee ya, he got all aroused stabbin' the victim in the neck, then took the crap to top it off.
Ew.
So you can make a phone call if you want.
I get one, right?
Just one shot.
Huh?
Nah, you got ten minutes, you could make ten one-minute calls if you want.
Can't believe you passed out before the 3 way.
Who do I call?
Dad lives on the other side of the country, and his hearing blows.
I'd be screaming the whole thing.
Roommate is useless.
I don't really have anyone to call...
Huh.
GYP 503-404

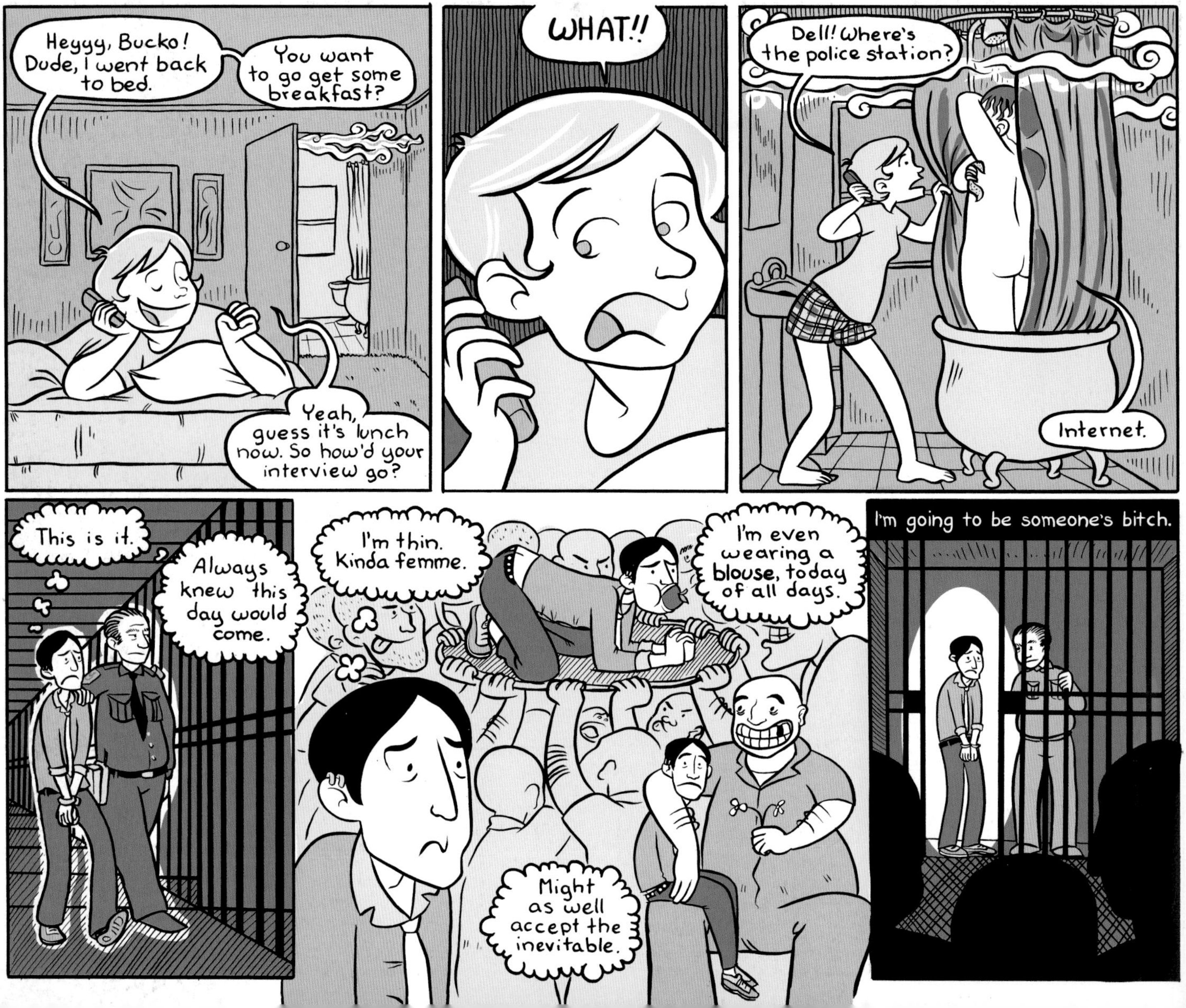
Heyyy, Bucko! Dude, I went back to bed.
You want to go get some breakfast?
Yeah, guess it's lunch now. So how'd your interview go?
WHAT!!
Dell! Where's the police station?
Internet.
This is it.
Always knew this day would come.
I'm thin. Kinda femme.
I'm even wearing a blouse, today of all days.
Might as well accept the inevitable.
I'm going to be someone's bitch.

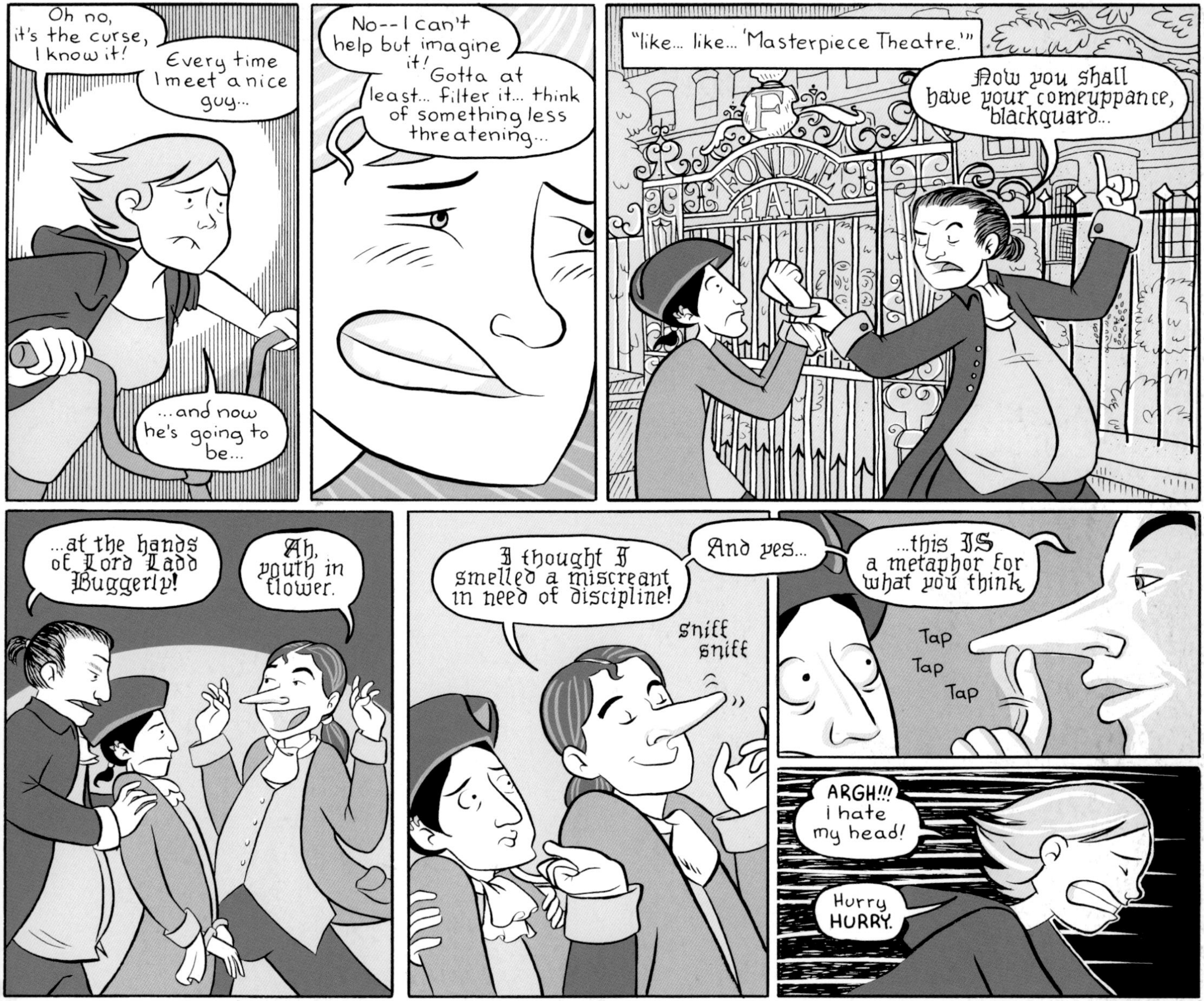
Oh no, it's the curse, I know it!
Every time I meet a nice guy...
...and now he's going to be...
No--I can't help but imagine it!
Gotta at least... filter it... think of something less threatening...
"like... like... 'Masterpiece Theatre.'"
FONDLE HALL
Now you shall have your comeuppance, blackguard...
...at the hands of Lord Ladd Buggerly!
Ah, youth in flower.
I thought I smelled a miscreant in need of discipline!
sniff sniff
And yes...
...this IS a metaphor for what you think.
Tap
Tap
Tap
ARGH!!! I hate my head!
Hurry HURRY.

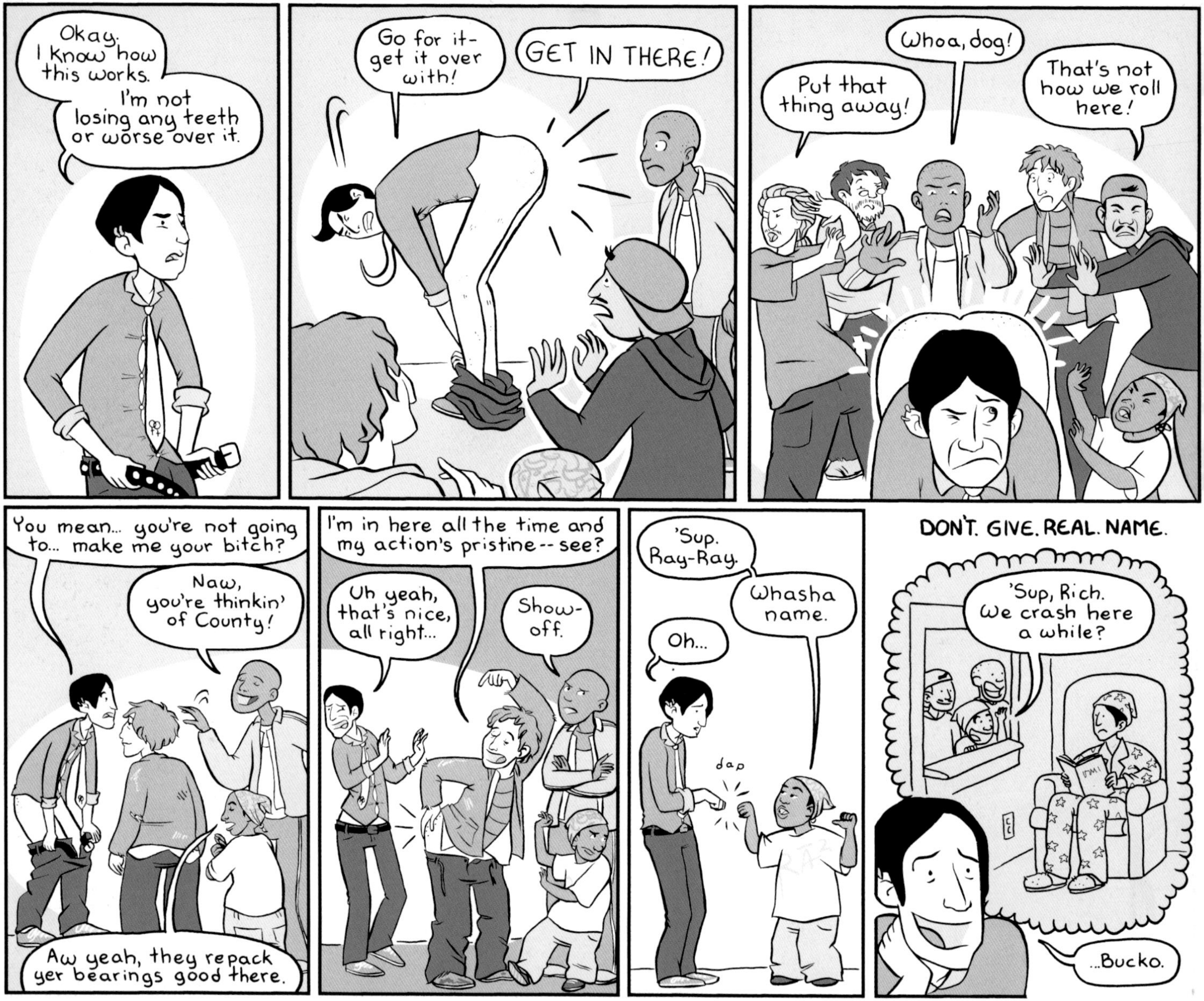
Okay. I know how this works.
I'm not losing any teeth or worse over it.
Go for it- get it over with!
GET IN THERE!
Put that thing away!
Whoa, dog!
That's not how we roll here!
You mean... you're not going to... make me your bitch?
Naw, you're thinkin' of County!
Aw yeah, they repack yer bearings good there.
I'm in here all the time and my action's pristine -- see?
Uh yeah, that's nice, all right...
Show-off.
'Sup. Ray-Ray.
Whasha name.
Oh...
dap
DON'T. GIVE. REAL. NAME.
'Sup, Rich. We crash here a while?
...Bucko.

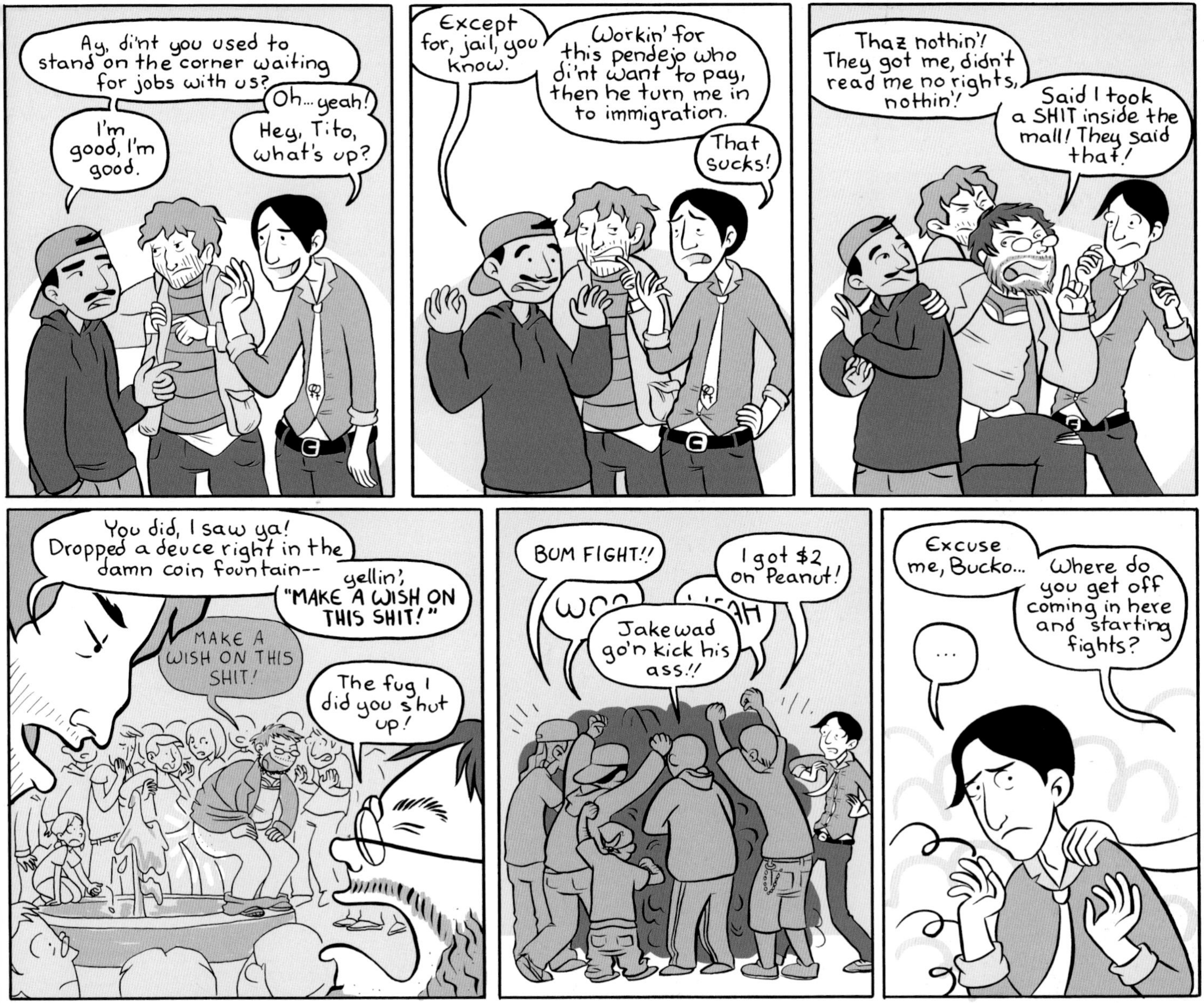
Ay, di'nt you used to stand on the corner waiting for jobs with us?
I'm good, I'm good.
Oh... yeah!
Hey, Tito, what's up?
Except for, jail, you know.
Workin' for this pendejo who di'nt want to pay, then he turn me in to immigration.
That sucks!
Thaz nothin'! They got me, didn't read me no rights, nothin'!
Said I took a SHIT inside the mall! They said that!
You did, I saw ya! Dropped a deuce right in the damn coin fountain--
yellin', "MAKE A WISH ON THIS SHIT!"
MAKE A WISH ON THIS SHIT!
The fug I did you shut up!
BUM FIGHT!!
I got $2 on Peanut!
Jakewad go'n kick his ass!!
Excuse me, Bucko...
Where do you get off coming in here and starting fights?
...

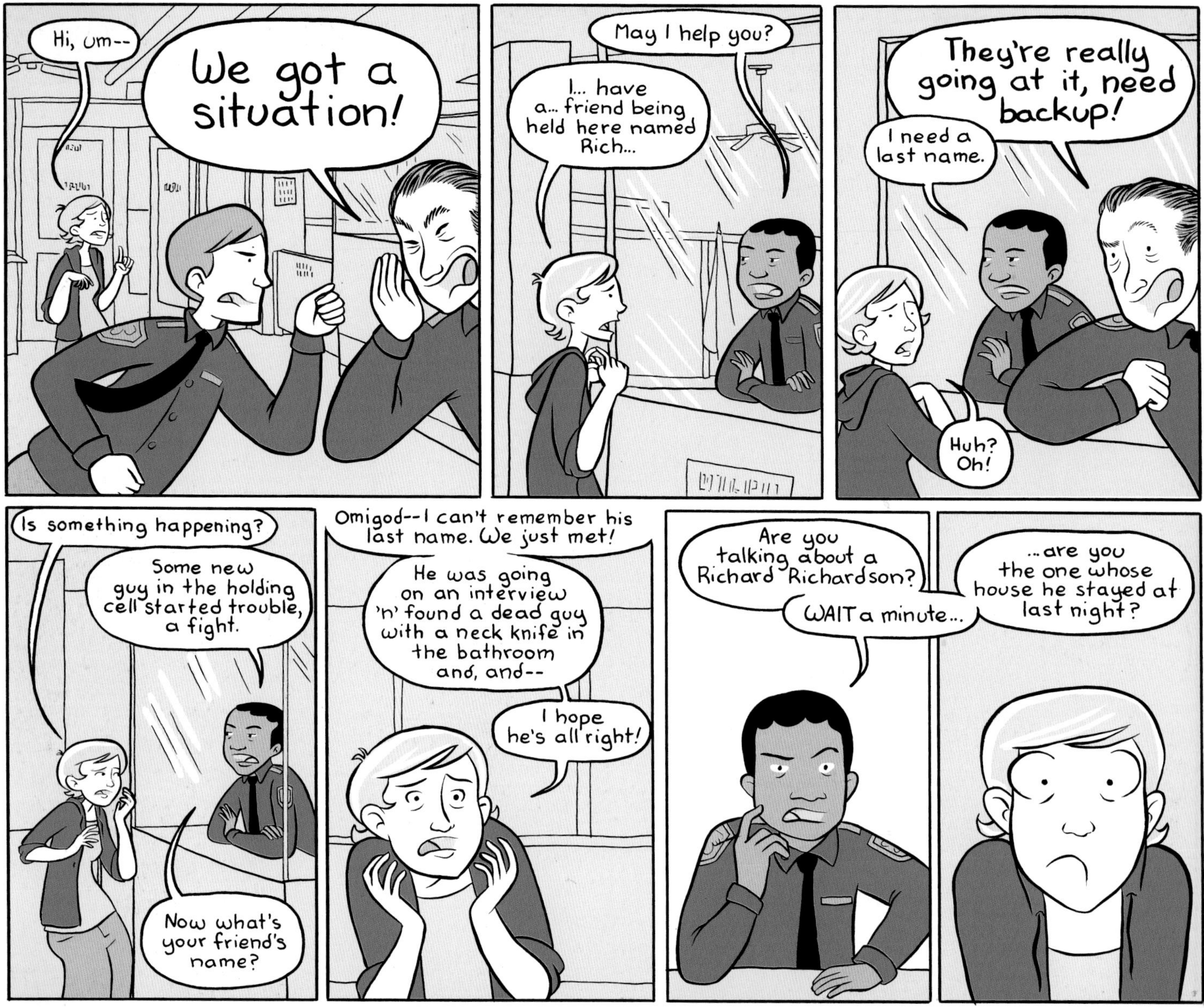
Hi, um--
We got a situation!
May I help you?
I... have a... friend being held here named Rich...
They're really going at it, need backup!
I need a last name.
Huh? Oh!
Is something happening?
Some new guy in the holding cell started trouble, a fight.
Now what's your friend's name?
Omigod--I can't remember his last name. We just met!
He was going on an interview 'n' found a dead guy with a neck knife in the bathroom and, and--
I hope he's all right!
Are you talking about a Richard Richardson?
WAIT a minute...
...are you the one whose house he stayed at last night?

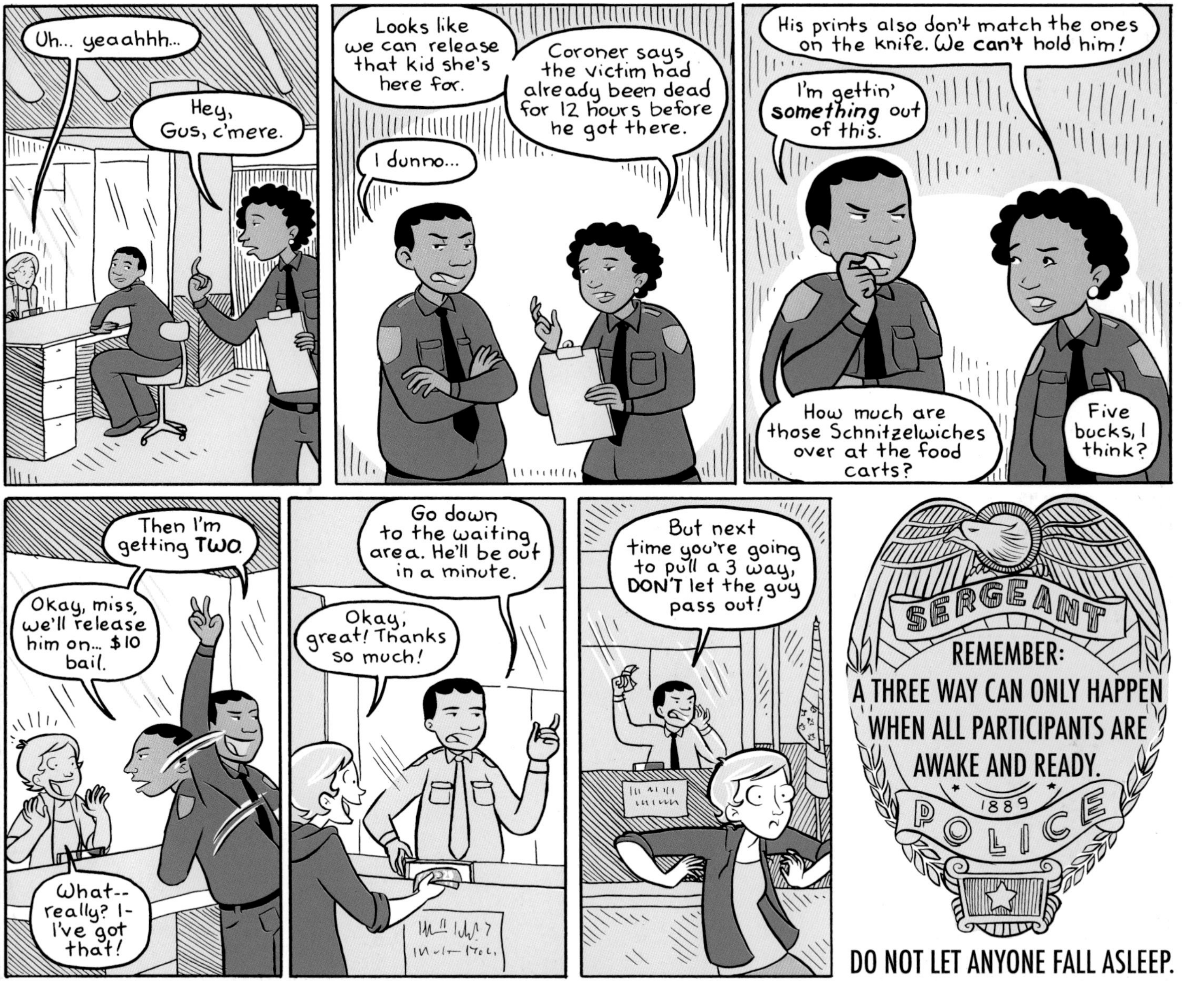
Uh... yeaahhh...
Hey, Gus, c'mere.
Looks like we can release that kid she's here for.
Coroner says the victim had already been dead for 12 hours before he got there.
I dunno...
His prints also don't match the ones on the knife. We **can't** hold him!
I'm gettin' ***something*** out of this.
How much are those Schnitzelwiches over at the food carts?
Five bucks, I think?
Then I'm getting **TWO**.
Okay, miss, we'll release him on... $10 bail.
What-- really? I- I've got that!
Go down to the waiting area. He'll be out in a minute.
Okay, great! Thanks so much!
But next time you're going to pull a 3 way, **DON'T** let the guy pass out!
SERGEANT
REMEMBER:
A THREE WAY CAN ONLY HAPPEN WHEN ALL PARTICIPANTS ARE AWAKE AND READY.
1889
POLICE
DO NOT LET ANYONE FALL ASLEEP.

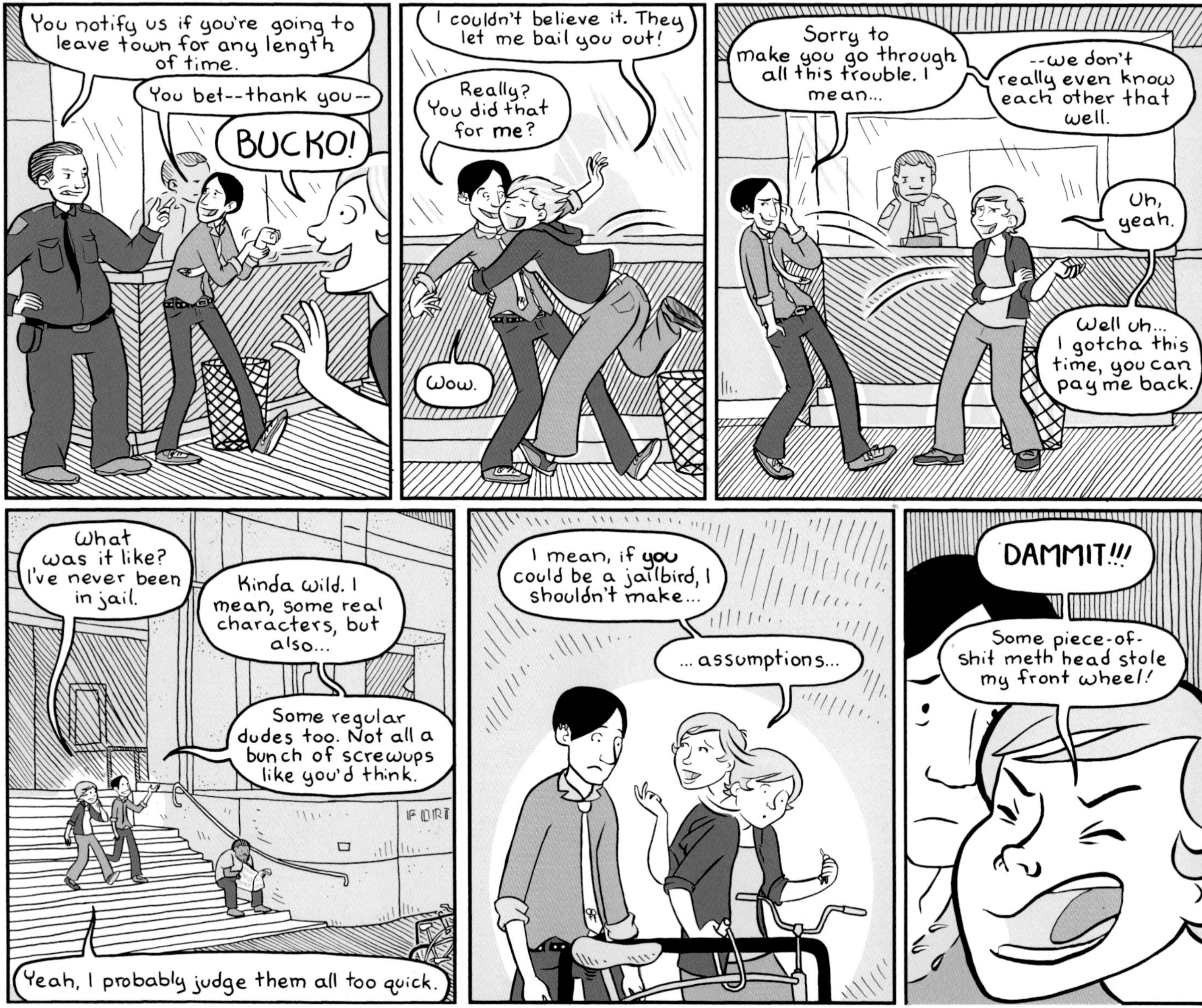
You notify us if you're going to leave town for any length of time.
You bet--thank you--
BUCKO!
I couldn't believe it. They let me bail you out!
Really? You did that for me?
Wow.
Sorry to make you go through all this trouble. I mean...
--we don't really even know each other that well.
Uh, yeah.
Well uh... I gotcha this time, you can pay me back.
What was it like? I've never been in jail.
Kinda wild. I mean, some real characters, but also...
Some regular dudes too. Not all a bunch of screwups like you'd think.
Yeah, I probably judge them all too quick.
I mean, if you could be a jailbird, I shouldn't make...
...assumptions...
DAMMIT!!!
Some piece-of-shit meth head stole my front wheel!

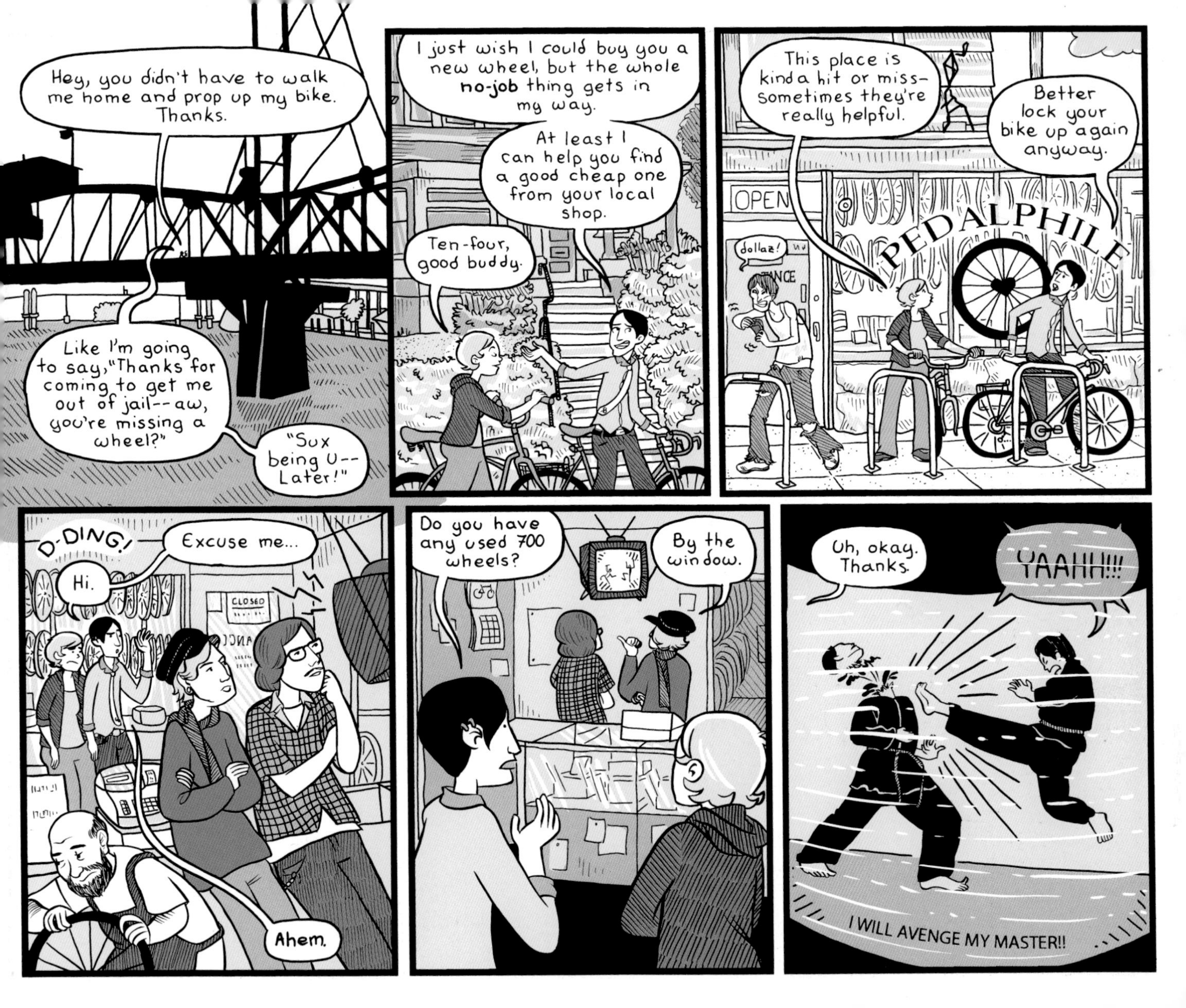
Hey, you didn't have to walk me home and prop up my bike. Thanks.
Like I'm going to say, "Thanks for coming to get me out of jail--aw, you're missing a wheel?"
"Sux being U--Later!"
I just wish I could buy you a new wheel, but the whole **no-job** thing gets in my way.
At least I can help you find a good cheap one from your local shop.
Ten-four, good buddy.
This place is kinda hit or miss-sometimes they're really helpful.
Better lock your bike up again anyway.
OPEN
PEDALPHILE
dollaz!
D-DING!
Excuse me...
Hi.
CLOSED
Ahem.
Do you have any used 700 wheels?
By the window.
Uh, okay. Thanks.
YAAHH!!!
I WILL AVENGE MY MASTER!!

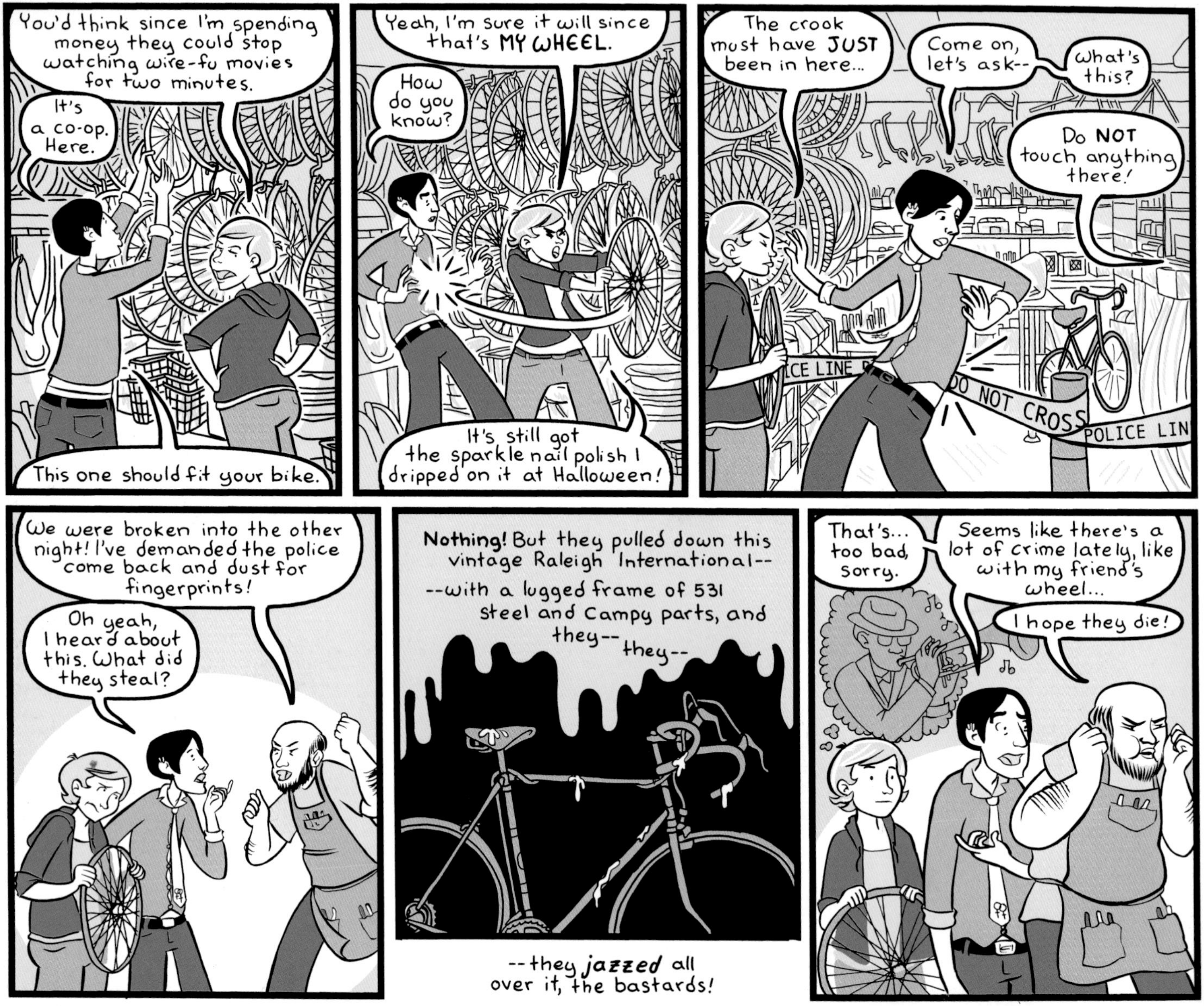
You'd think since I'm spending money they could stop watching wire-fu movies for two minutes.
It's a co-op. Here.
This one should fit your bike.
Yeah, I'm sure it will since that's MY WHEEL.
How do you know?
It's still got the sparkle nail polish I dripped on it at Halloween!
The crook must have JUST been in here...
Come on, let's ask--
What's this?
Do NOT touch anything there!
ICE LINE
DO NOT CROSS
POLICE LIN
We were broken into the other night! I've demanded the police come back and dust for fingerprints!
Oh yeah, I heard about this. What did they steal?
Nothing! But they pulled down this vintage Raleigh International--
--with a lugged frame of 531 steel and Campy parts, and they-- they--
--they jazzed all over it, the bastards!
That's... too bad, sorry.
Seems like there's a lot of crime lately, like with my friend's wheel...
I hope they die!

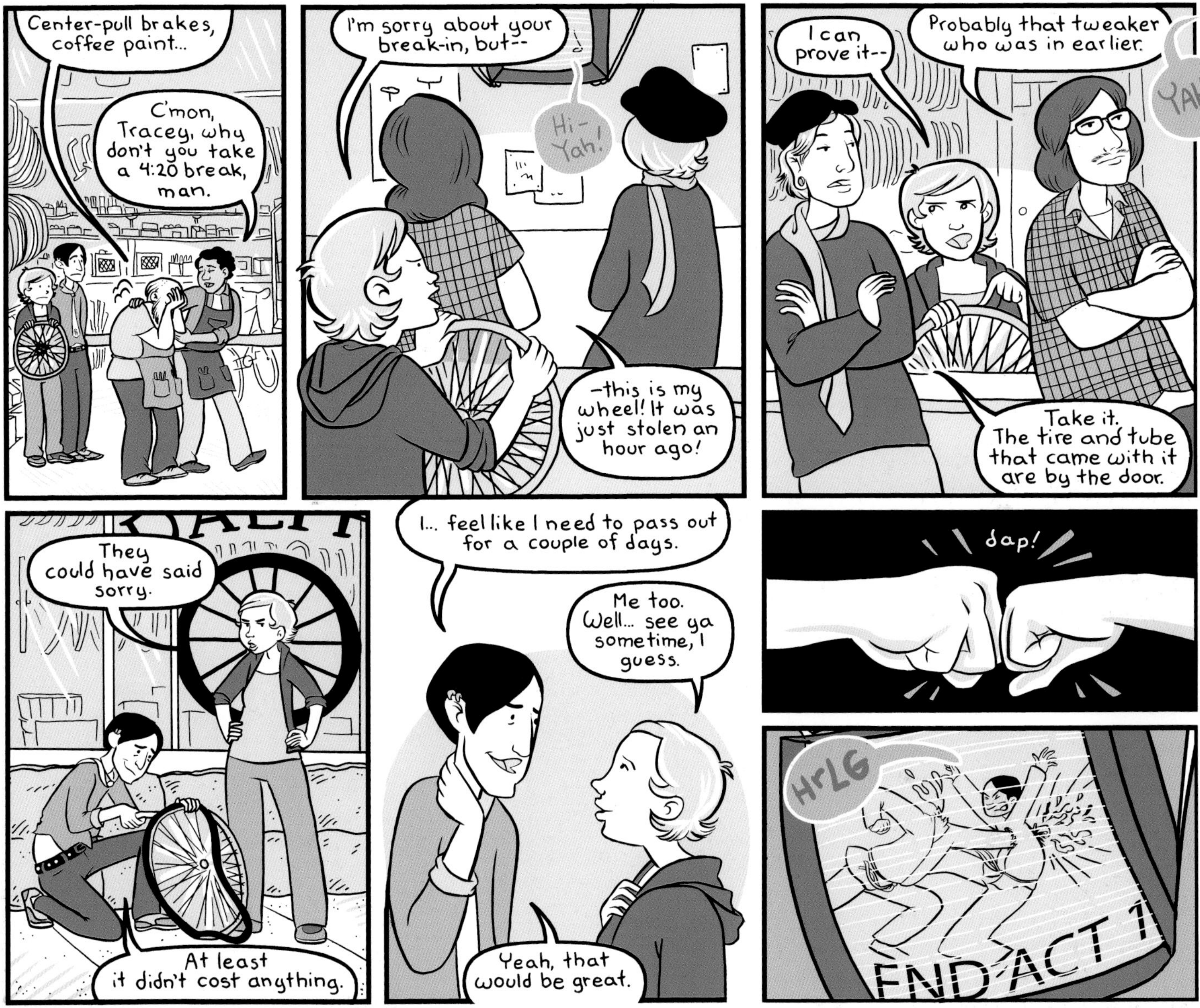
Center-pull brakes, coffee paint...
C'mon, Tracey, why don't you take a 4:20 break, man.
I'm sorry about your break-in, but--
Hi-Yah!
-this is my wheel! It was just stolen an hour ago!
I can prove it--
Probably that tweaker who was in earlier.
YAH!
Take it. The tire and tube that came with it are by the door.
They could have said sorry.
At least it didn't cost anything.
I... feel like I need to pass out for a couple of days.
Me too. Well... see ya sometime, I guess.
Yeah, that would be great.
dap!
HrLG
END ACT 1

INTERMISSION

boners . . . on the go!

At some point before we went live with *Bucko* and were still building up our buffer of strips, Erika and I got completely fired up about making a website called *BonersOnTheGo.com*. I don't remember why it came up, but we were both certain that it needed to exist and tie into the strip. We talked about making a big fake ad for it on the sidebar, and when you clicked through to it, you would see several stock photos of people smiling and in a hurry, professional types mostly, who looked like they had busy yet fulfilling lives.

But for some reason these people "just didn't have time for boners." And the solution would be Boners on the Go. I think we were just in love with all the "oh" sounds in the phrase. The site wouldn't offer any solutions or explain what exactly BonersOnTheGo.com provided; it would just link back to BuckoComic.com.

No, no, the tagline was, "For people who just *don't have the time*." And you'd have to furrow your brow and hold out your hands in an I'm-just-so-overworked shrug while you said it. Oh jeez, I better reregister BonersOnTheGo .com before this book goes to print, so some asshole doesn't snap it up and get free advertising from us talking about it here.

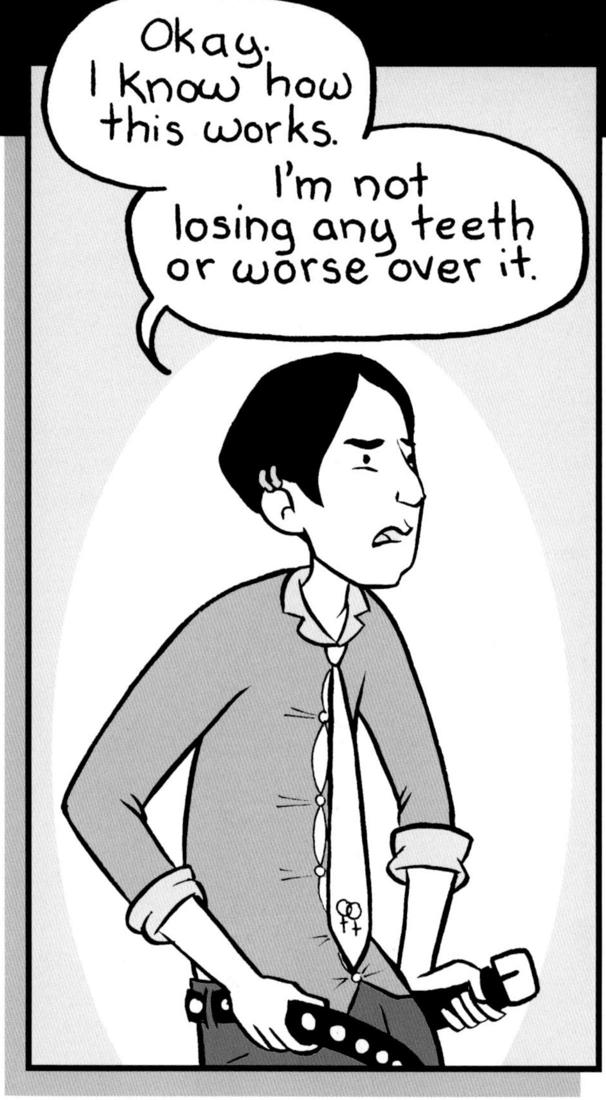
Okay. I know how this works.
I'm not losing any teeth or worse over it.

Oh yeah, I went and bought it that night; it was such a sure thing. Goodbye, twenty dollars.

I think we also were going to take pictures of our friends smiling and running around with briefcases to slip in among the stock photos. And then try to spread it around the Internet, viral style. Possibly even make videos to go with it. Like all big plans, it had to face the reality of us having many deadlines of our own and being lucky to just get the twice-weekly comic updated.

toning and interns

Before we launched, we had worked up a giant buffer of strips, probably way more than most webcomics begin with, and we still managed to dwindle it down to being just one or two ahead in a couple of months. I think around this time Erika started letting the interns add in the color tones on the strip. She would of course change things to be more like she wanted, but it still saved some time.

Have you heard of interns? They are *the best*. If you don't have some, you should get some. At Periscope Studio we always have two interns doing three-month shifts with us, often receiving college credit for an art degree. Or they at least get as much advice and guidance as we can offer. They most definitely do not get money: hence, they are interns. Sometimes when they've really had to pitch in we get them lunch and coffees.

Oh my goodness, I cannot function without the interns. God bless them.

And, like gods, we do. Most of our members conduct workshops and talks according to our specialties, and we regularly go through their portfolios and help them figure out what to include, badger them to write and draw short stories that we advise on, and so forth. I chime in a lot on their layouts, but my workshop talk is usually about writing and thinking visually in story. Erika often takes the tough subject of how to promote your work online and at comics shows, filling orders, and many other networking points commercial artists need. Also, the 'terns watch how we go about getting jobs, handling them, the kinds of things we complain about, the importance of invoicing quickly—all the things a cartoonist would find out the hard way otherwise.

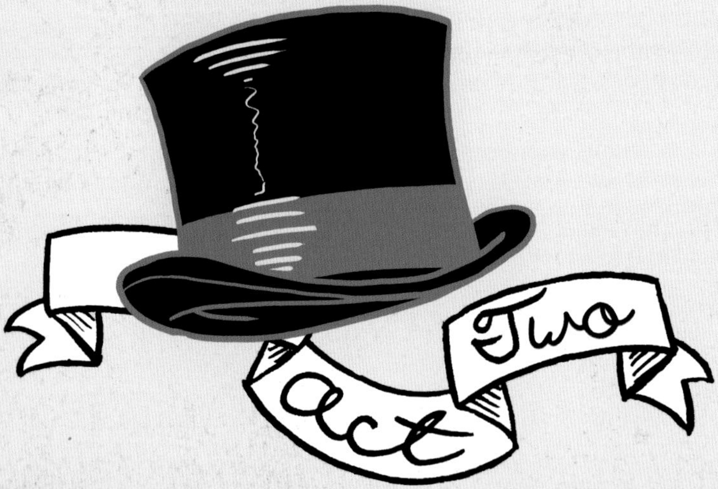
act Two

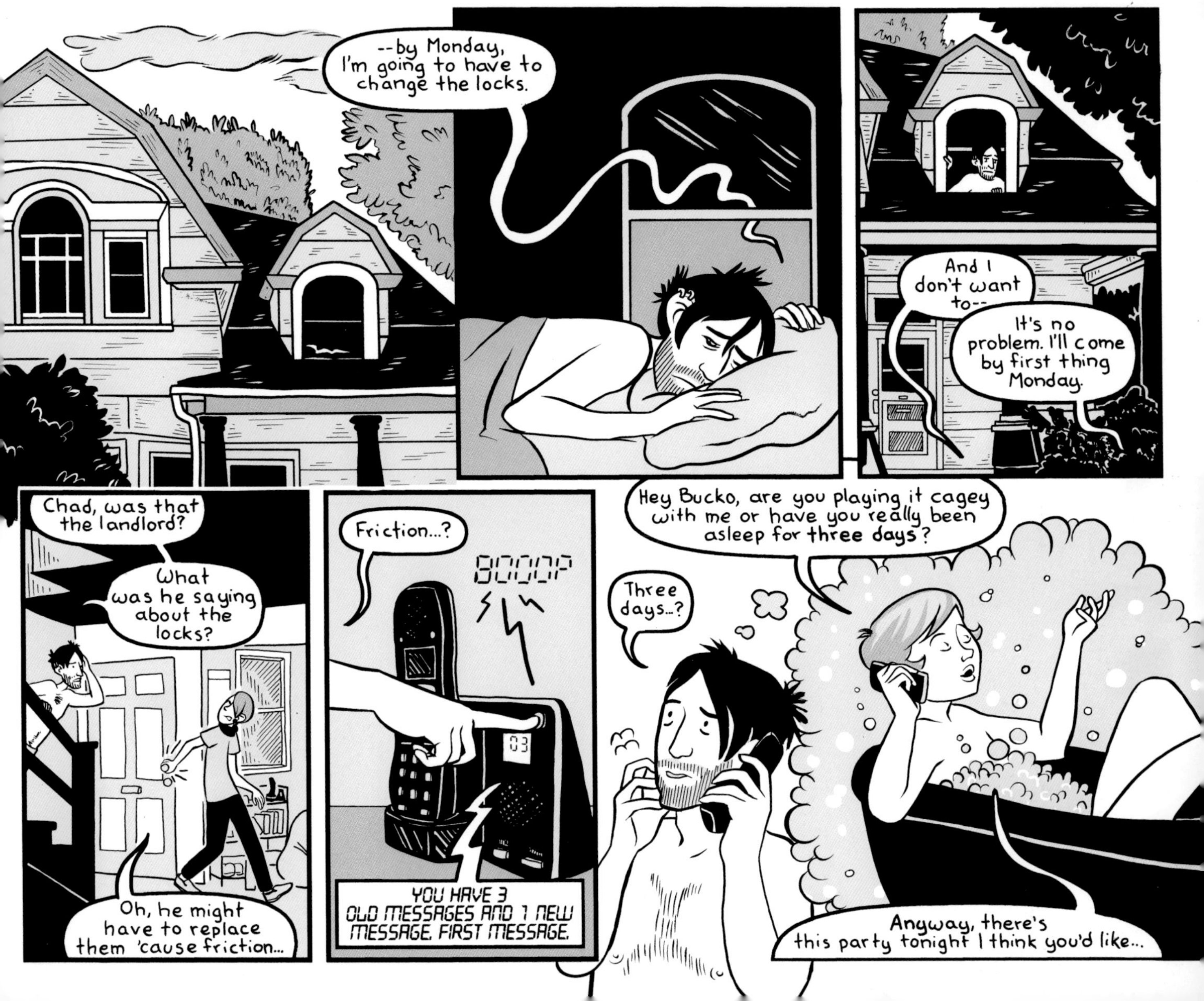
--by Monday, I'm going to have to change the locks.
And I don't want to--
It's no problem. I'll come by first thing Monday.
Chad, was that the landlord?
What was he saying about the locks?
Oh, he might have to replace them 'cause friction...
Friction...?
BOOOP
03
YOU HAVE 3 OLD MESSAGES AND 1 NEW MESSAGE. FIRST MESSAGE.
Hey Bucko, are you playing it cagey with me or have you really been asleep for three days?
Three days...?
Anyway, there's this party tonight I think you'd like...

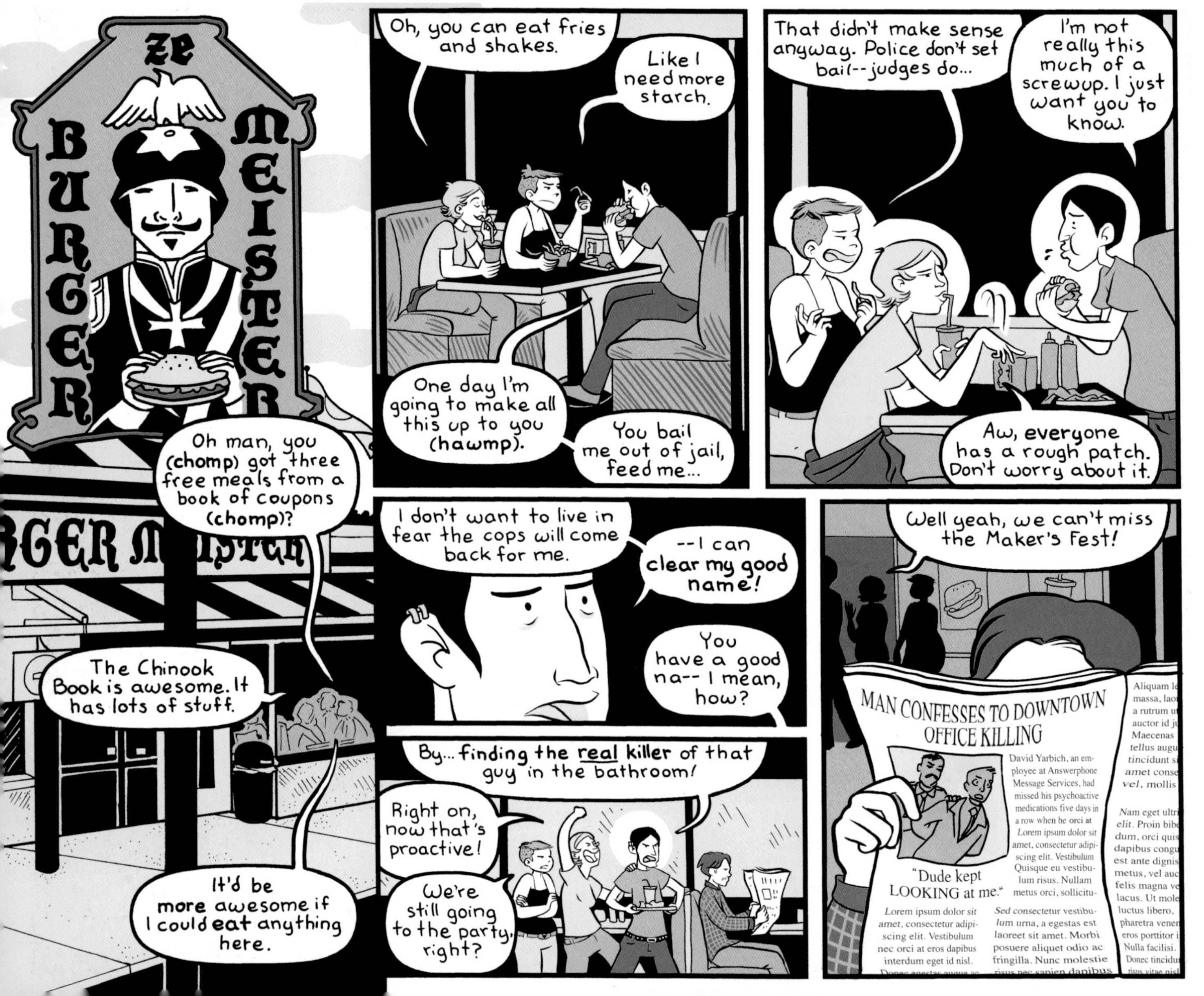
ZE
BURGER MEISTER
Oh man, you (chomp) got three free meals from a book of coupons (chomp)?
The Chinook Book is awesome. It has lots of stuff.
It'd be more awesome if I could eat anything here.
Oh, you can eat fries and shakes.
Like I need more starch.
One day I'm going to make all this up to you (hawmp).
You bail me out of jail, feed me...
That didn't make sense anyway. Police don't set bail--judges do...
I'm not really this much of a screwup. I just want you to know.
Aw, everyone has a rough patch. Don't worry about it.
I don't want to live in fear the cops will come back for me.
--I can clear my good name!
You have a good na-- I mean, how?
By... finding the real killer of that guy in the bathroom!
Right on, now that's proactive!
We're still going to the party, right?
Well yeah, we can't miss the Maker's Fest!
MAN CONFESSES TO DOWNTOWN OFFICE KILLING
David Yarbich, an employee at Answerphone Message Services, had missed his psychoactive medications five days in a row when he orci at
"Dude kept LOOKING at me."

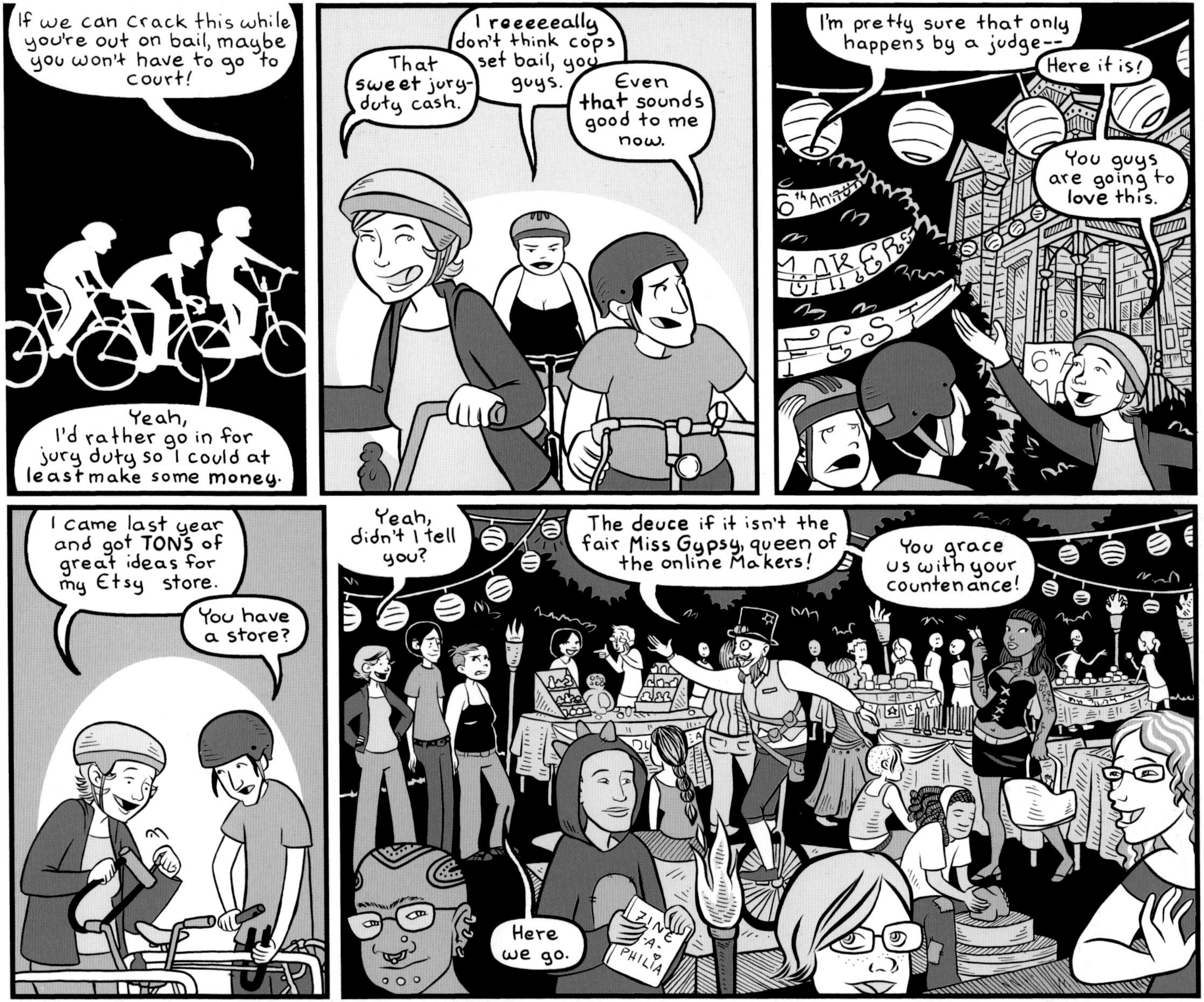

If we can crack this while you're out on bail, maybe you won't have to go to court!
Yeah, I'd rather go in for jury duty so I could at least make some money.
That sweet jury-duty cash.
I reeeeeally don't think cops set bail, you guys.
Even that sounds good to me now.
I'm pretty sure that only happens by a judge--
Here it is!
You guys are going to love this.
I came last year and got TONS of great ideas for my Etsy store.
You have a store?
Yeah, didn't I tell you?
The deuce if it isn't the fair Miss Gypsy, queen of the online Makers!
You grace us with your countenance!
Here we go.
ZINE-A-PHILIA

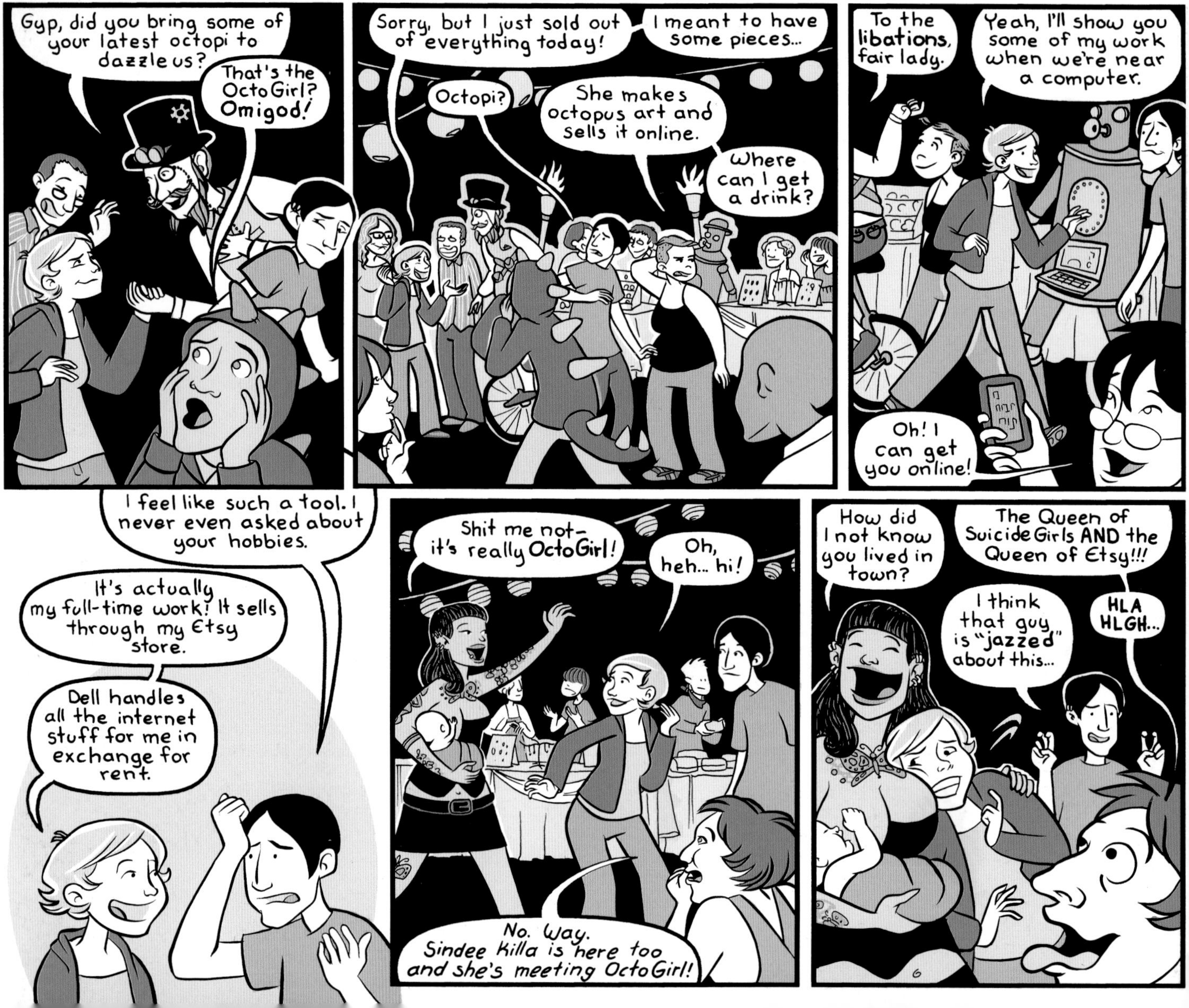
Gyp, did you bring some of your latest octopi to dazzle us?
That's the OctoGirl? Omigod!
Sorry, but I just sold out of everything today!
I meant to have some pieces...
Octopi?
She makes octopus art and sells it online.
Where can I get a drink?
To the libations, fair lady.
Yeah, I'll show you some of my work when we're near a computer.
Oh! I can get you online!
I feel like such a tool. I never even asked about your hobbies.
It's actually my full-time work! It sells through my Etsy store.
Dell handles all the internet stuff for me in exchange for rent.
Shit me not—it's really OctoGirl!
Oh, heh... hi!
No. Way. Sindee Killa is here too and she's meeting OctoGirl!
How did I not know you lived in town?
The Queen of SuicideGirls AND the Queen of Etsy!!!
I think that guy is "jazzed" about this...
HLA HLGH...
6

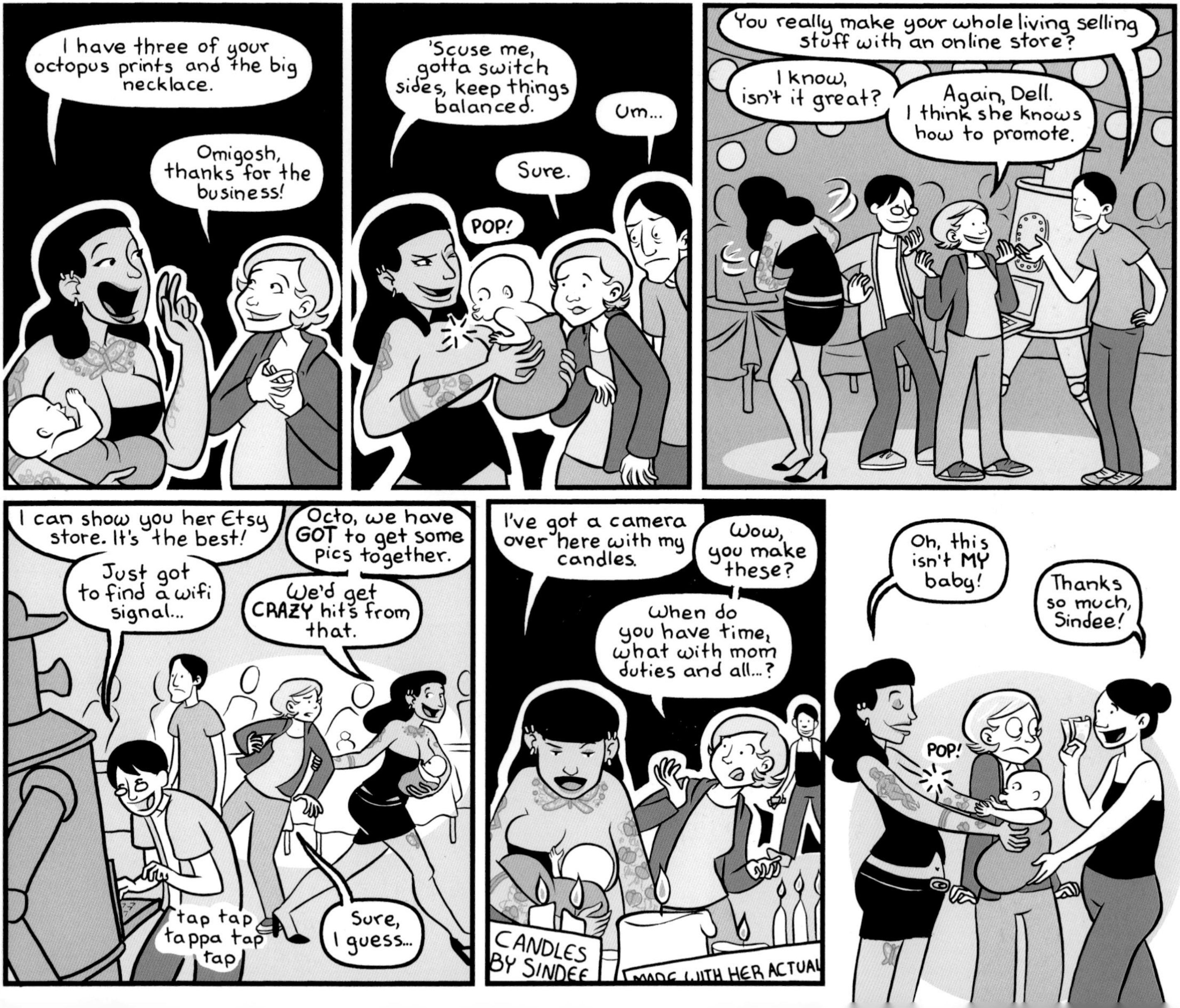

I have three of your octopus prints and the big necklace.
Omigosh, thanks for the business!
'Scuse me, gotta switch sides, keep things balanced.
Um...
Sure.
POP!
You really make your whole living selling stuff with an online store?
I know, isn't it great?
Again, Dell. I think she knows how to promote.
I can show you her Etsy store. It's the best!
Octo, we have GOT to get some pics together.
Just got to find a wifi signal...
We'd get CRAZY hits from that.
tap tap tappa tap tap
Sure, I guess...
I've got a camera over here with my candles.
Wow, you make these?
When do you have time, what with mom duties and all...?
CANDLES BY SINDEE
MADE WITH HER ACTUAL
Oh, this isn't MY baby!
Thanks so much, Sindee!
POP!

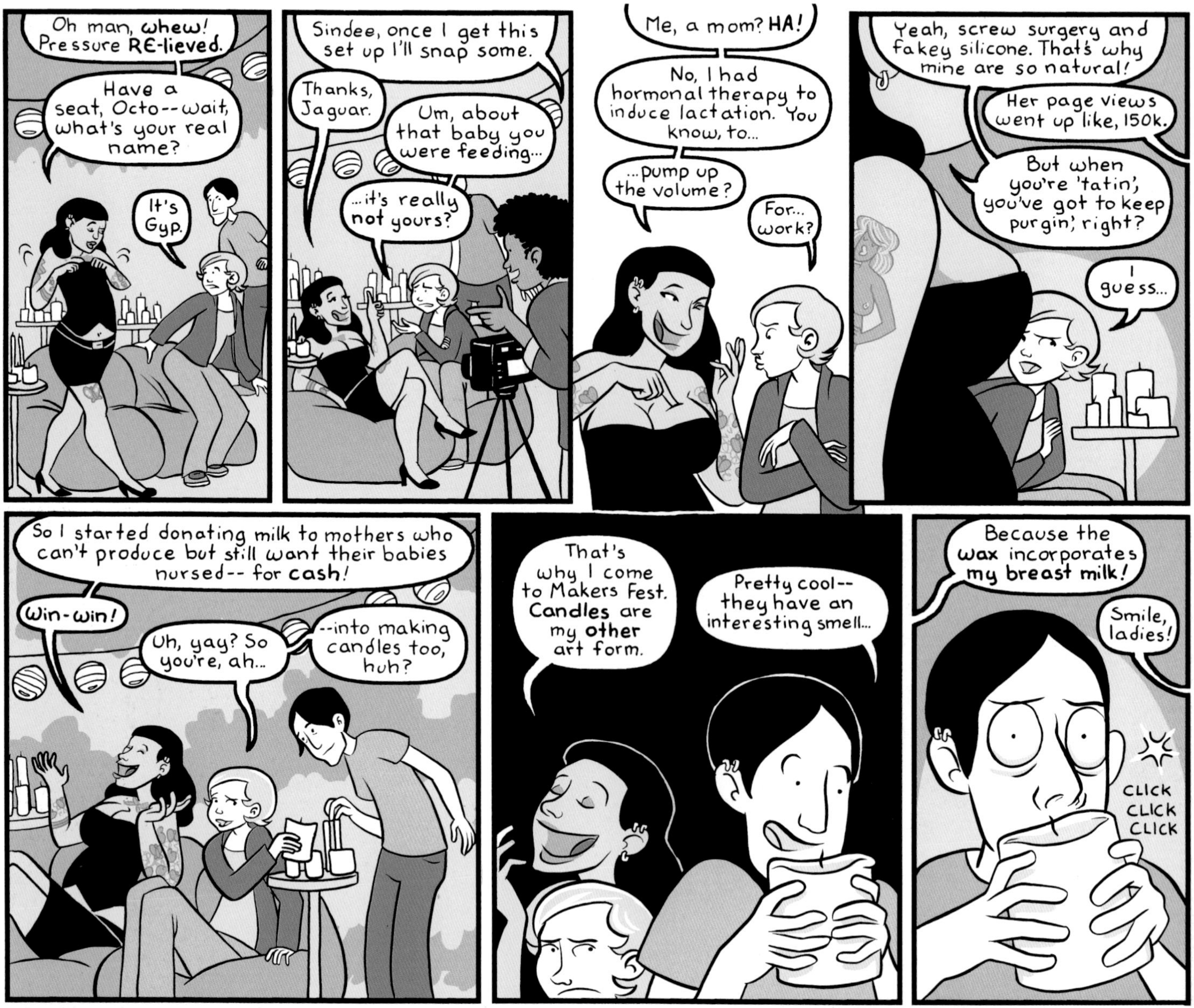

Oh man, **whew**! Pressure **RE-lieved**.
Have a seat, Octo--wait, what's your real name?
It's Gyp.
Sindee, once I get this set up I'll snap some.
Thanks, Jaguar.
Um, about that baby you were feeding...
...it's really **not** yours?
Me, a mom? **HA**!
No, I had hormonal therapy to induce lactation. You know, to...
...pump up the volume?
For... work?
Yeah, screw surgery and fakey silicone. That's why mine are so natural!
Her page views went up like, 150k.
But when you're 'tatin', you've got to keep purgin', right?
I guess...
So I started donating milk to mothers who can't produce but still want their babies nursed-- for **cash**!
Win-win!
Uh, yay? So you're, ah...
--into making candles too, huh?
That's why I come to Makers Fest. **Candles** are my **other** art form.
Pretty cool-- they have an interesting smell...
Because the **wax** incorporates **my breast milk**!
Smile, ladies!
CLICK CLICK CLICK

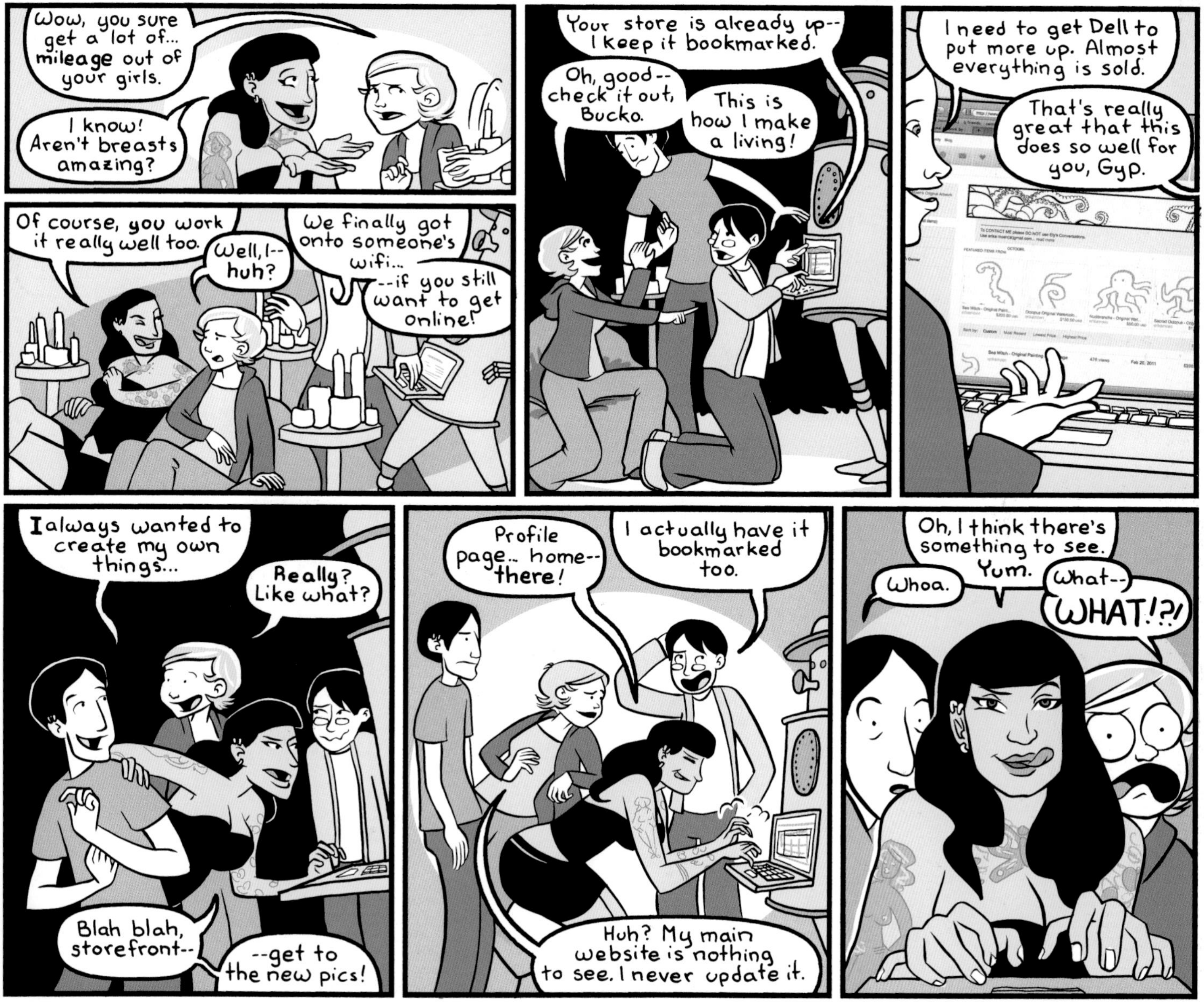
Wow, you sure get a lot of... mileage out of your girls.
I know! Aren't breasts amazing?
Your store is already up-- I keep it bookmarked.
Oh, good-- check it out, Bucko.
This is how I make a living!
I need to get Dell to put more up. Almost everything is sold.
That's really great that this does so well for you, Gyp.
Of course, you work it really well too.
Well, I-- huh?
We finally got onto someone's wifi...
--if you still want to get online!
I always wanted to create my own things...
Really? Like what?
Blah blah, storefront--
--get to the new pics!
Profile page... home-- there!
I actually have it bookmarked too.
Huh? My main website is nothing to see. I never update it.
Oh, I think there's something to see. Yum.
Whoa.
What-- WHAT!?!

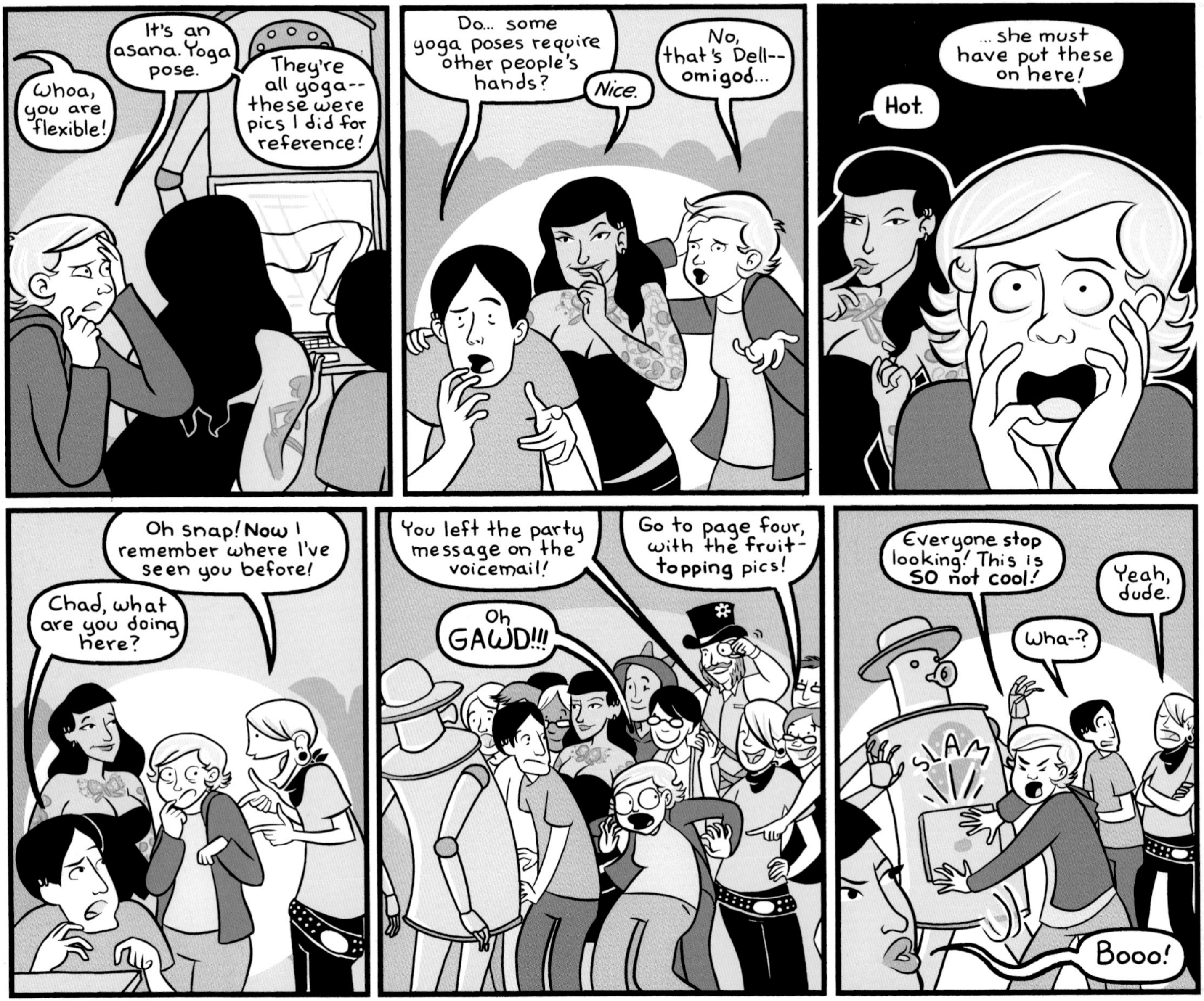
Whoa, you are flexible!
It's an asana. Yoga pose.
They're all yoga--these were pics I did for reference!
Do... some yoga poses require other people's hands?
Nice.
No, that's Dell--omigod...
Hot.
...she must have put these on here!
Oh snap! Now I remember where I've seen you before!
Chad, what are you doing here?
You left the party message on the voicemail!
Go to page four, with the fruit-topping pics!
Oh GAWD!!!
Everyone stop looking! This is SO not cool!
Yeah, dude.
Wha--?
SLAM
Booo!

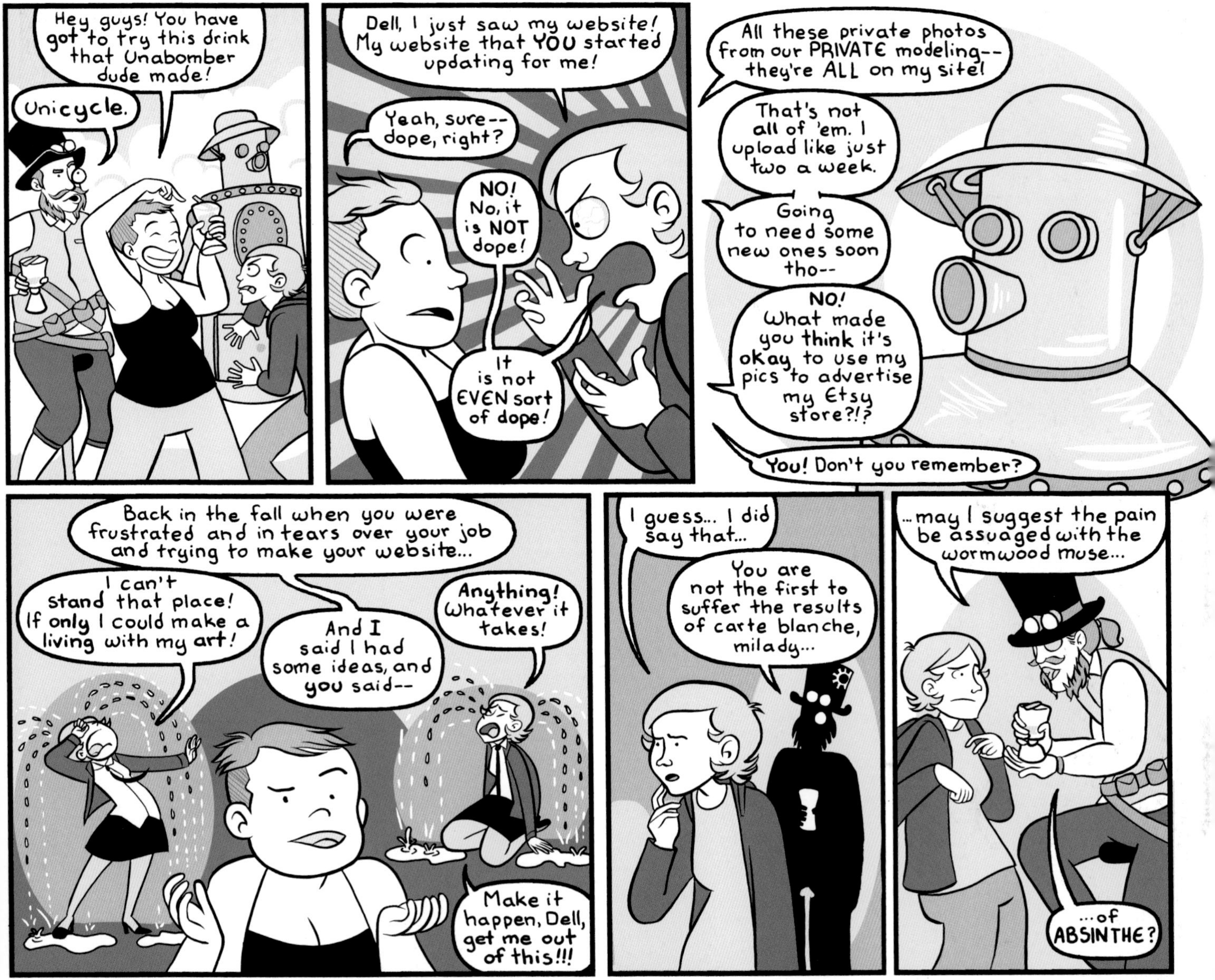
Hey guys! You have got to try this drink that Unabomber dude made!
Unicycle.
Dell, I just saw my website! My website that YOU started updating for me!
Yeah, sure-- dope, right?
NO! No, it is NOT dope!
It is not EVEN sort of dope!
All these private photos from our PRIVATE modeling-- they're ALL on my site!
That's not all of 'em. I upload like just two a week.
Going to need some new ones soon tho--
NO! What made you think it's okay to use my pics to advertise my Etsy store?!?
You! Don't you remember?
Back in the fall when you were frustrated and in tears over your job and trying to make your website...
I can't stand that place! If only I could make a living with my art!
And I said I had some ideas, and you said--
Anything! Whatever it takes!
Make it happen, Dell, get me out of this!!!
I guess... I did say that...
You are not the first to suffer the results of carte blanche, milady...
...may I suggest the pain be assuaged with the wormwood muse...
...of ABSINTHE?

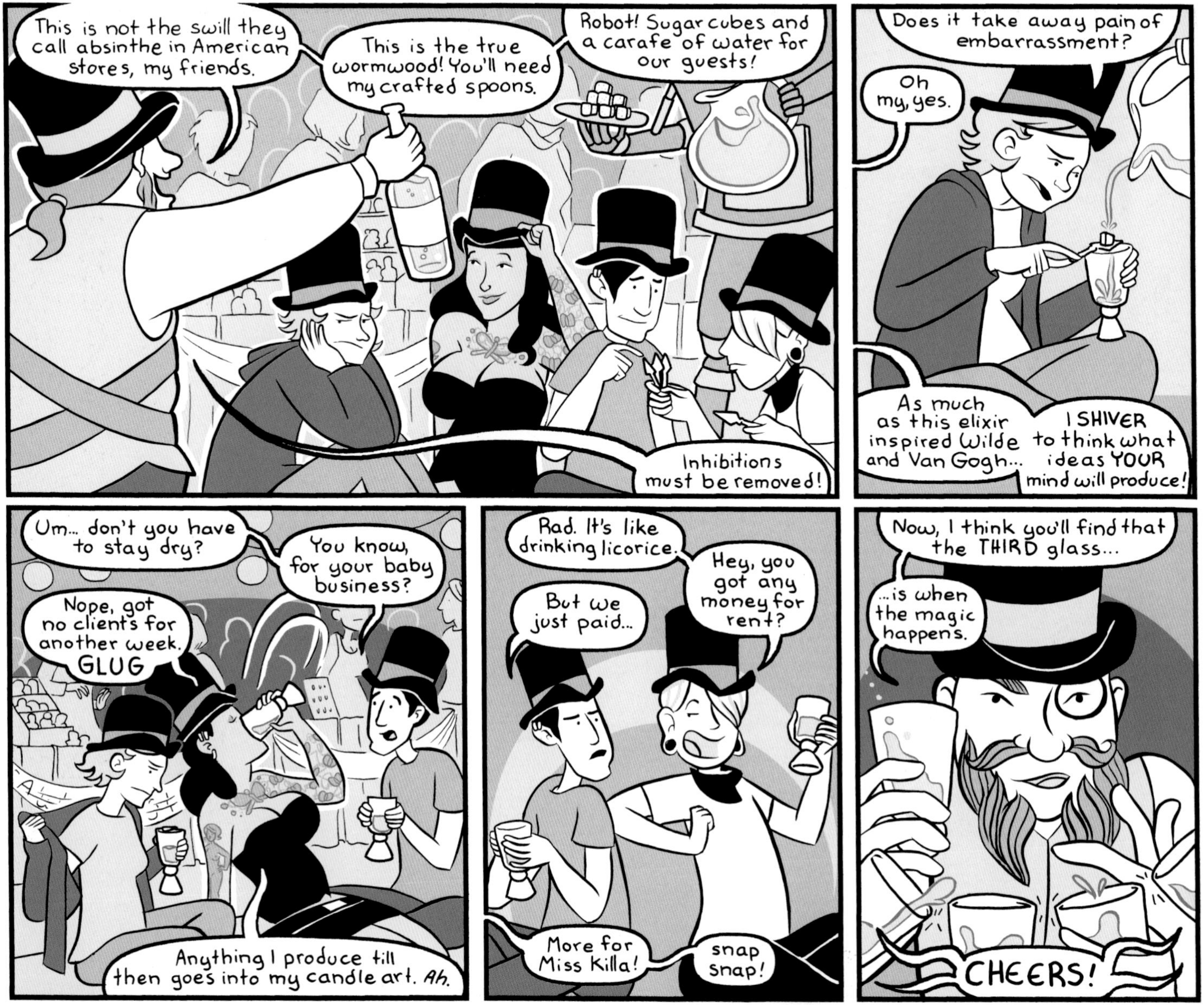

This is not the swill they call absinthe in American stores, my friends.
This is the true wormwood! You'll need my crafted spoons.
Robot! Sugar cubes and a carafe of water for our guests!
Inhibitions must be removed!
Does it take away pain of embarrassment?
Oh my, yes.
As much as this elixir inspired Wilde and Van Gogh...
I SHIVER to think what ideas YOUR mind will produce!
Um... don't you have to stay dry?
You know, for your baby business?
Nope, got no clients for another week.
GLUG
Anything I produce till then goes into my candle art. Ah.
Rad. It's like drinking licorice.
Hey, you got any money for rent?
But we just paid...
More for Miss Killa!
snap snap!
Now, I think you'll find that the THIRD glass...
...is when the magic happens.
CHEERS!

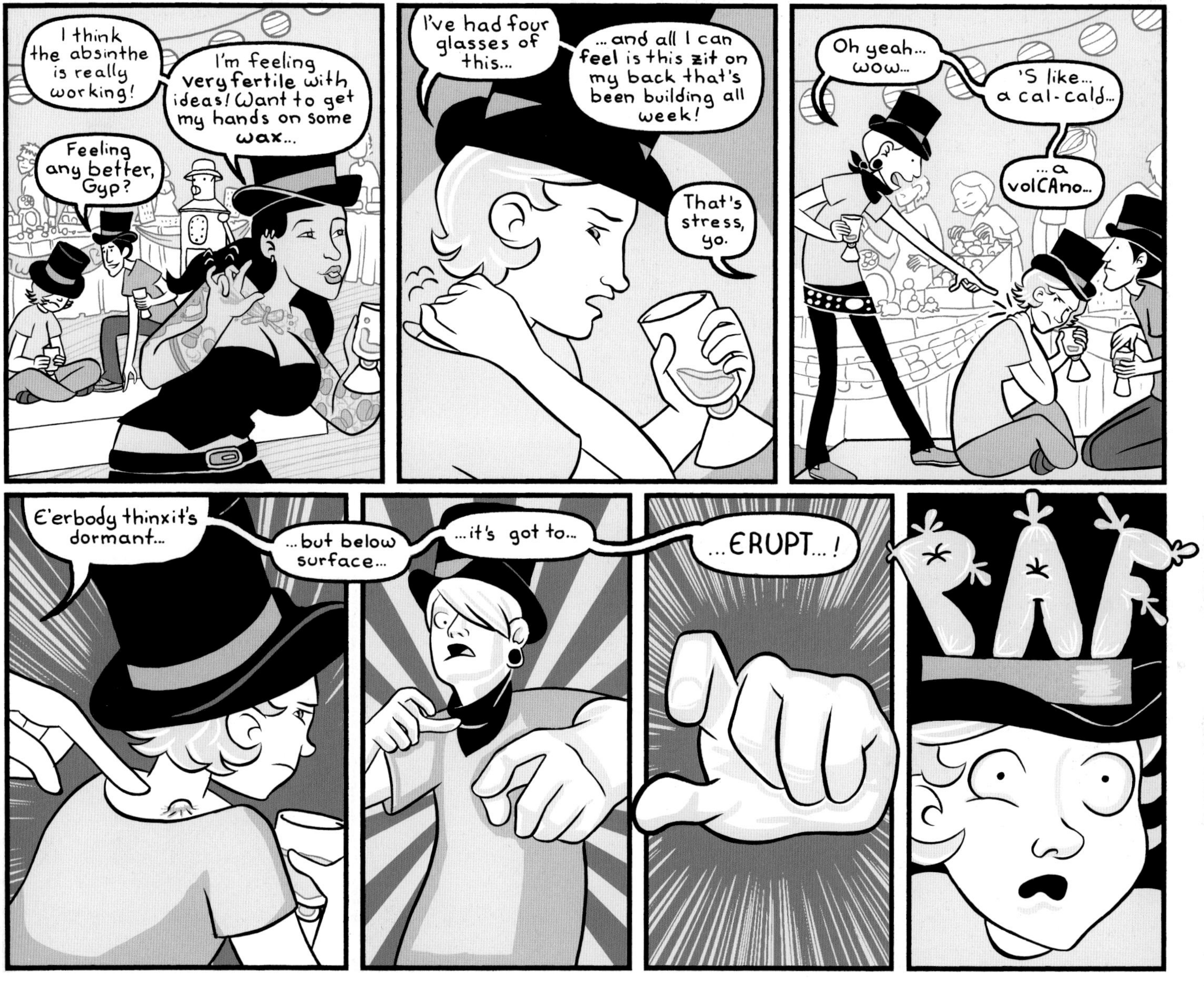
I think the absinthe is really working!
I'm feeling very fertile with ideas! Want to get my hands on some wax...
Feeling any better, Gyp?
I've had four glasses of this...
... and all I can feel is this zit on my back that's been building all week!
That's stress, yo.
Oh yeah... wow...
'S like... a cal-cald...
... a volCAno...
E'erbody thinxit's dormant...
...but below surface...
...it's got to...
...ERUPT...!
PAF

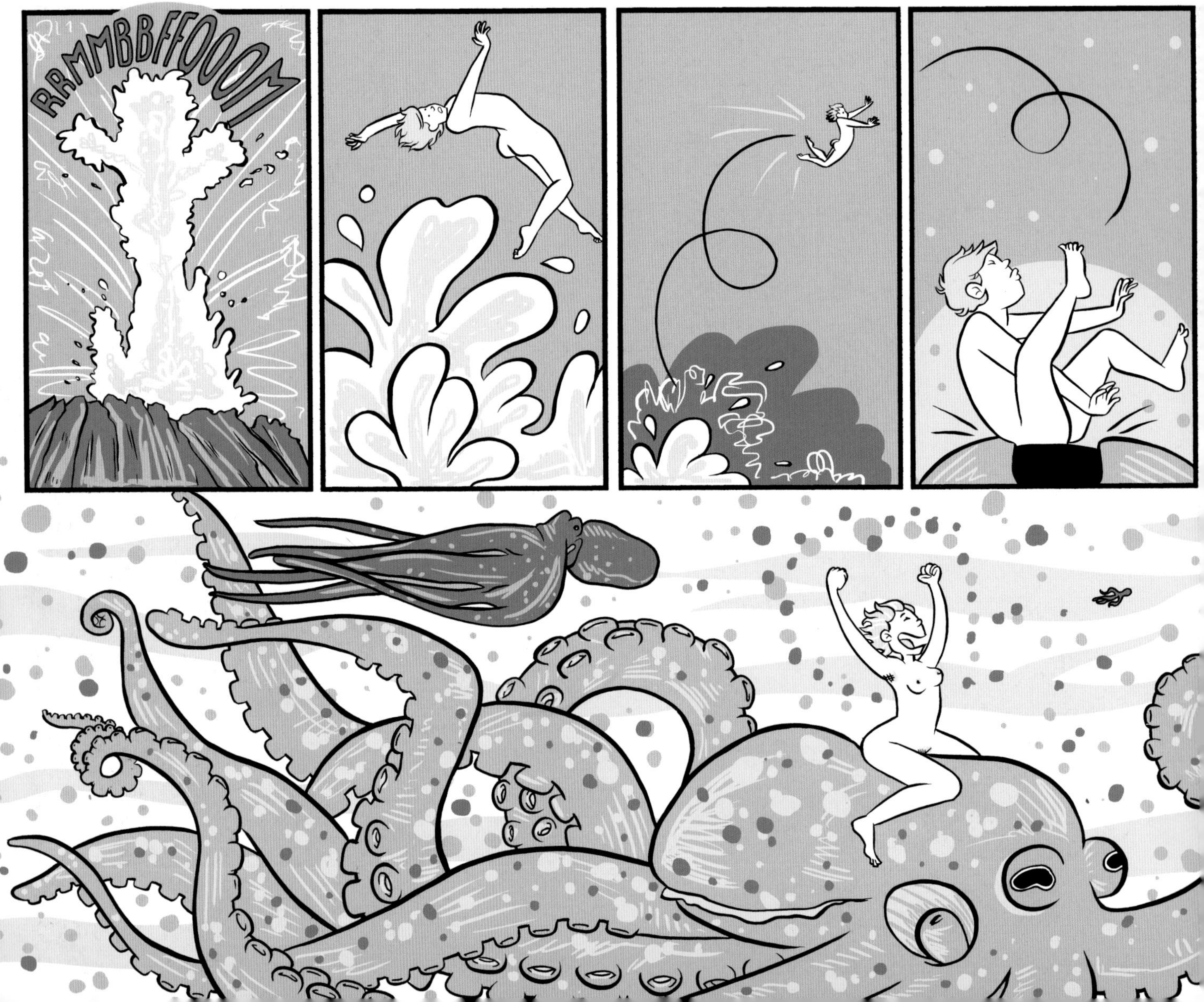
RRMMBBFFOOOM

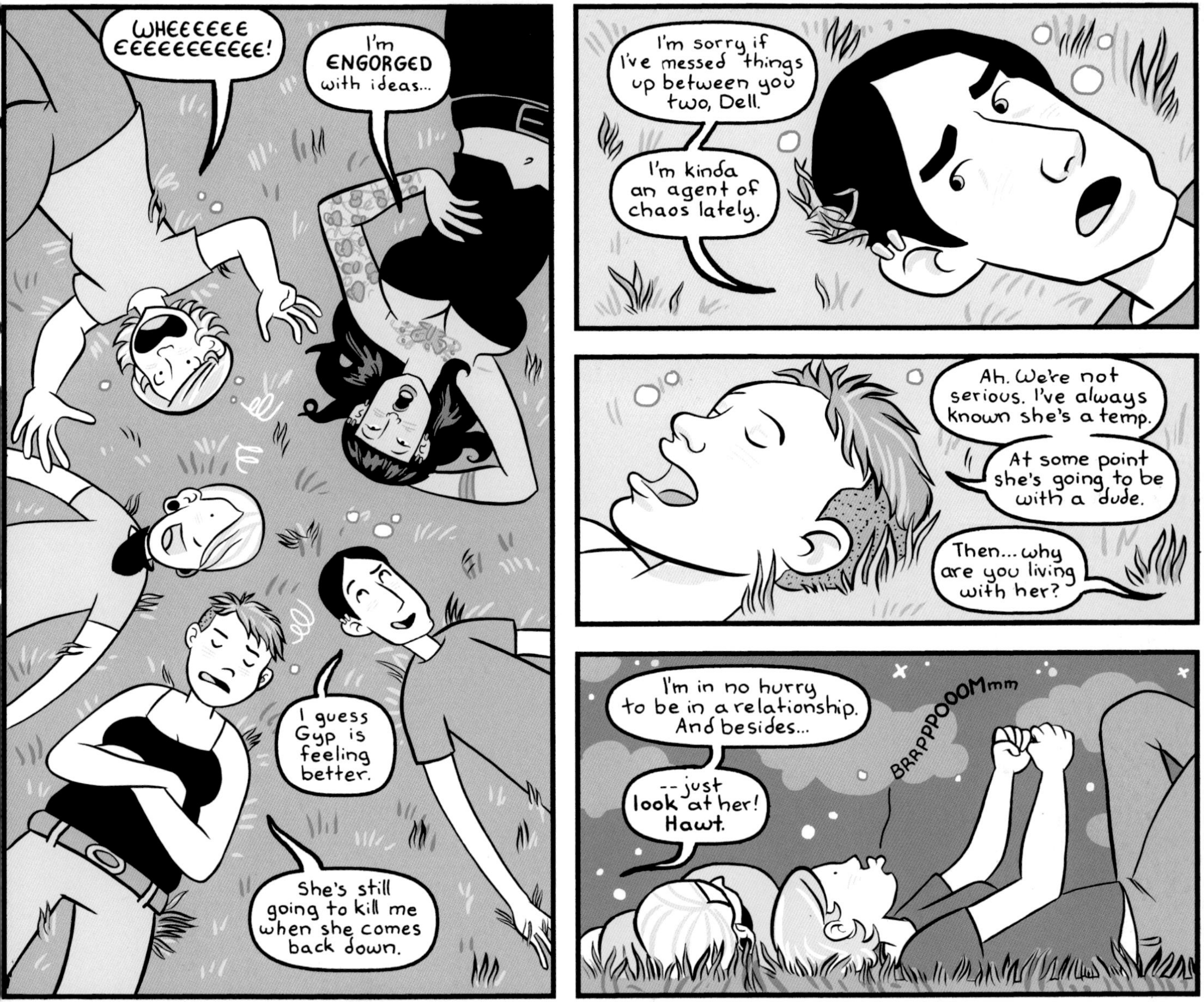
WHEEEEEE EEEEEEEEEEE!
I'm ENGORGED with ideas...
I guess Gyp is feeling better.
She's still going to kill me when she comes back down.
I'm sorry if I've messed things up between you two, Dell.
I'm kinda an agent of chaos lately.
Ah. We're not serious. I've always known she's a temp.
At some point she's going to be with a dude.
Then... why are you living with her?
I'm in no hurry to be in a relationship. And besides...
-- just look at her! Hawt.
BRRPPOOOMmm

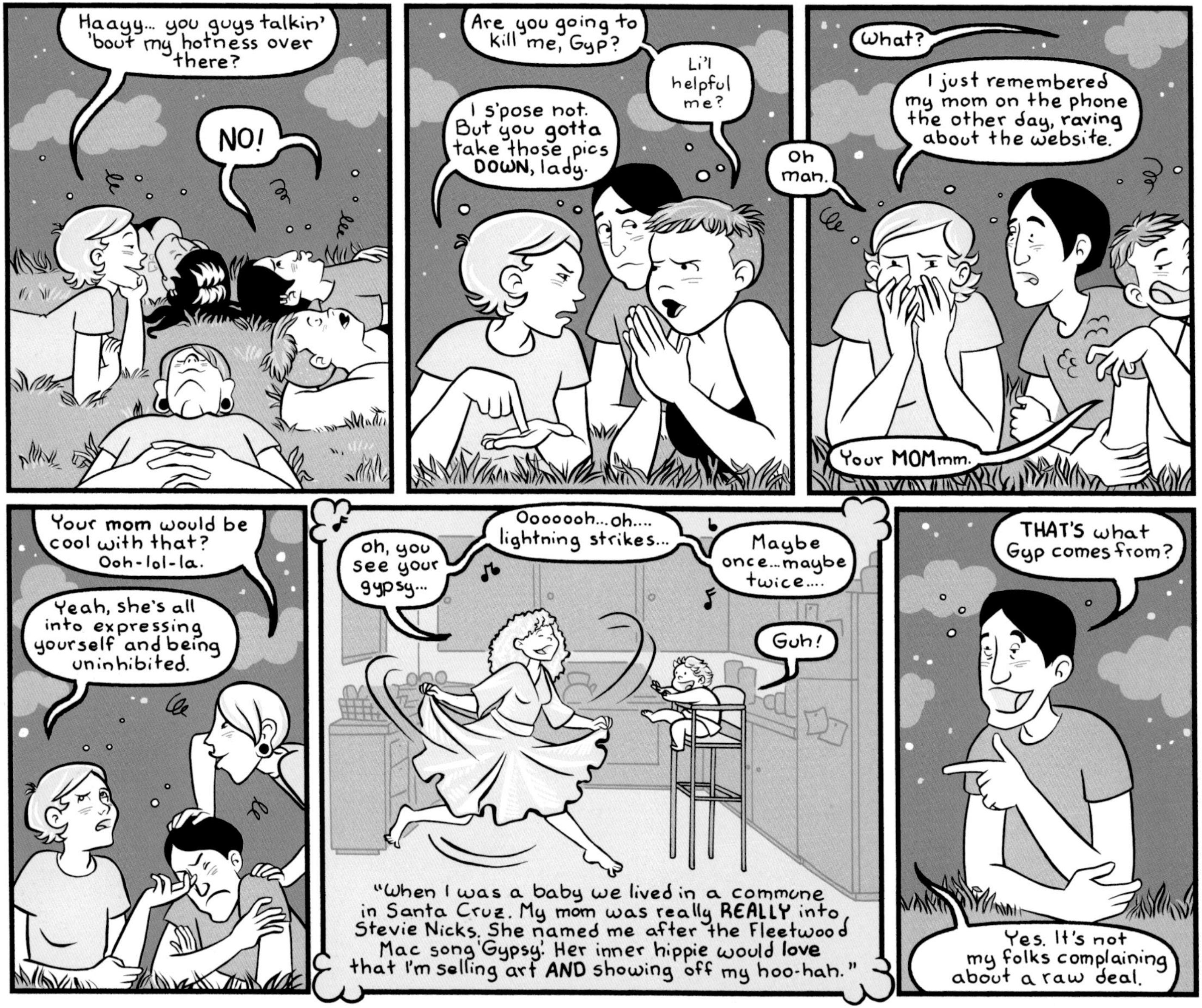
Haayy... you guys talkin' 'bout my hotness over there?
NO!
Are you going to kill me, Gyp?
Li'l helpful me?
I s'pose not. But you gotta take those pics DOWN, lady.
Oh man.
What?
I just remembered my mom on the phone the other day, raving about the website.
Your MOMmm.
Your mom would be cool with that? Ooh-lol-la.
Yeah, she's all into expressing yourself and being uninhibited.
oh, you see your gypsy...
Ooooooh...oh.... lightning strikes...
Maybe once...maybe twice....
Guh!
"When I was a baby we lived in a commune in Santa Cruz. My mom was really REALLY into Stevie Nicks. She named me after the Fleetwood Mac song 'Gypsy.' Her inner hippie would love that I'm selling art AND showing off my hoo-hah."
THAT'S what Gyp comes from?
Yes. It's not my folks complaining about a raw deal.

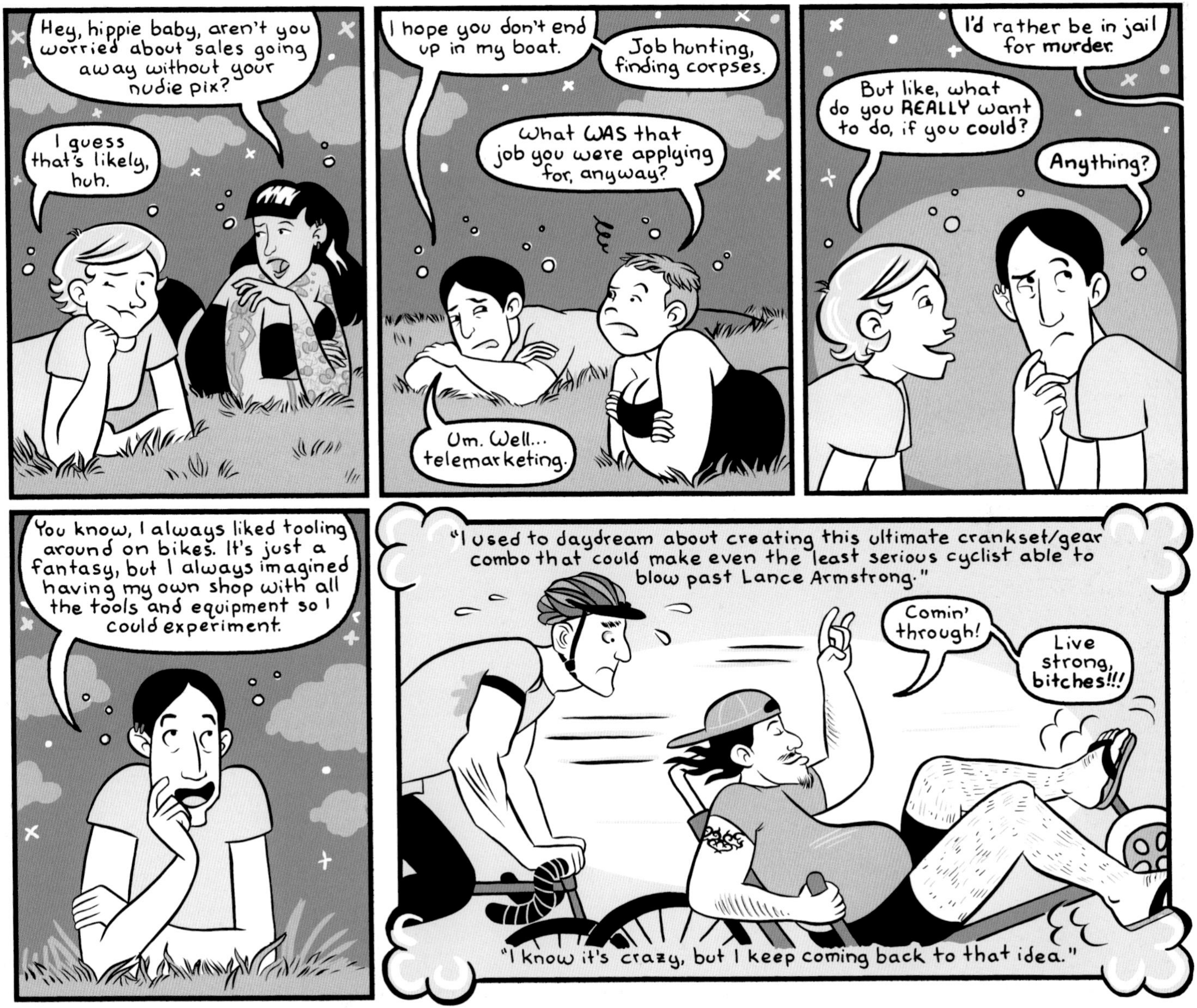

Hey, hippie baby, aren't you worried about sales going away without your nudie pix?
I guess that's likely, huh.
I hope you don't end up in my boat.
Job hunting, finding corpses.
What WAS that job you were applying for, anyway?
Um. Well... telemarketing.
I'd rather be in jail for murder.
But like, what do you REALLY want to do, if you could?
Anything?
You know, I always liked tooling around on bikes. It's just a fantasy, but I always imagined having my own shop with all the tools and equipment so I could experiment.
"I used to daydream about creating this ultimate crankset/gear combo that could make even the least serious cyclist able to blow past Lance Armstrong."
Comin' through!
Live strong, bitches!!!
"I know it's crazy, but I keep coming back to that idea."

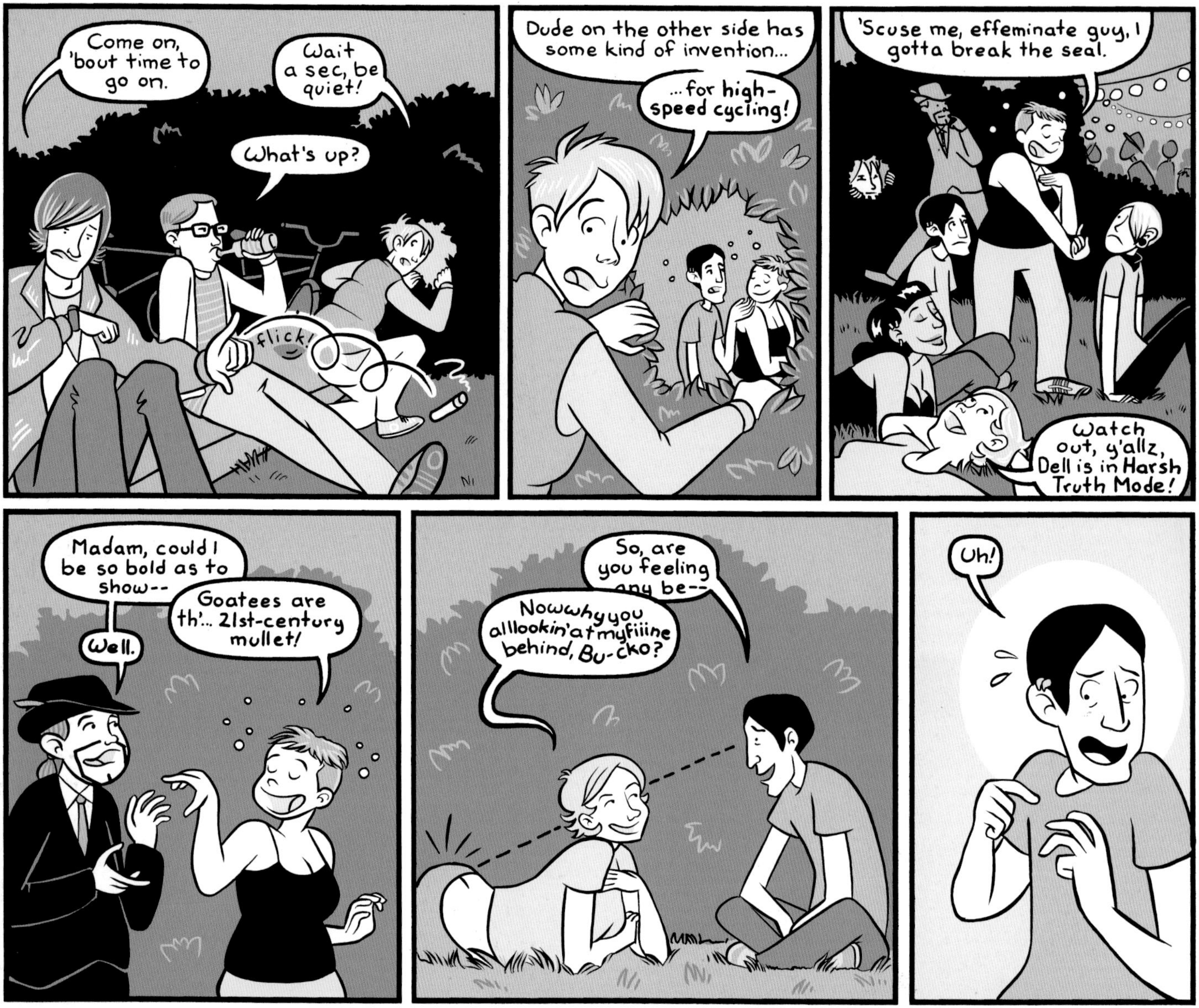

Come on, 'bout time to go on.
Wait a sec, be quiet!
What's up?
flick!
Dude on the other side has some kind of invention...
...for high-speed cycling!
'Scuse me, effeminate guy, I gotta break the seal.
Watch out, y'allz, Dell is in Harsh Truth Mode!
Madam, could I be so bold as to show--
Well.
Goatees are th'... 21st-century mullet!
So, are you feeling any be--
Nowwhyyou alllookin'atmyfiiine behind, Bu-cko?
Uh!

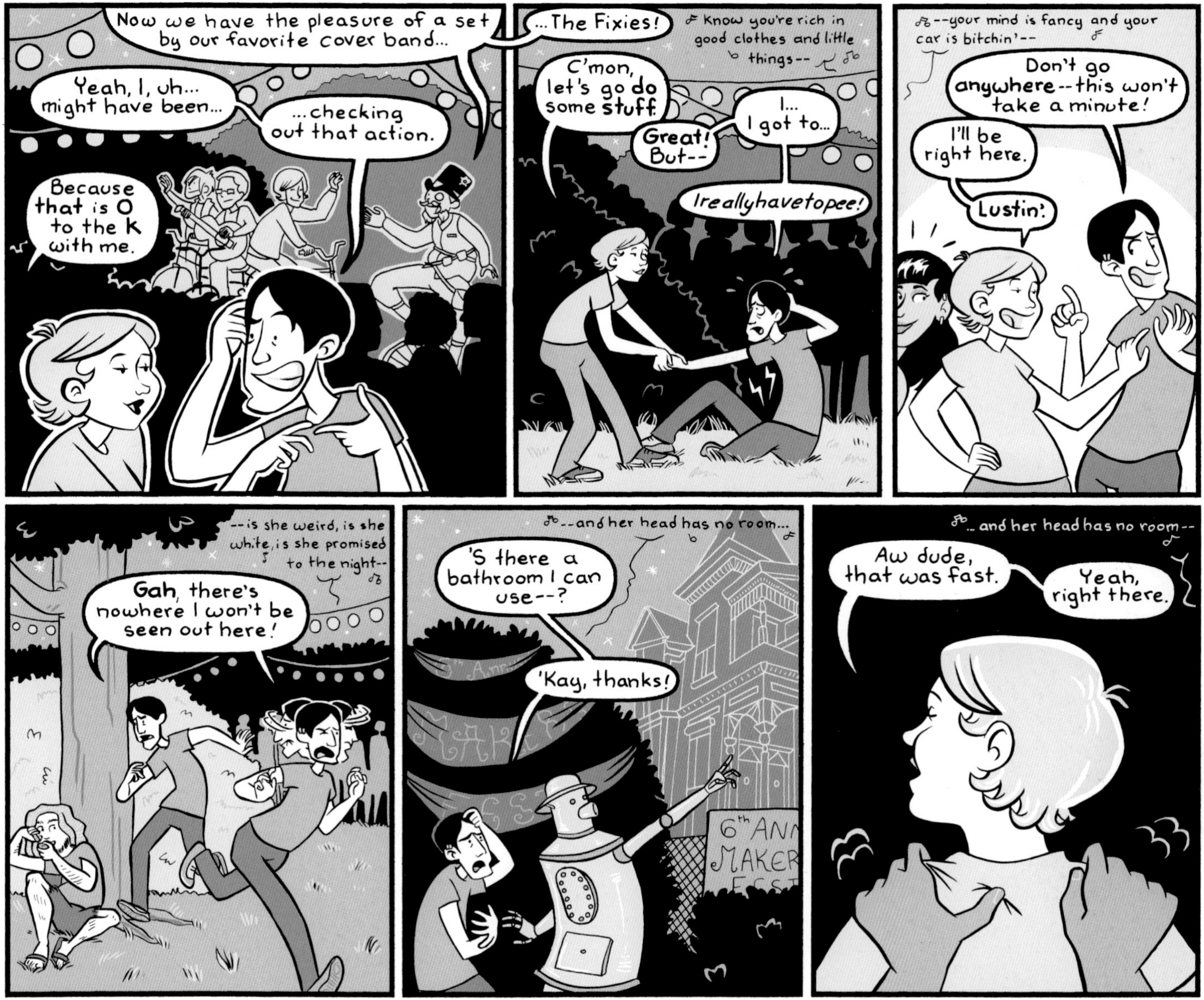
Now we have the pleasure of a set by our favorite cover band...
...The Fixies!
Yeah, I, uh... might have been...
...checking out that action.
Because that is O to the K with me.
Know you're rich in good clothes and little things--
C'mon, let's go do some stuff.
Great! But--
I... I got to...
Ireallyhavetopee!
--your mind is fancy and your car is bitchin'--
Don't go anywhere--this won't take a minute!
I'll be right here.
Lustin'.
--is she weird, is she white, is she promised to the night--
Gah, there's nowhere I won't be seen out here!
--and her head has no room...
'S there a bathroom I can use--?
'Kay, thanks!
6th ANN MAKER FEST
... and her head has no room--
Aw dude, that was fast.
Yeah, right there.

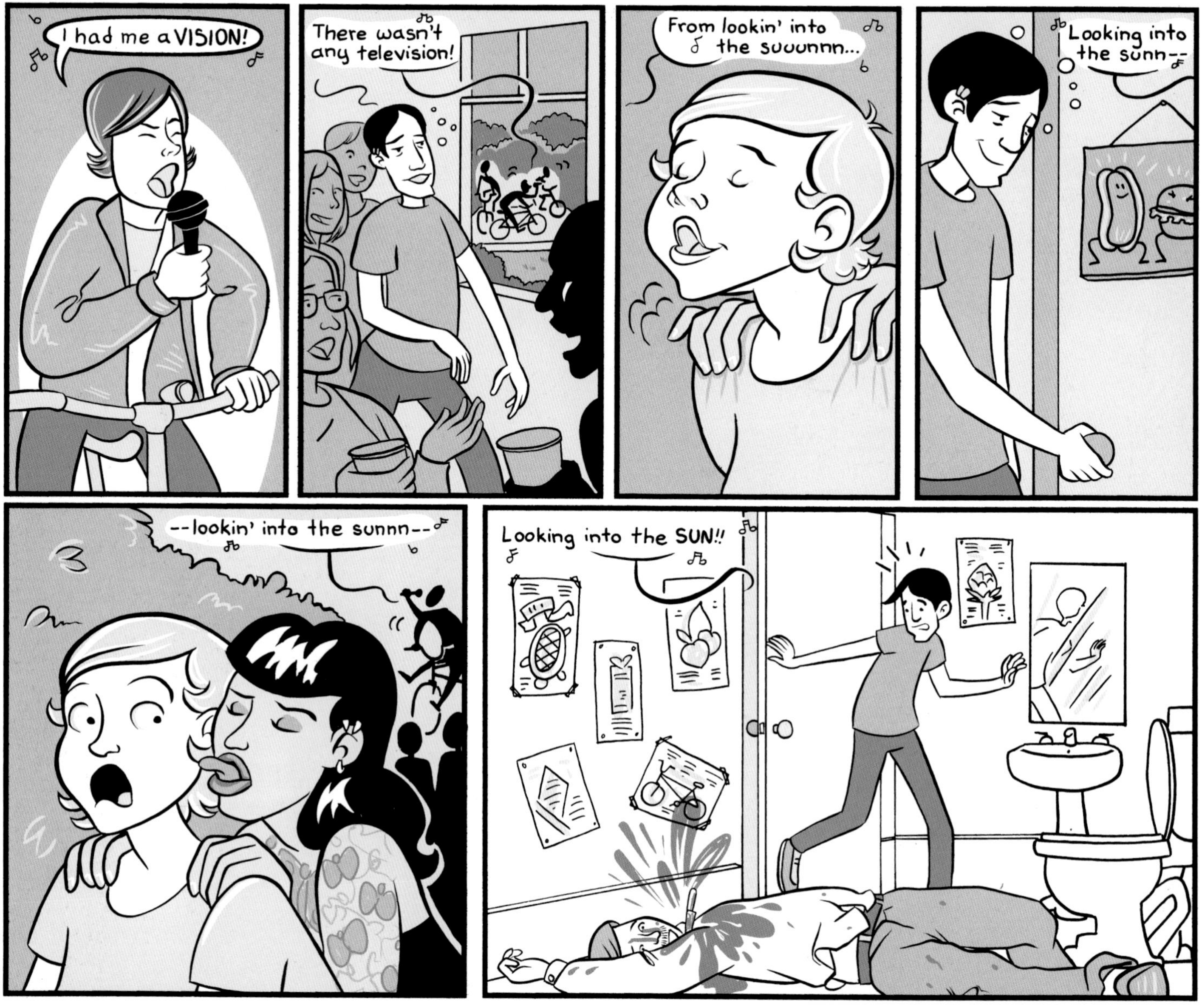
I had me a VISION!
There wasn't any television!
From lookin' into the suuunnn...
Looking into the sunn--
--lookin' into the sunnn--
Looking into the SUN!!

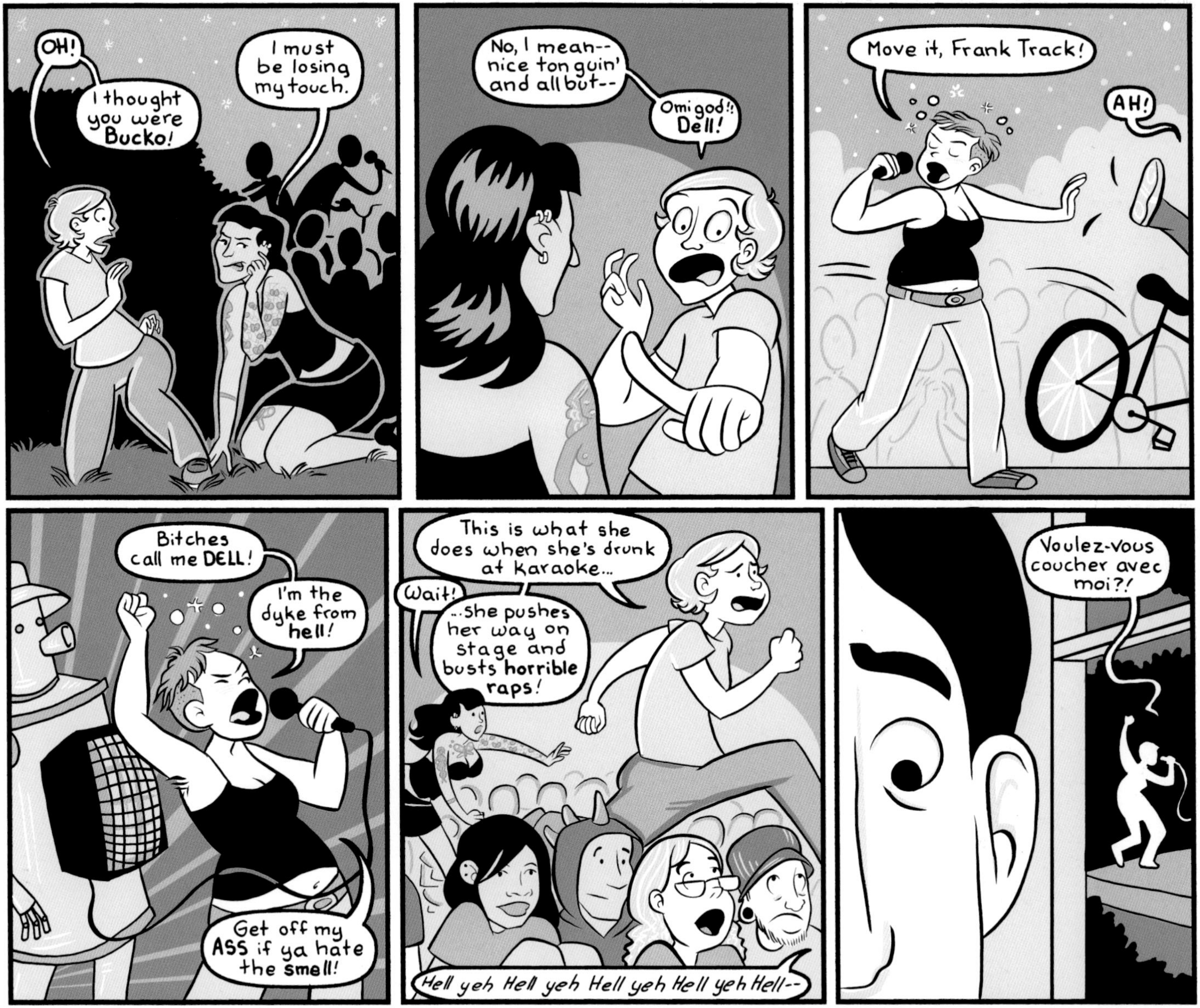
OH!
I thought you were Bucko!
I must be losing my touch.
No, I mean-- nice ton guin' and all but--
Omigod!! Dell!
Move it, Frank Track!
AH!
Bitches call me DELL!
I'm the dyke from hell!
Get off my ASS if ya hate the smell!
This is what she does when she's drunk at karaoke...
Wait!
...she pushes her way on stage and busts horrible raps!
Hell yeh Hell yeh Hell yeh Hell yeh Hell--
Voulez-vous coucher avec moi?!

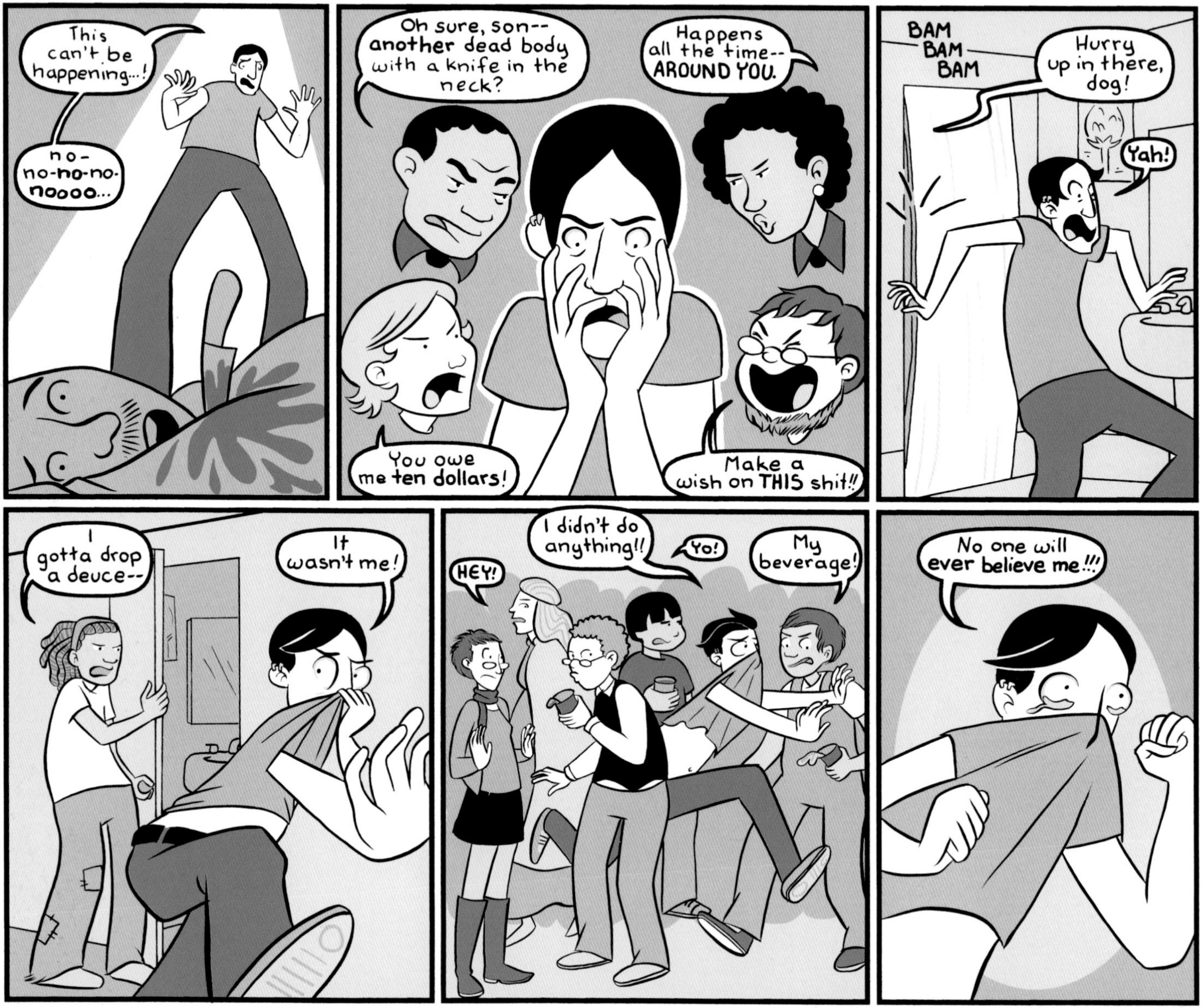
This can't be happening...!
no-no-no-no-noooo...
Oh sure, son-- another dead body with a knife in the neck?
Happens all the time-- AROUND YOU.
You owe me ten dollars!
Make a wish on THIS shit!!
BAM BAM BAM
Hurry up in there, dog!
Yah!
I gotta drop a deuce--
It wasn't me!
HEY!
I didn't do anything!!
YO!
My beverage!
No one will ever believe me!!!

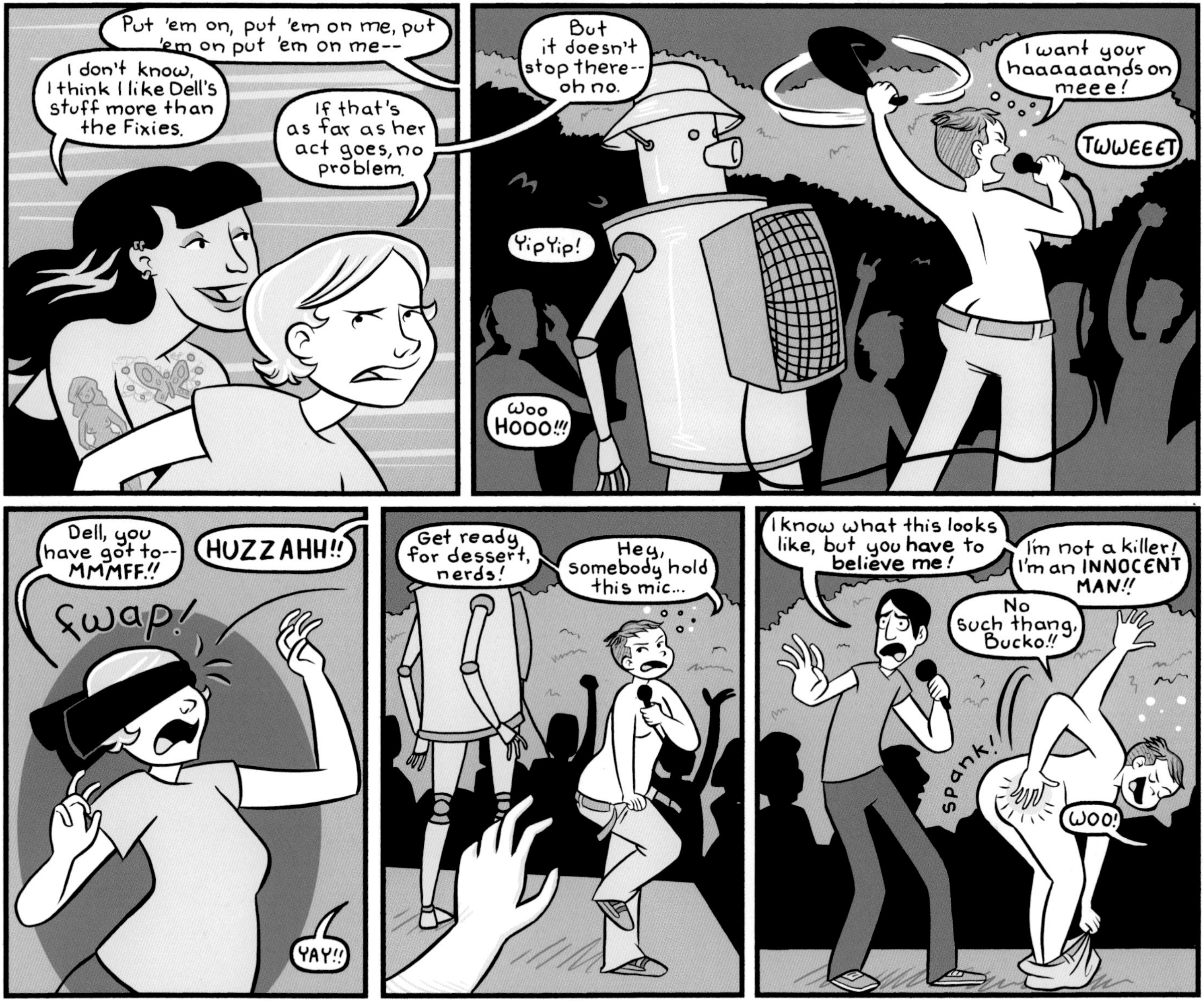

Put 'em on, put 'em on me, put 'em on put 'em on me--
I don't know, I think I like Dell's stuff more than the Fixies.
If that's as far as her act goes, no problem.
But it doesn't stop there--oh no.
I want your haaaaaands on meee!
TWWEEET
YipYip!
Woo HOOO!!!
Dell, you have got to--MMMFF!!
HUZZAHH!!
fwap!
YAY!!
Get ready for dessert, nerds!
Hey, somebody hold this mic...
I know what this looks like, but you have to believe me!
I'm not a killer! I'm an INNOCENT MAN!!
No such thang, Bucko!!
spank!
WOO!

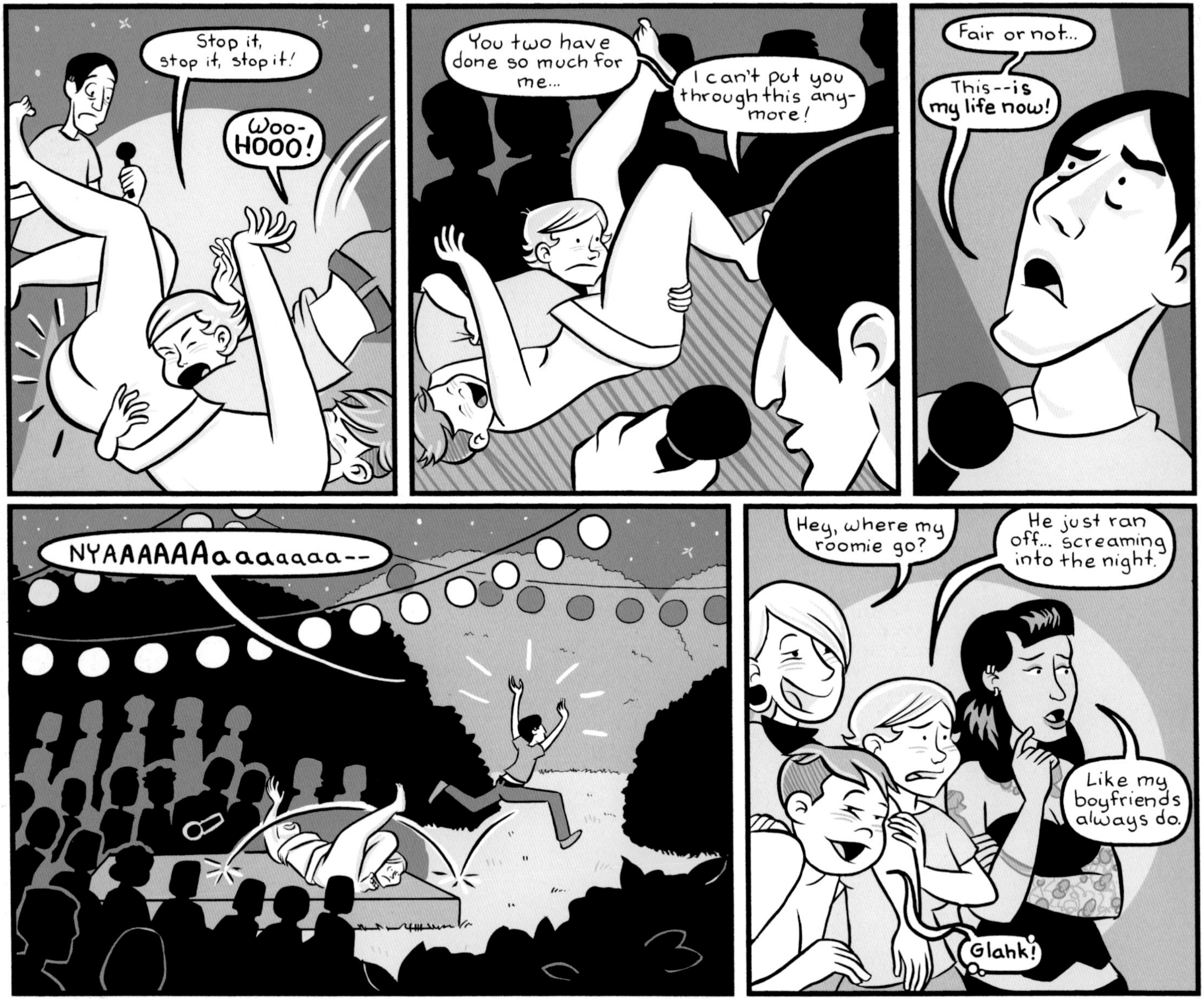
Stop it, stop it, stop it!
Woo-HOOO!
You two have done so much for me...
I can't put you through this any-more!
Fair or not...
This--is my life now!
NYAAAAAAaaaaaa--
Hey, where my roomie go?
He just ran off... screaming into the night.
Like my boyfriends always do.
Glahk!

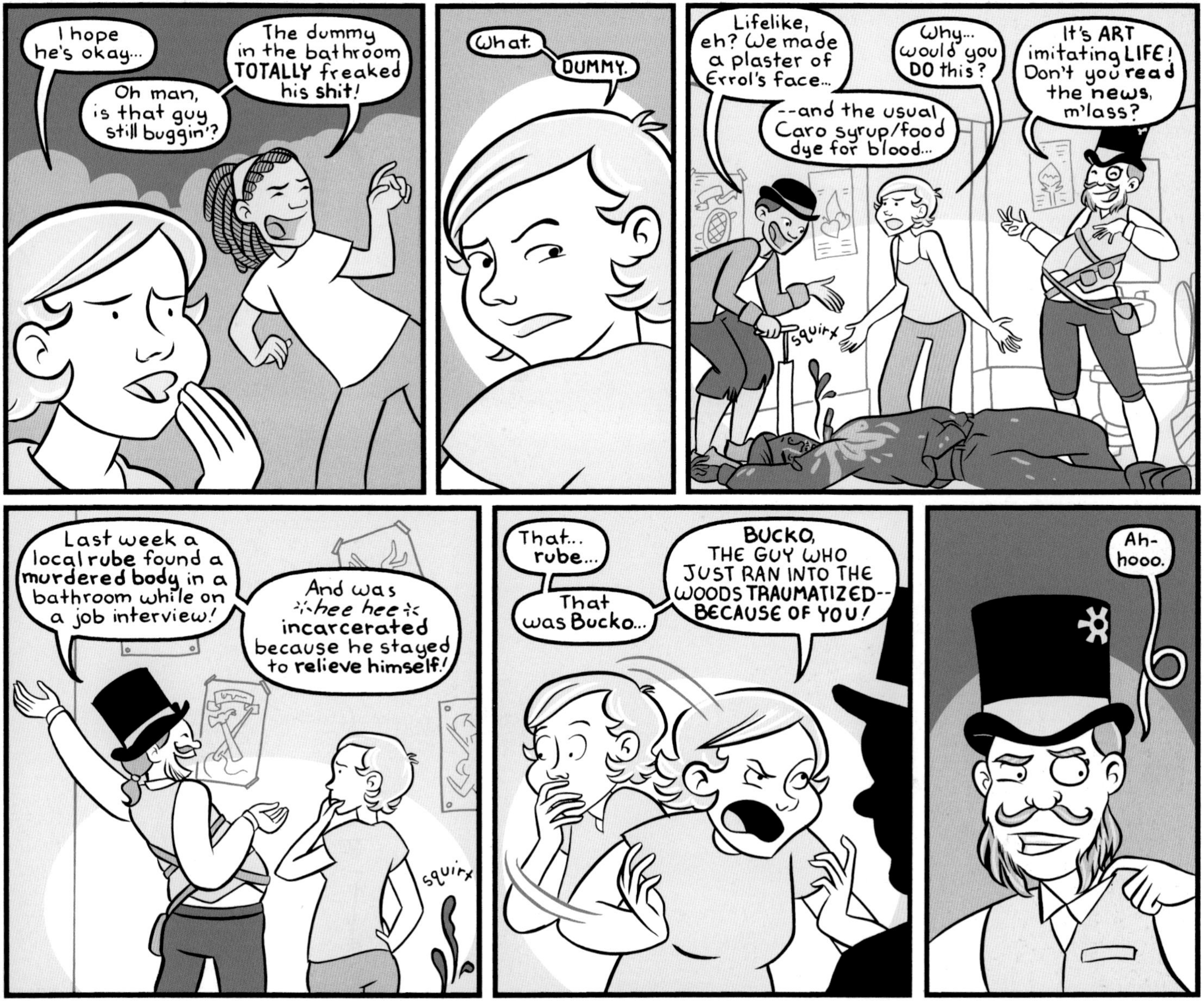
I hope he's okay...
Oh man, is that guy still buggin'?
The dummy in the bathroom TOTALLY freaked his shit!
What.
DUMMY.
Lifelike, eh? We made a plaster of Errol's face...
--and the usual Caro syrup/food dye for blood...
Why... would you DO this?
It's ART imitating LIFE! Don't you read the news, m'lass?
squirt
Last week a local rube found a murdered body in a bathroom while on a job interview!
And was hee hee incarcerated because he stayed to relieve himself!
squirt
That... rube...
That was Bucko...
BUCKO, THE GUY WHO JUST RAN INTO THE WOODS TRAUMATIZED-- BECAUSE OF YOU!
Ah-hooo.

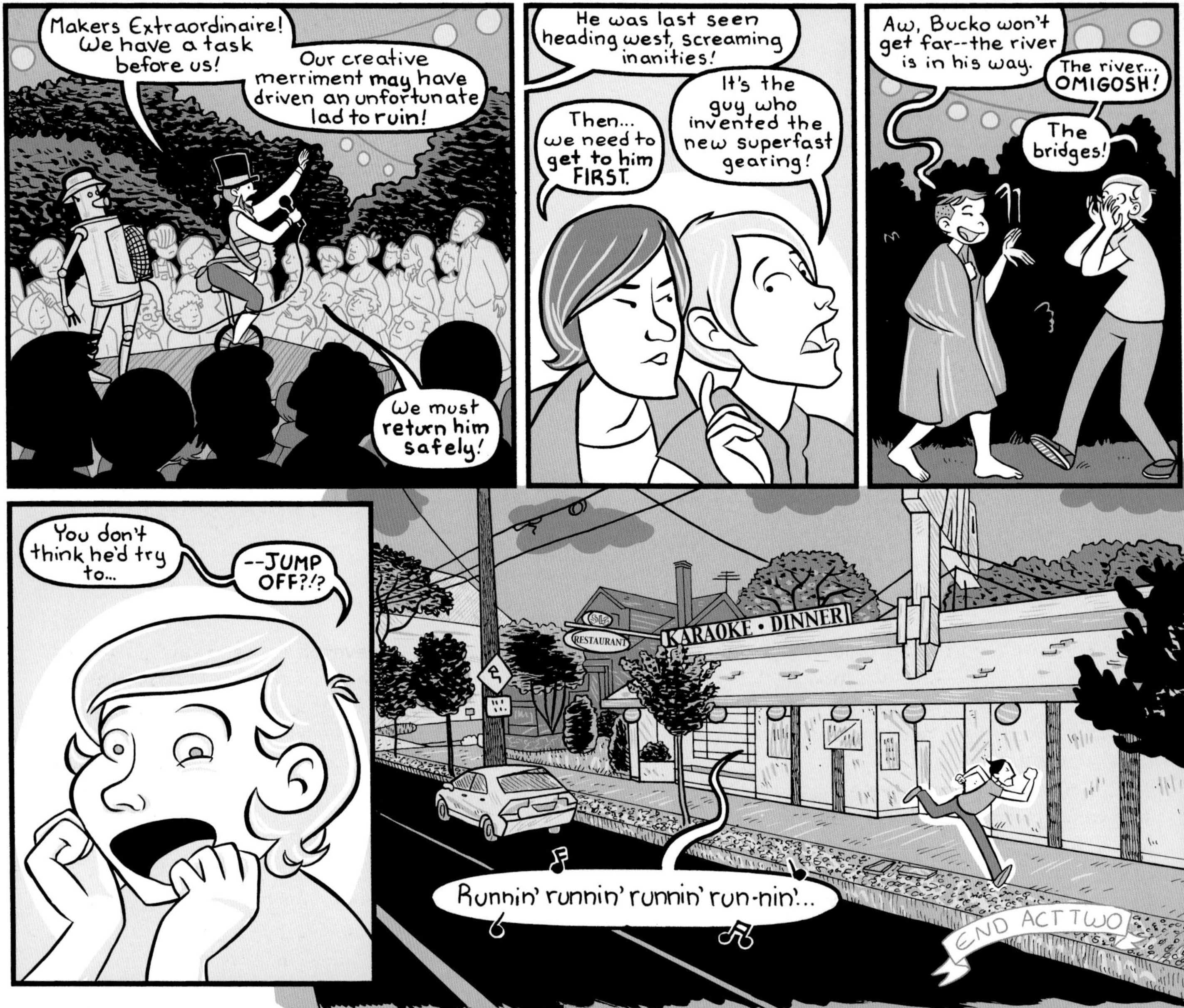
Makers Extraordinaire! We have a task before us!
Our creative merriment may have driven an unfortunate lad to ruin!
We must return him safely!
He was last seen heading west, screaming inanities!
Then... we need to get to him FIRST.
It's the guy who invented the new superfast gearing!
Aw, Bucko won't get far--the river is in his way.
The river... OMIGOSH!
The bridges!
You don't think he'd try to...
--JUMP OFF?!?
RESTAURANT
KARAOKE • DINNER
Runnin' runnin' runnin' run-nin'...
END ACT TWO

INTERMISSION

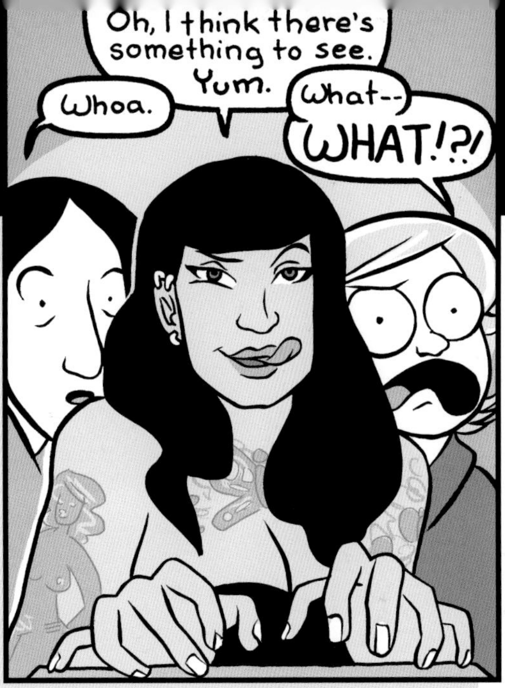
Oh, I think there's something to see. Yum.
Whoa.
What--
WHAT!?!

no room, no time

Since we planned *Bucko* to be done in a year, before our tiny attention spans could sabotage the story, I had to trim out a few scenes and ideas along the way to keep everything moving.

Ray-Ray the Dwarf Gangsta: He appears in the jail scene, and I meant to use him more but realized it'd be taking us down the worn path of dwarf jokes and turn into some Adam Sandler film instead of the *Bucko* humor. I think I put him in because I saw some homemade video with a little rapper. *Au revoir*, Ray-Ray.

The Disease of Lust: When Erika attended the Toronto Comics Art Festival, she was hounded by some old Gandhi-looking dude who kept making observations about her art, clothes, and hair, drawing the conclusion that she had "the disease of lust." It required you hearing an imitation of his mannerisms and voice to get the gist, so it wouldn't translate well to the cartoon, but I wanted to acknowledge it.

Nudity 'n' Sex: Hey, we had strong language and could put whatever we wanted in here—why nobody Gettin' It On? I know, right? Because Erika can draw the hell out of that action! But I've seen this happen in strips and books where the hot content upstages the story and readers start to expect it. Then each check-in becomes all about whether there are sexy times happening, and I didn't want that dynamic. Also, we were playing meta style with the idea that readers might expect it, and then we subvert expectations, as with the failed three way. In short, we're dicks.

Food Cartlandia: Never had time for the gang to eat at some food carts, which are now the one thing people from other areas know exists in Portland. And that was fine, because I didn't really want it to be about Portland, or we would have named the city; it all still applies to similar cities infested with "creatives" everywhere. Also, about the time we started the strip, the show *Portlandia* began airing, and while we shared a lot of things on a Venn diagram, we became conscious of staying distinct from the show. It's quite funny, but we didn't want to be the webcomic version of it. I only regret not showing an American South/Middle Eastern fusion cart called *Bubba Ganoosh*.

Snaps: Meant to stop the story and have a "Your Momma So . . ."-off between some characters, but it just never worked out.

A Ghost: Just kidding; there were no plans to put a ghost in *Bucko*.

ACT THREE

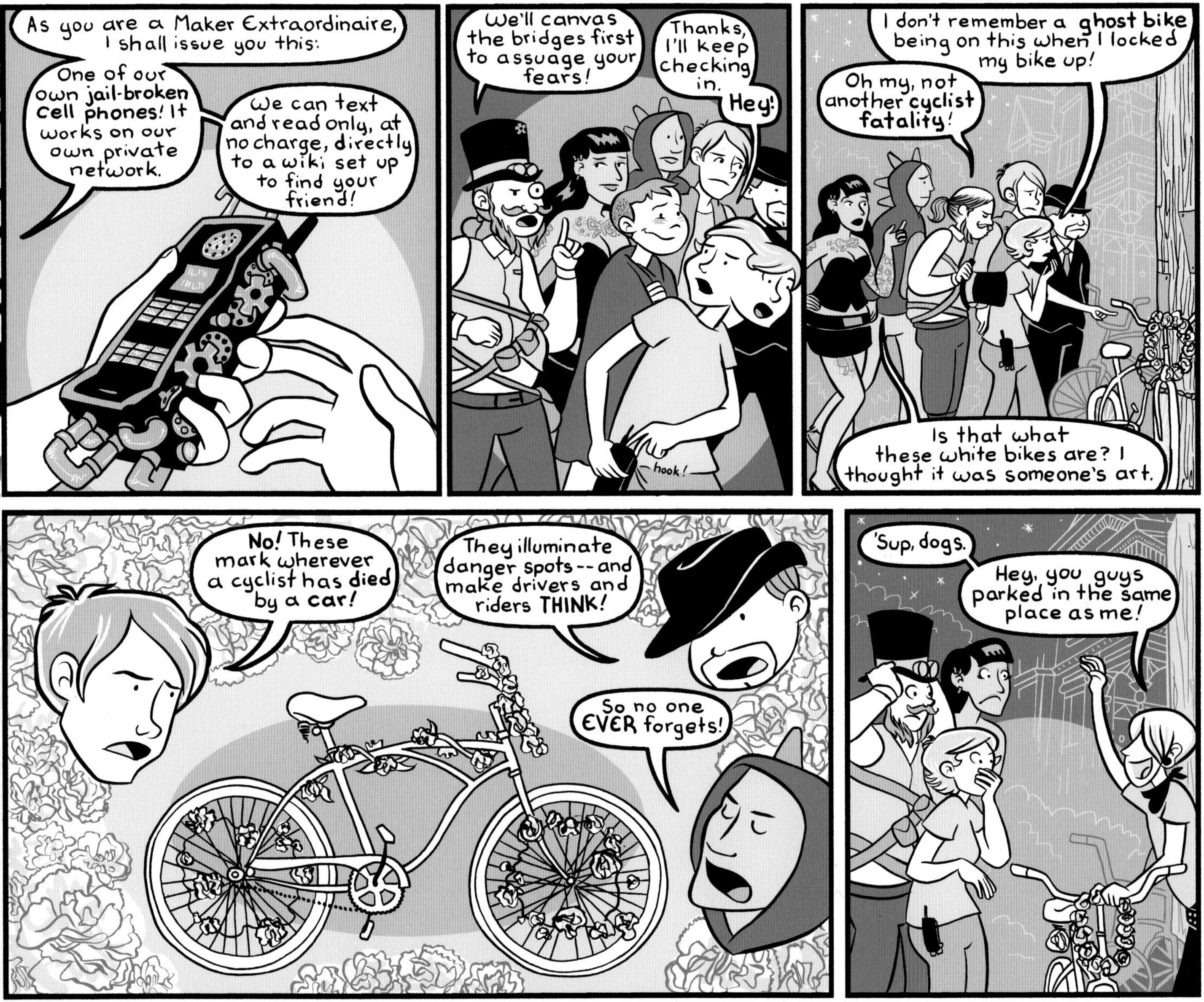

As you are a Maker Extraordinaire, I shall issue you this:
One of our own jail-broken cell phones! It works on our own private network.
We can text and read only, at no charge, directly to a wiki set up to find your friend!
We'll canvas the bridges first to assuage your fears!
Thanks, I'll keep checking in.
Hey!
hook!
I don't remember a ghost bike being on this when I locked my bike up!
Oh my, not another cyclist fatality!
Is that what these white bikes are? I thought it was someone's art.
No! These mark wherever a cyclist has died by a car!
They illuminate danger spots--and make drivers and riders THINK!
So no one EVER forgets!
'Sup, dogs.
Hey, you guys parked in the same place as me!

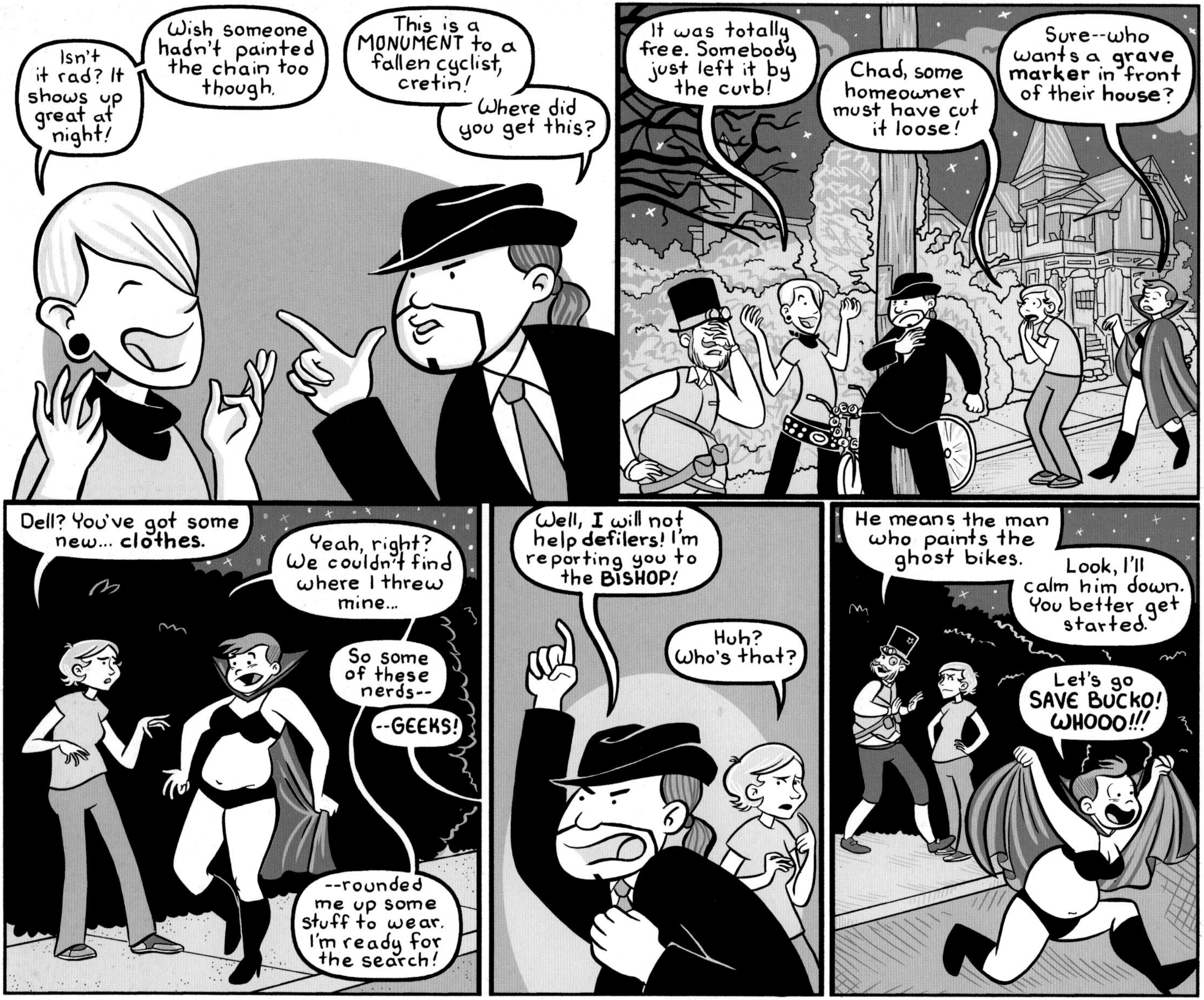

Isn't it rad? It shows up great at night!
Wish someone hadn't painted the chain too though.
This is a MONUMENT to a fallen cyclist, cretin!
Where did you get this?
It was totally free. Somebody just left it by the curb!
Chad, some homeowner must have cut it loose!
Sure--who wants a grave marker in front of their house?
Dell? You've got some new... clothes.
Yeah, right? We couldn't find where I threw mine...
So some of these nerds--
--GEEKS!
--rounded me up some stuff to wear. I'm ready for the search!
Well, I will not help defilers! I'm reporting you to the BISHOP!
Huh? Who's that?
He means the man who paints the ghost bikes.
Look, I'll calm him down. You better get started.
Let's go SAVE BUCKO! WHOOO!!!

It had to be the one that went missing off the Schuyler corner!

Well, you're supposed to be helping them search, right?

Keep tabs on their location. Don't lose them.

I'll send... SOME GUYS.

smak

This is the first bridge he could have reached!

I dunno. It's a drawbridge.

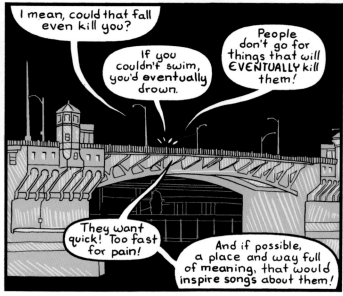

I mean, could that fall even kill you?

If you couldn't swim, you'd eventually drown.

People don't go for things that will EVENTUALLY kill them!

They want quick! Too fast for pain!

And if possible, a place and way full of meaning, that would inspire songs about them!

I AM a SuicideGirl, duh!

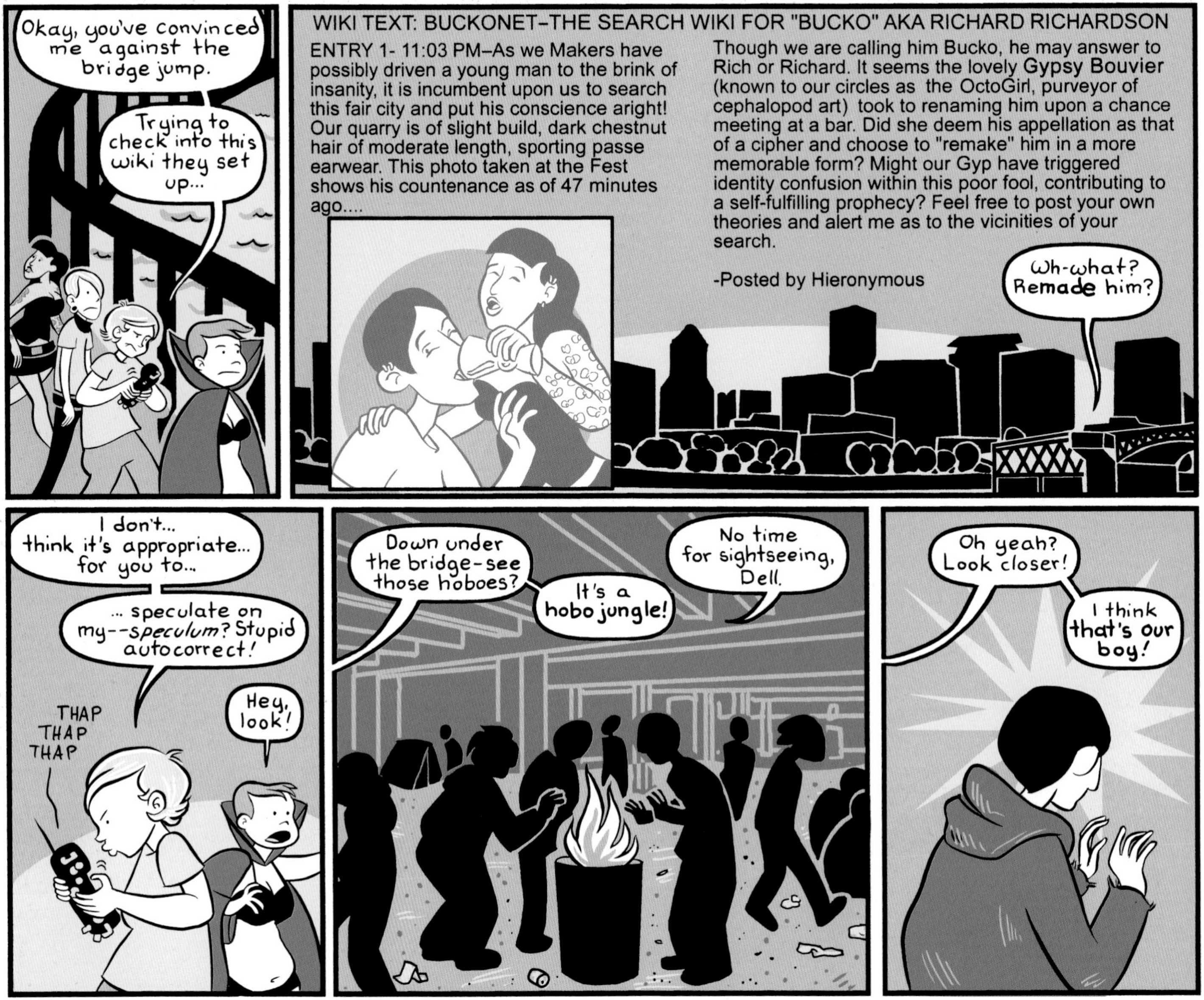
Okay, you've convinced me against the bridge jump.
Trying to check into this wiki they set up...
WIKI TEXT: BUCKONET–THE SEARCH WIKI FOR "BUCKO" AKA RICHARD RICHARDSON
ENTRY 1- 11:03 PM–As we Makers have possibly driven a young man to the brink of insanity, it is incumbent upon us to search this fair city and put his conscience aright! Our quarry is of slight build, dark chestnut hair of moderate length, sporting passe earwear. This photo taken at the Fest shows his countenance as of 47 minutes ago....
Though we are calling him Bucko, he may answer to Rich or Richard. It seems the lovely Gypsy Bouvier (known to our circles as the OctoGirl, purveyor of cephalopod art) took to renaming him upon a chance meeting at a bar. Did she deem his appellation as that of a cipher and choose to "remake" him in a more memorable form? Might our Gyp have triggered identity confusion within this poor fool, contributing to a self-fulfilling prophecy? Feel free to post your own theories and alert me as to the vicinities of your search.
-Posted by Hieronymous
Wh-what? Remade him?
I don't... think it's appropriate... for you to...
... speculate on my--speculum? Stupid autocorrect!
THAP THAP THAP
Hey, look!
Down under the bridge-see those hoboes?
It's a hobo jungle!
No time for sightseeing, Dell.
Oh yeah? Look closer!
I think that's our boy!

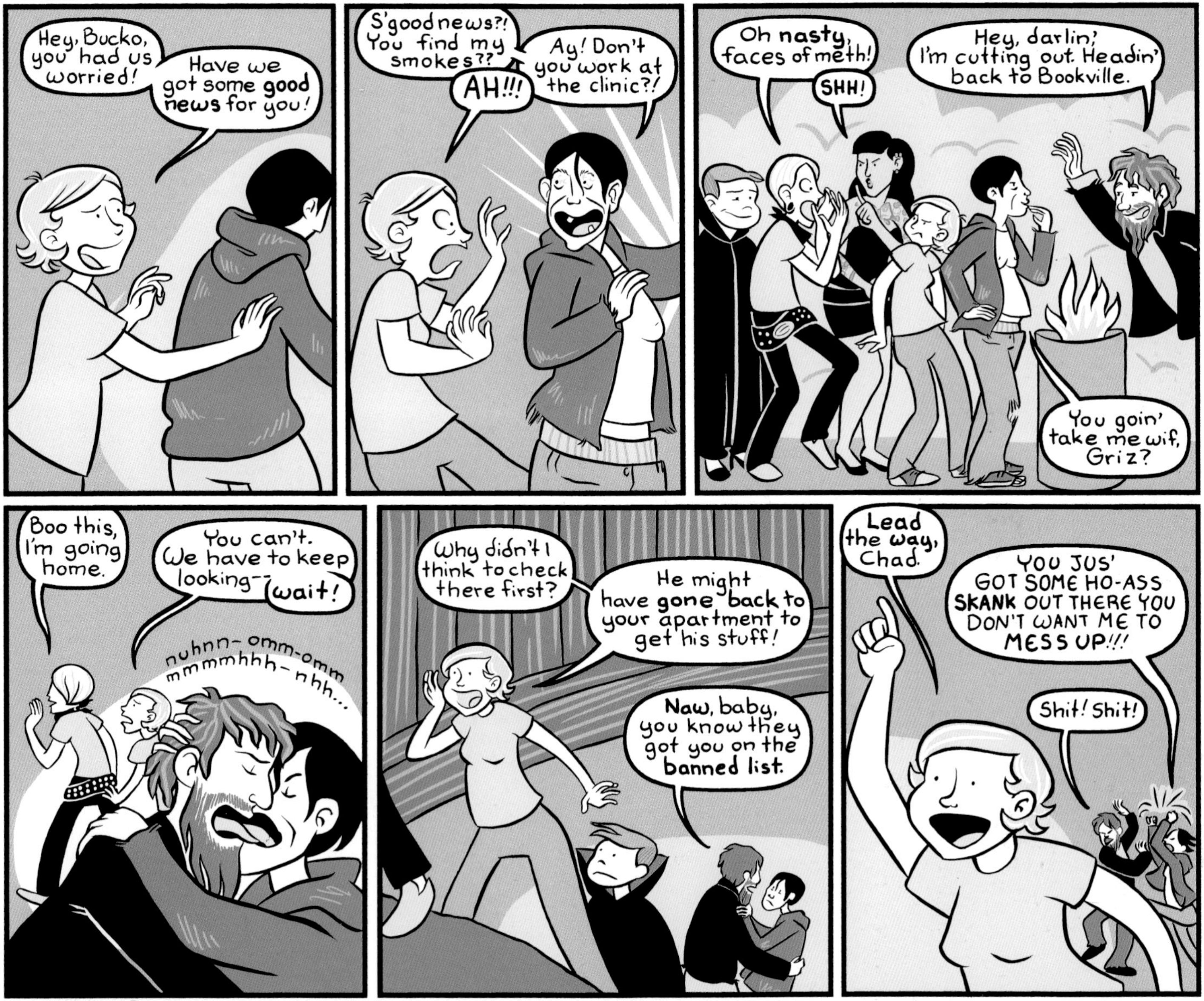

Hey, Bucko, you had us worried!
Have we got some **good news** for you!
S'good news?! You find my smokes??
Ay! Don't you work at the clinic?!
AH!!!
Oh **nasty**, faces of meth!
SHH!
Hey, darlin,' I'm cutting out. Headin' back to Bookville.
You goin' take me wif, Griz?
Boo this, I'm going home.
You can't. We have to keep looking--
wait!
nuhnn-omm-omm mmmmhhh-nhh...
Why didn't I think to check there first?
He might have **gone back** to your apartment to get his stuff!
Naw, baby, you know they got you on the **banned list**.
Lead the **way**, Chad.
YOU JUS' GOT SOME HO-ASS **SKANK** OUT THERE YOU DON'T WANT ME TO **MESS UP**!!!
Shit! Shit!

BUCKONET WIKI

12:07- Okay everybody, so we've given up on searching around the bridges since Sindee convinced me Bucko wouldn't kill himself that way. Based on her knowing him for an hour and a half, I guess. Anyhoo, it's too problematic to search the water at night. And I was probably being a little hysterectomy because of the absinthe I drank.

@@@@@DAMN-IT. **HYSTERICAL.** How do I turn the autocorrect off on this stupid steampunk phone!!!?

So we're going for a logical place to check- Chad is leading us to the house where he and B rent rooms. Maybe B went there to get his stuff and hit the open road? Maybe we'll catch him in time and tell him there's no extra dead body! I will update as soon as we get there.

Posted by GYP

My swank pad, ladies!

If the THREE of you want to come in and get comfortable, I can--

Just open the door, Chad.

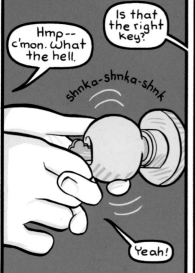

Hmp-- c'mon. What the hell.

Is that the right key?

shnka-shnka-shnk

Yeah!

I can solve this mystery if you cast your gaze this way.

Whatcha got, Dell?

VOILÀ! Your stuff!

Which has been removed from the rooms by your landlord...

...who then CHANGED THE LOCK!!!

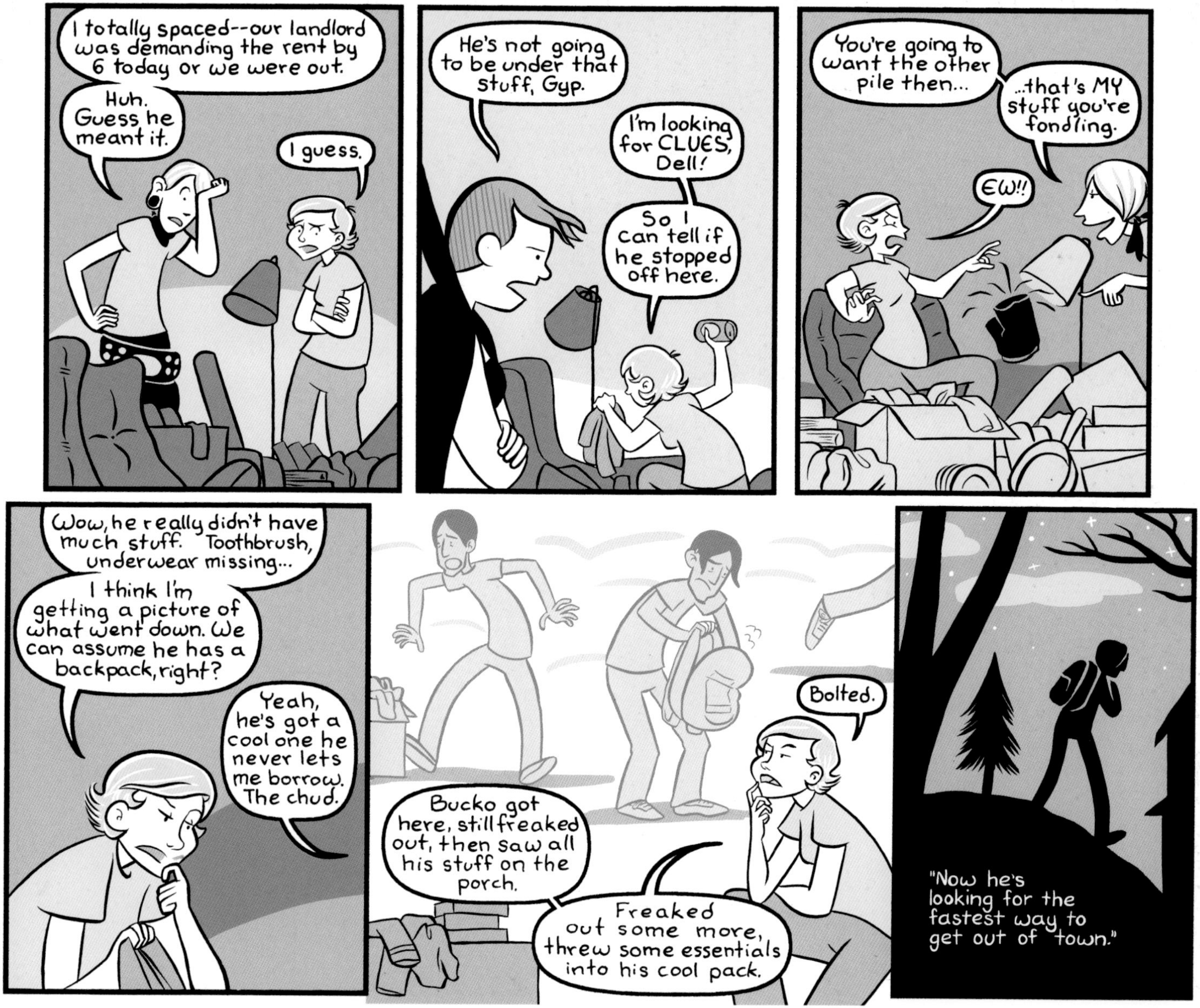

I totally spaced--our landlord was demanding the rent by 6 today or we were out.
Huh. Guess he meant it.
I guess.
He's not going to be under that stuff, Gyp.
I'm looking for CLUES, Dell!
So I can tell if he stopped off here.
You're going to want the other pile then...
...that's MY stuff you're fondling.
EW!!
Wow, he really didn't have much stuff. Toothbrush, underwear missing...
I think I'm getting a picture of what went down. We can assume he has a backpack, right?
Yeah, he's got a cool one he never lets me borrow. The chud.
Bucko got here, still freaked out, then saw all his stuff on the porch.
Freaked out some more, threw some essentials into his cool pack.
Bolted.
"Now he's looking for the fastest way to get out of town."

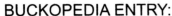

BUCKOPEDIA ENTRY:

Since we know Bucko came by his former apartment, we are now circling the area in an ever-widening spiral. - GYP

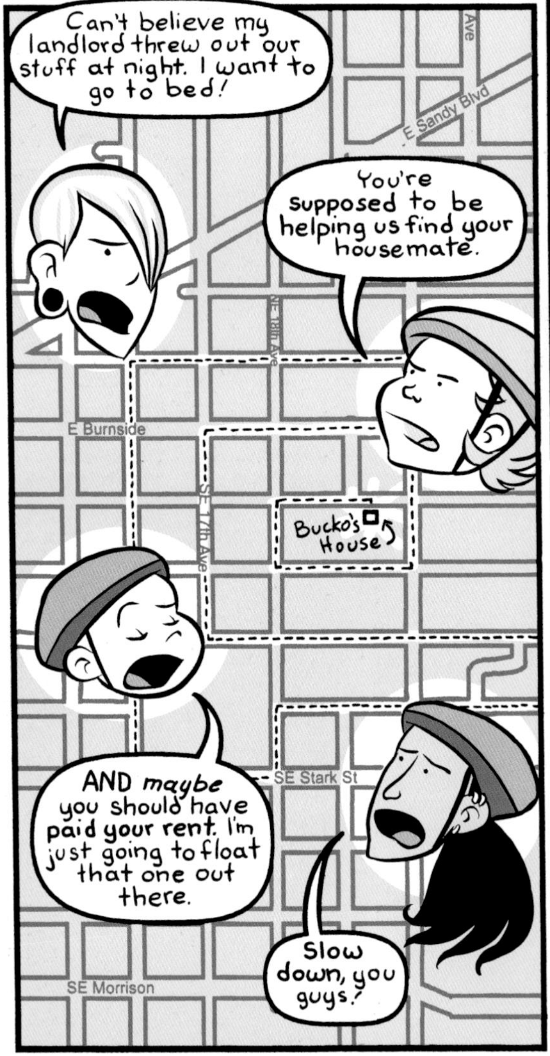

Can't believe my landlord threw out our stuff at night. I want to go to bed!
You're supposed to be helping us find your housemate.
Ave
E Sandy Blvd
NE 18th Ave
E Burnside
SE 17th Ave
Bucko's House
SE Stark St
SE Morrison
AND *maybe* you should have paid your rent. I'm just going to float that one out there.
Slow down, you guys!

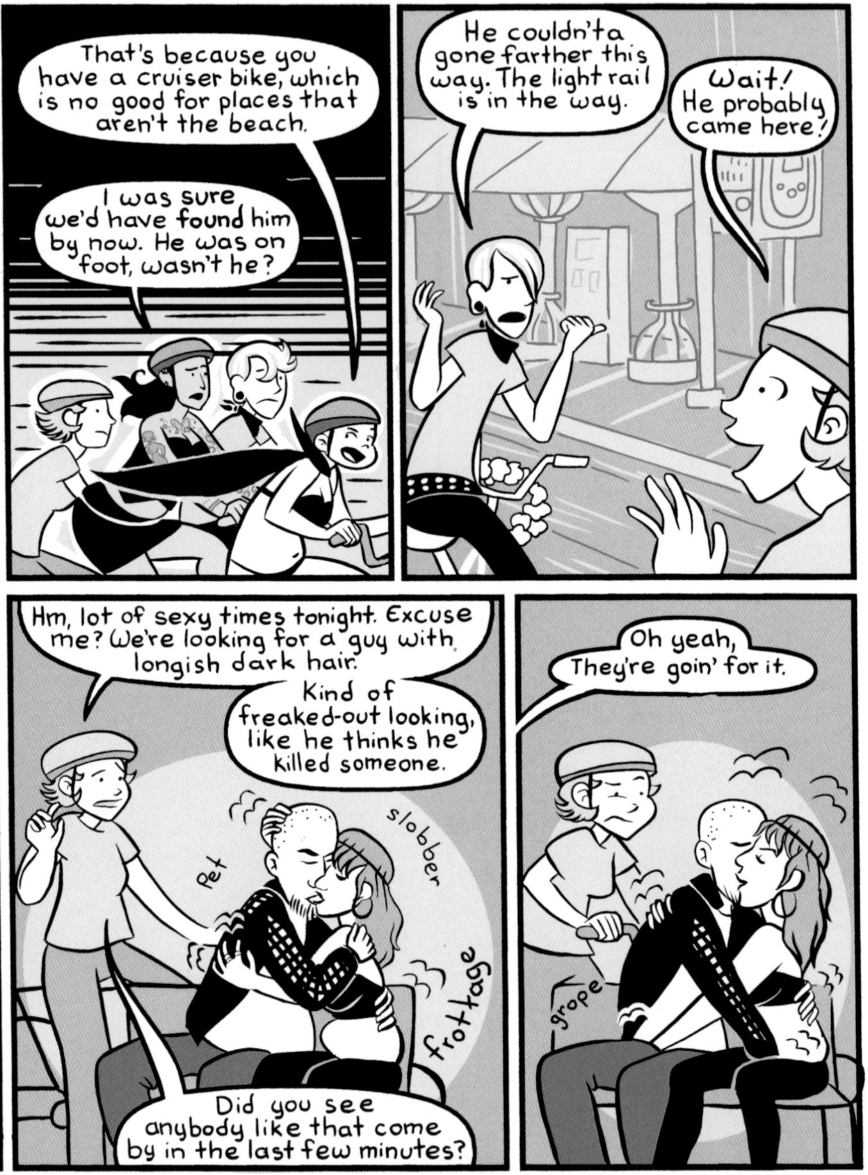

That's because you have a cruiser bike, which is no good for places that aren't the beach.
I was sure we'd have found him by now. He was on foot, wasn't he?
He couldn't'a gone farther this way. The light rail is in the way.
Wait! He probably came here!
Hm, lot of sexy times tonight. Excuse me? We're looking for a guy with longish dark hair.
Kind of freaked-out looking, like he thinks he killed someone.
pet
slobber
frottage
Did you see anybody like that come by in the last few minutes?
Oh yeah, They're goin' for it.
grope

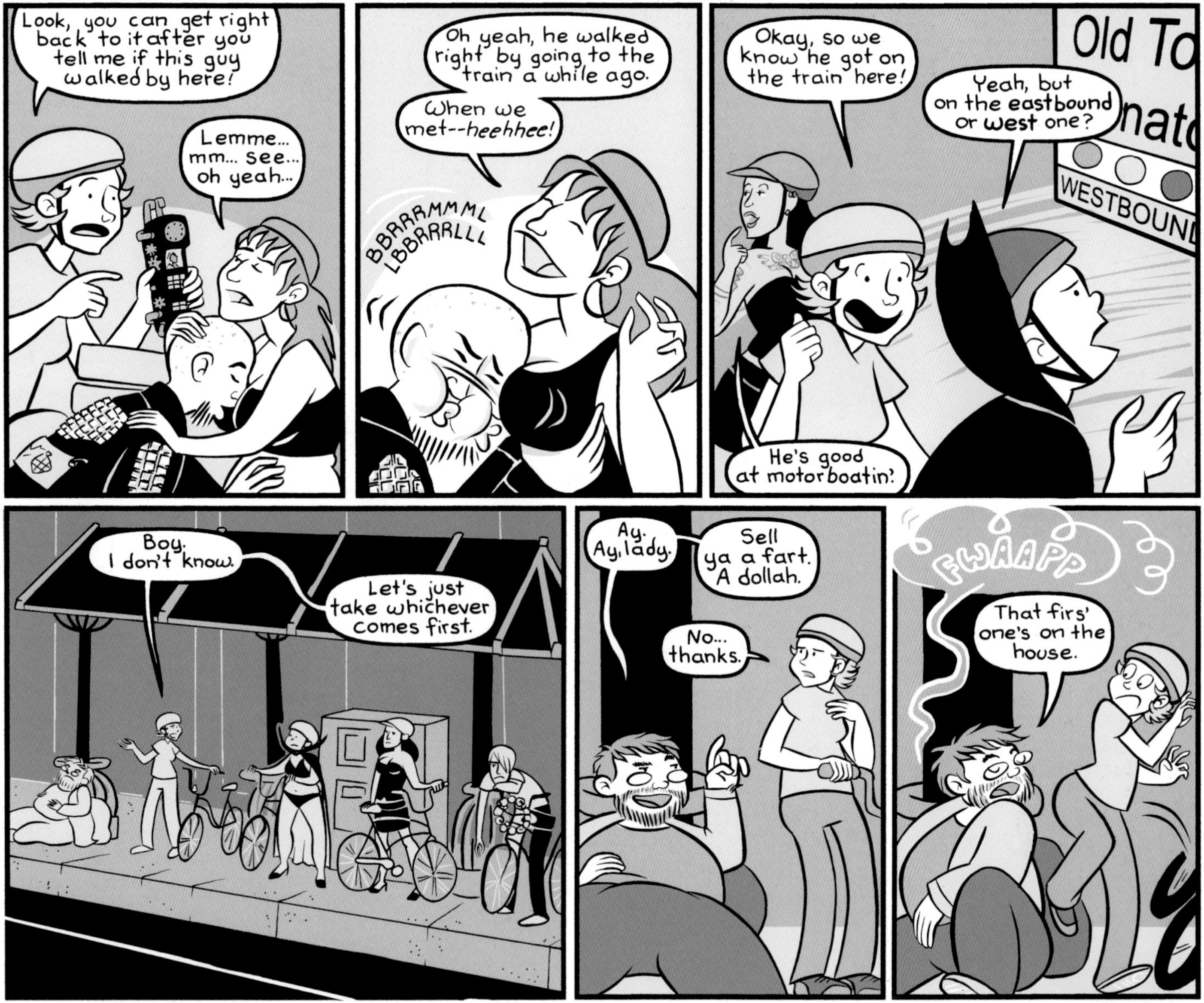
Look, you can get right back to it after you tell me if this guy walked by here!
Lemme... mm... see... oh yeah...
Oh yeah, he walked right by going to the train a while ago.
When we met--*heehhee!*
BBRRRMMML LBBRRRLLL
Okay, so we know he got on the train here!
Yeah, but on the **eastbound** or **west** one?
Old To
nato
WESTBOUND
He's good at motorboatin'.
Boy. I don't know.
Let's just take whichever comes first.
Ay. Ay, lady.
Sell ya a fart. A dollah.
No... thanks.
FWAAAPP
That firs' one's on the house.

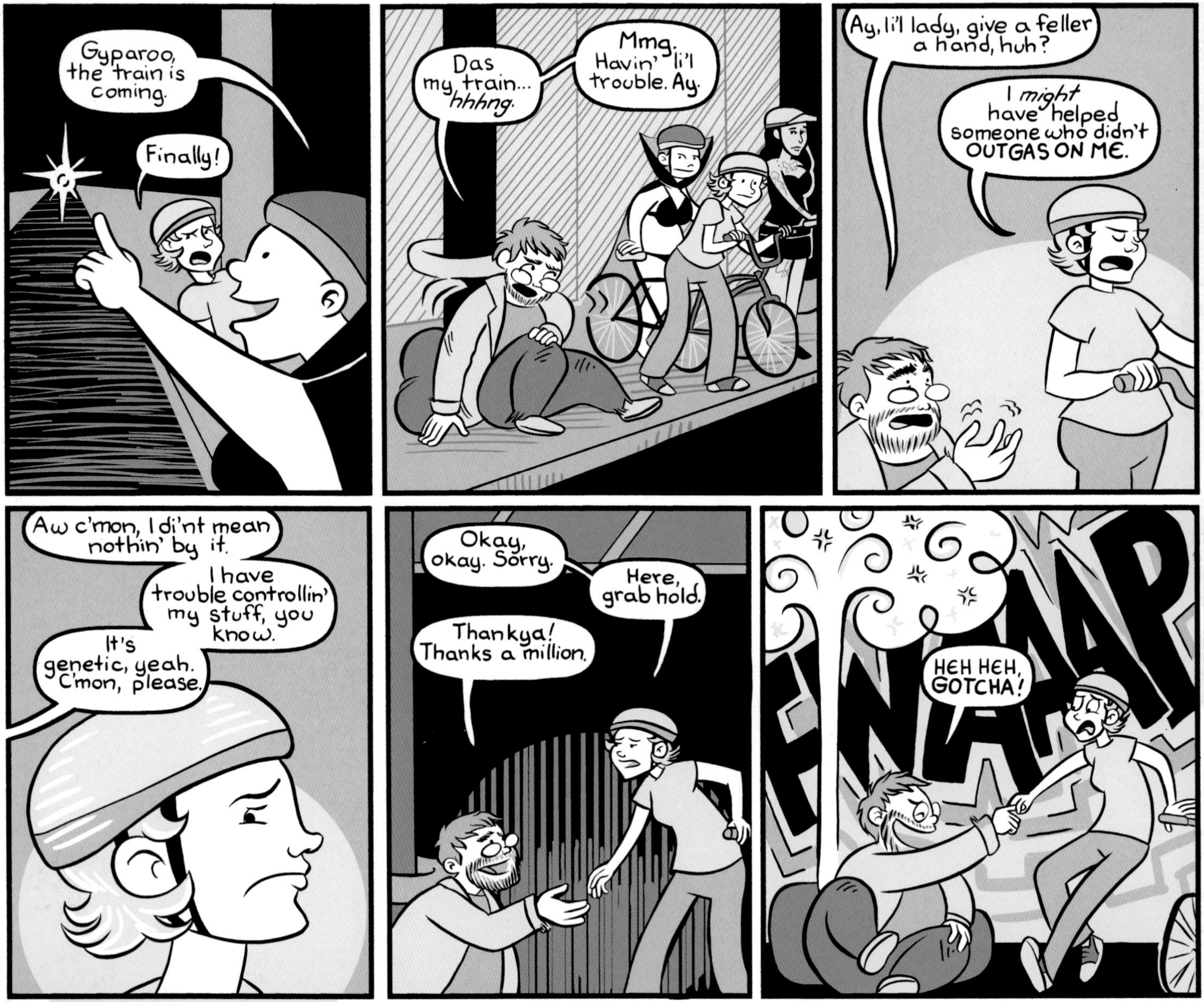
Gyparoo, the train is coming.
Finally!
Das my train... hhhng.
Mmg. Havin' li'l trouble. Ay.
Ay, li'l lady, give a feller a hand, huh?
I might have helped someone who didn't OUTGAS ON ME.
Aw c'mon, I di'nt mean nothin' by it.
I have trouble controllin' my stuff, you know.
It's genetic, yeah. C'mon, please.
Okay, okay. Sorry.
Here, grab hold.
Thankya! Thanks a million.
FNAAP
HEH HEH, GOTCHA!

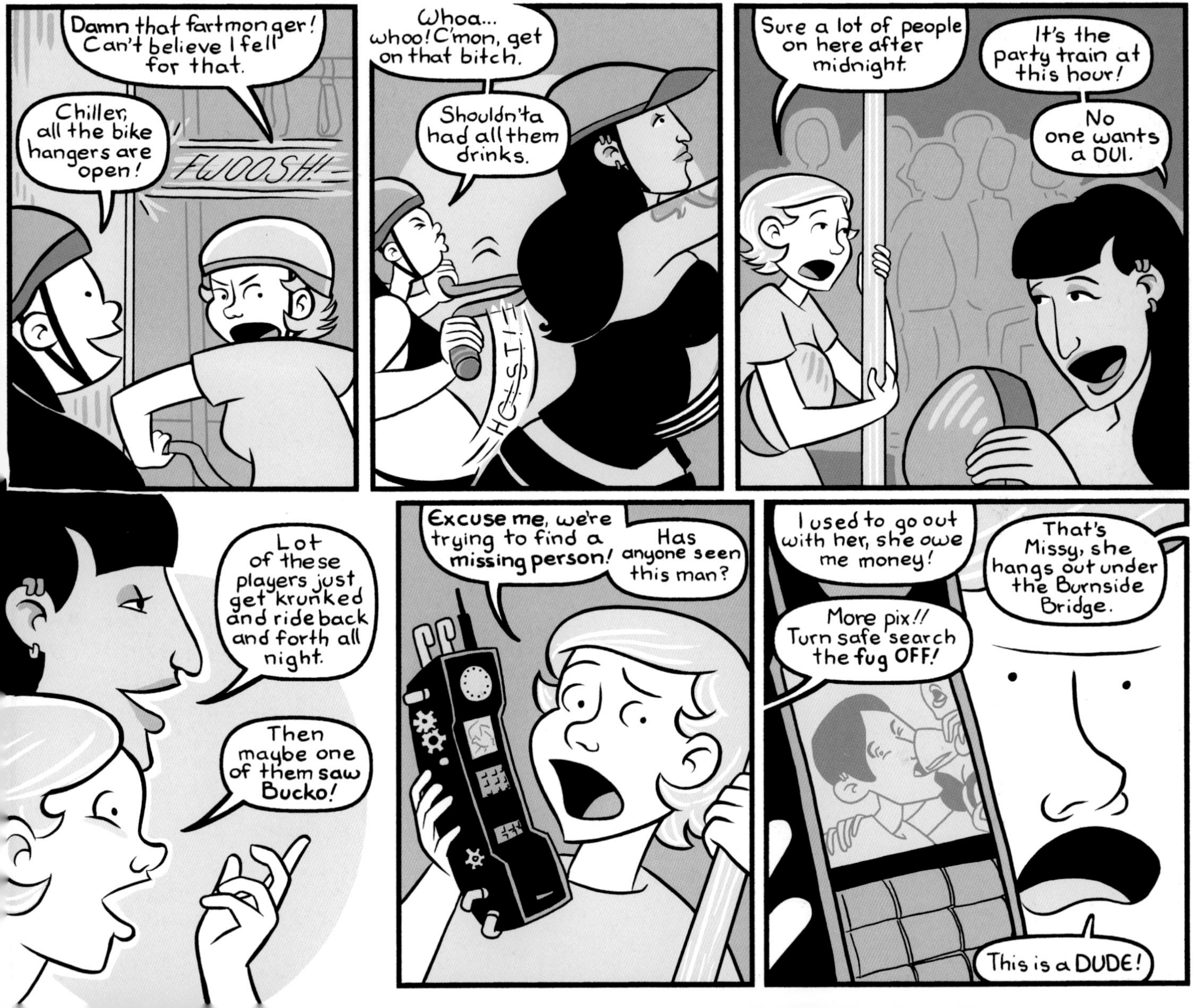
Damn that fartmonger! Can't believe I fell for that.
Chiller, all the bike hangers are open!
FWOOSH!
Whoa... whoo! C'mon, get on that bitch.
Shouldn'ta had all them drinks.
HOIST!
Sure a lot of people on here after midnight.
It's the party train at this hour!
No one wants a DUI.
Lot of these players just get krunked and ride back and forth all night.
Then maybe one of them saw Bucko!
Excuse me, we're trying to find a missing person!
Has anyone seen this man?
I used to go out with her, she owe me money!
More pix!! Turn safe search the fug OFF!
That's Missy, she hangs out under the Burnside Bridge.
This is a DUDE!

appellation as that of a cipher and choose to "r
confusion within this poor fool, contributing to a
the vicinities of your search.
-Posted by Hieronymous

12:07- Okay everybody, so we've given up on s
himself that way. Based on her knowing him fo
night. And I was probably being a little hystered

@@@@@DAMN-IT. **HYSTERICAL**. How do I
So we're going for a logical place to check- Ch
get his stuff and hit the open road? Maybe we'l
as we get there.
-Posted by GYP

1:00 - Have placed agents on both Canadian a
country.
-Posted by thirdmike

1:15 - After little time have also secured assista
pretty lady" to come to any harm.
-Posted by thirdmike

2:32am - I think I saw him in a gas station on I-
-johnca

3:00am - I just saw a mysterious, battered, wail
could have gotten this far?
-Delora

6:00am- Does he go by the street-name "Twizte
said to say "MMFWCL, fuckeroos."

17:41 PM, 8/24/2052 - Did you folks ever find h

4:18 I saw this fellow down by the harbor, perha

12:12 - I checked down by the froggery, but I di
cow fields.

8:35pm- Sighted near a Taco Bell in Fairless Hi

7:47 pm - Checked with the Bigfoot Research C
mounting up.
-mecowgill

7:55 pm - Called the Portland police to update t
-mecowgill

10:33 pm - I just woke up from a dream where I
Romeo's!
-mstrawbridge

10:45 pm - Not sure where he is now, but here's

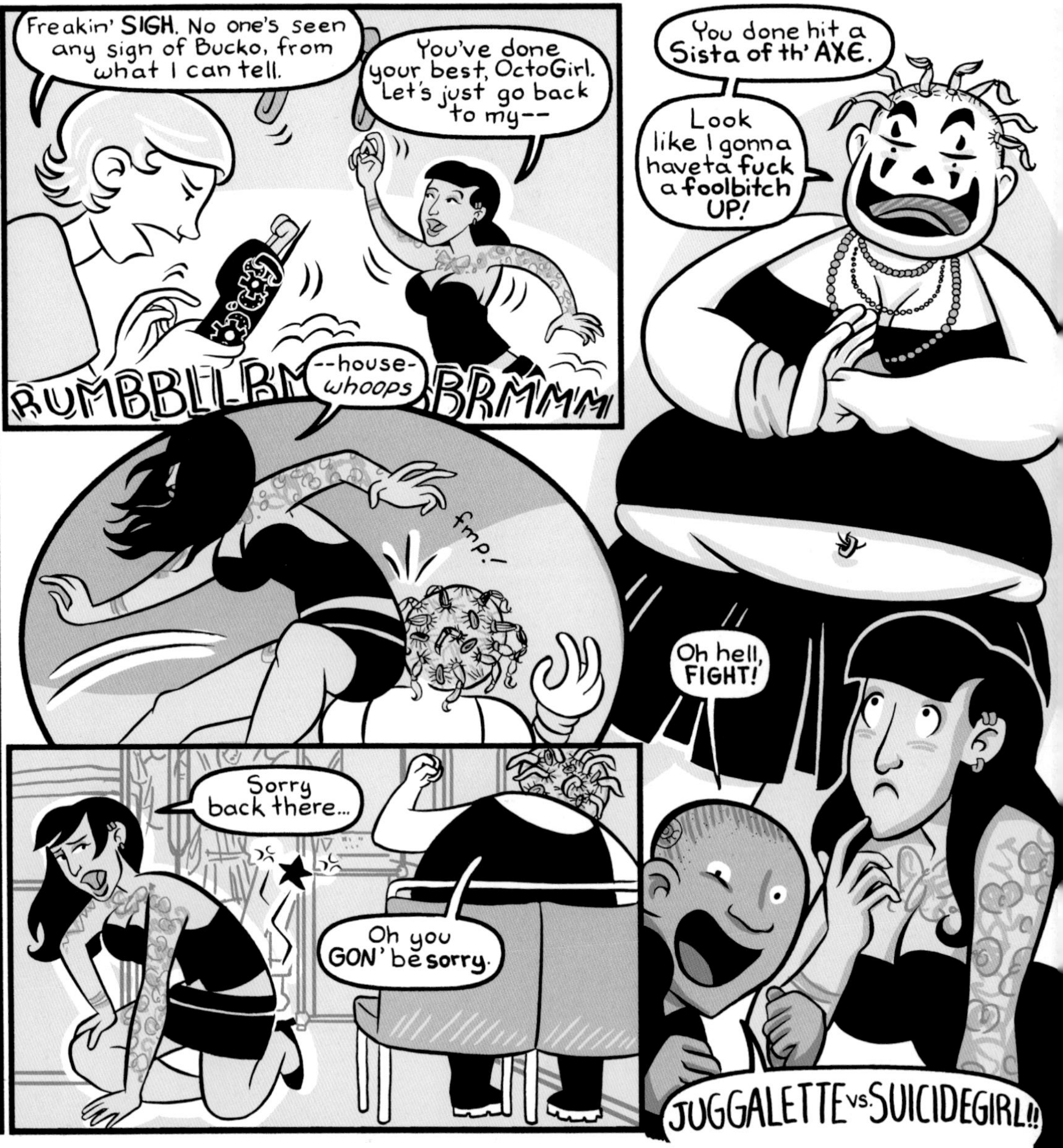

Freakin' SIGH. No one's seen any sign of Bucko, from what I can tell.
You've done your best, OctoGirl. Let's just go back to my--
RUMBBLLBM
--house-- whoops
BRMMM
You done hit a Sista of th' AXE.
Look like I gonna haveta fuck a foolbitch UP!
fmp!
Sorry back there...
Oh you GON' be sorry.
Oh hell, FIGHT!
JUGGALETTE vs. SUICIDEGIRL!!

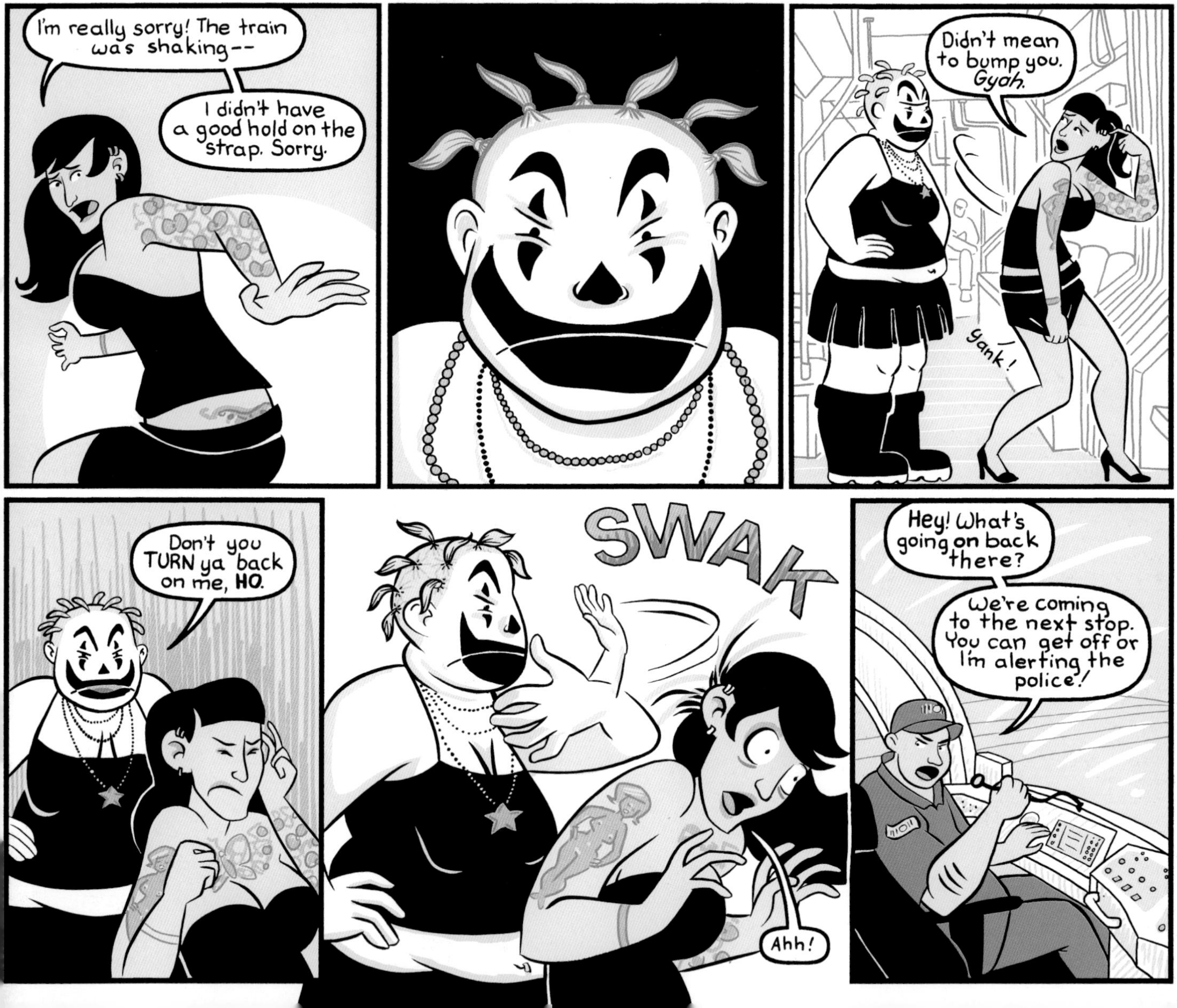
I'm really sorry! The train was shaking--
I didn't have a good hold on the strap. Sorry.
Didn't mean to bump you. Gyah.
Yank!
Don't you TURN ya back on me, HO.
SWAK
Ahh!
Hey! What's going on back there?
We're coming to the next stop. You can get off or I'm alerting the police!

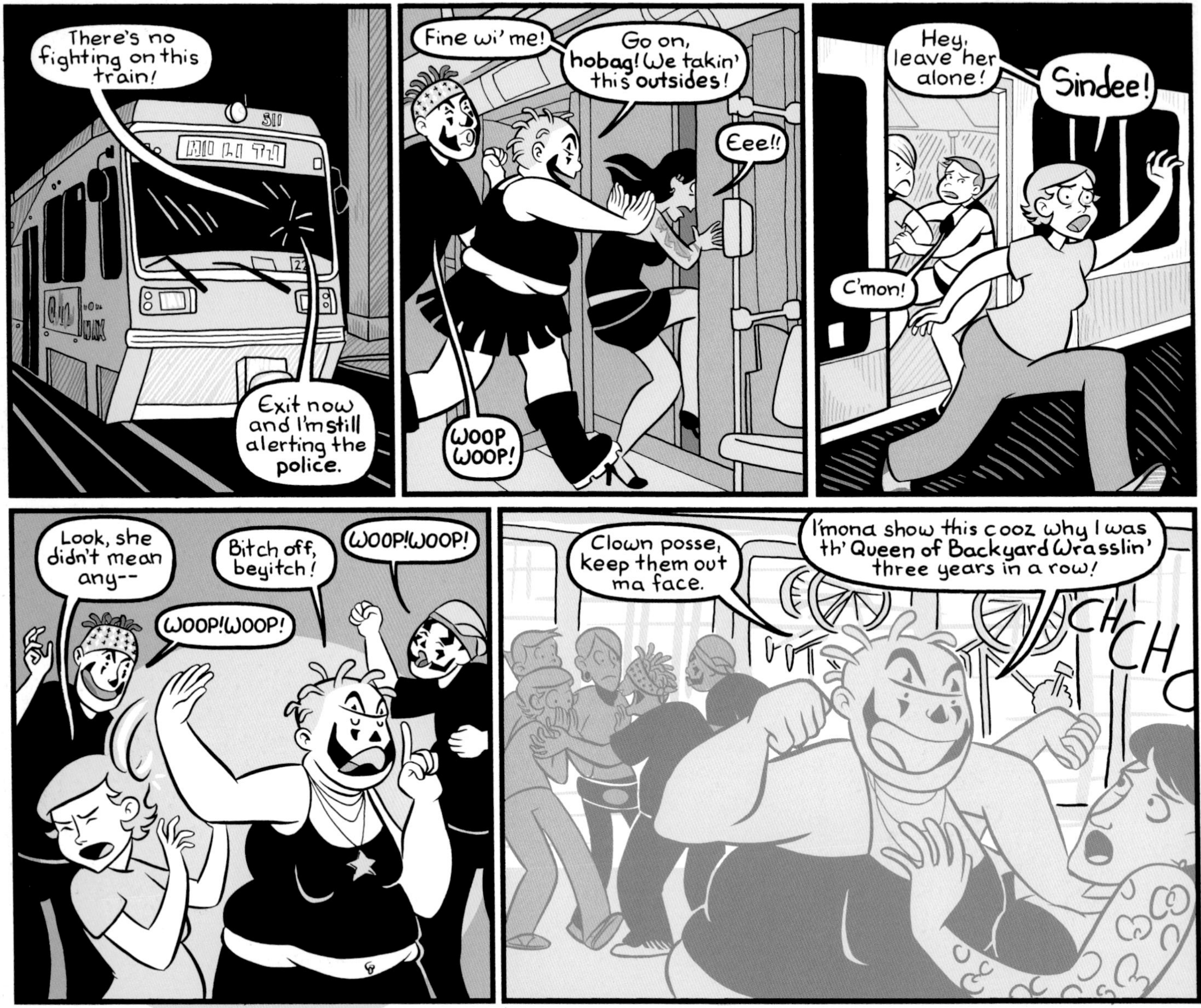
There's no fighting on this train!
Exit now and I'm still alerting the police.
Fine wi' me!
Go on, hobag! We takin' this outsides!
Eee!!
WOOP WOOP!
Hey, leave her alone!
Sindee!
C'mon!
Look, she didn't mean any--
WOOP!WOOP!
Bitch off, beyitch!
WOOP!WOOP!
Clown posse, keep them out ma face.
I'mona show this cooz why I was th' Queen of Backyard Wrasslin' three years in a row!
CH CH

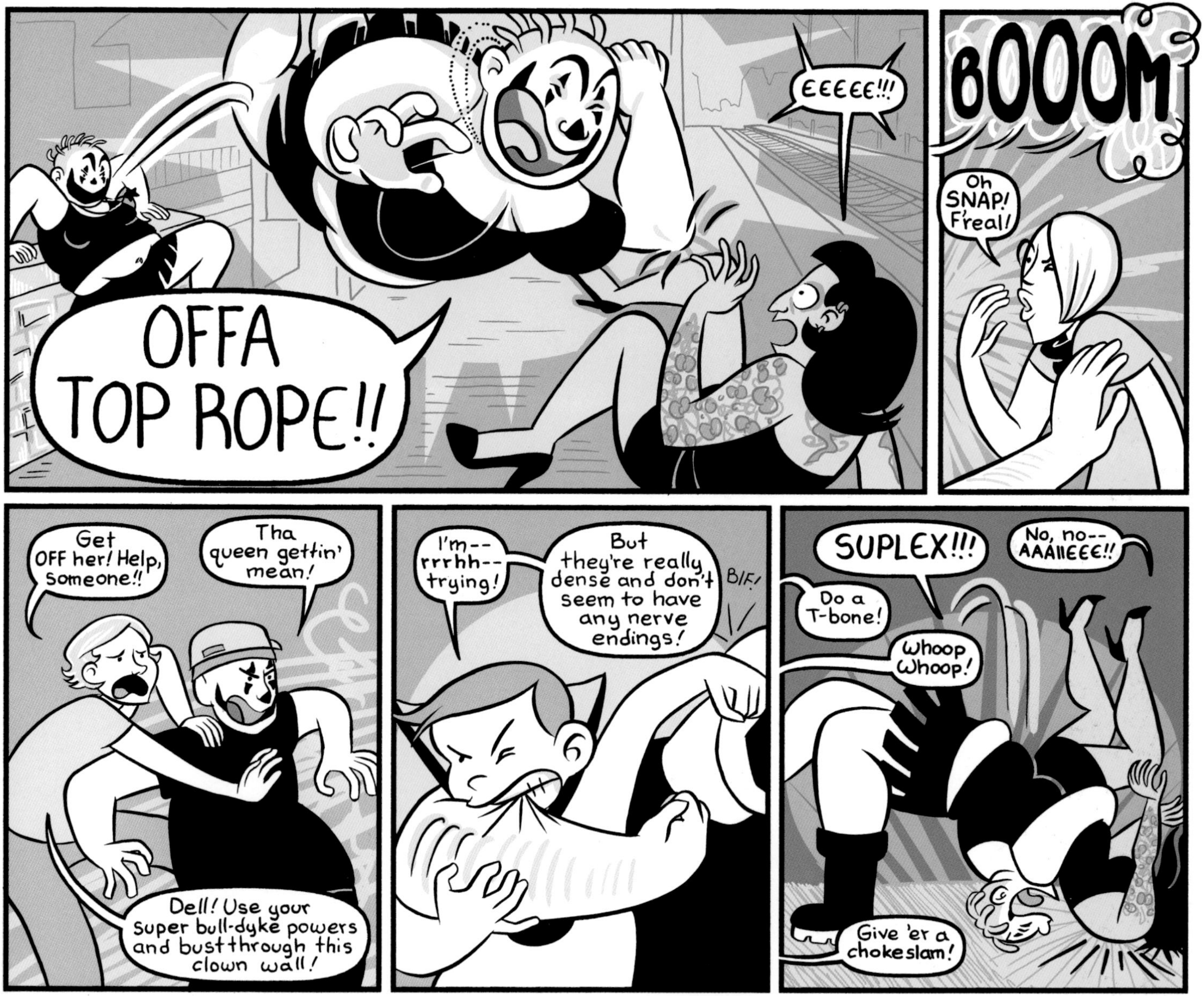
OFFA TOP ROPE!!
EEEEE!!!
BOOOM!
Oh SNAP! F'real!
Get OFF her! Help, someone!!
Tha queen gettin' mean!
Dell! Use your super bull-dyke powers and bust through this clown wall!
I'm--rrrhh--trying!
But they're really dense and don't seem to have any nerve endings!
BIF!
SUPLEX!!!
No, no--AAAIIEEE!!
Do a T-bone!
Whoop Whoop!
Give 'er a chokeslam!

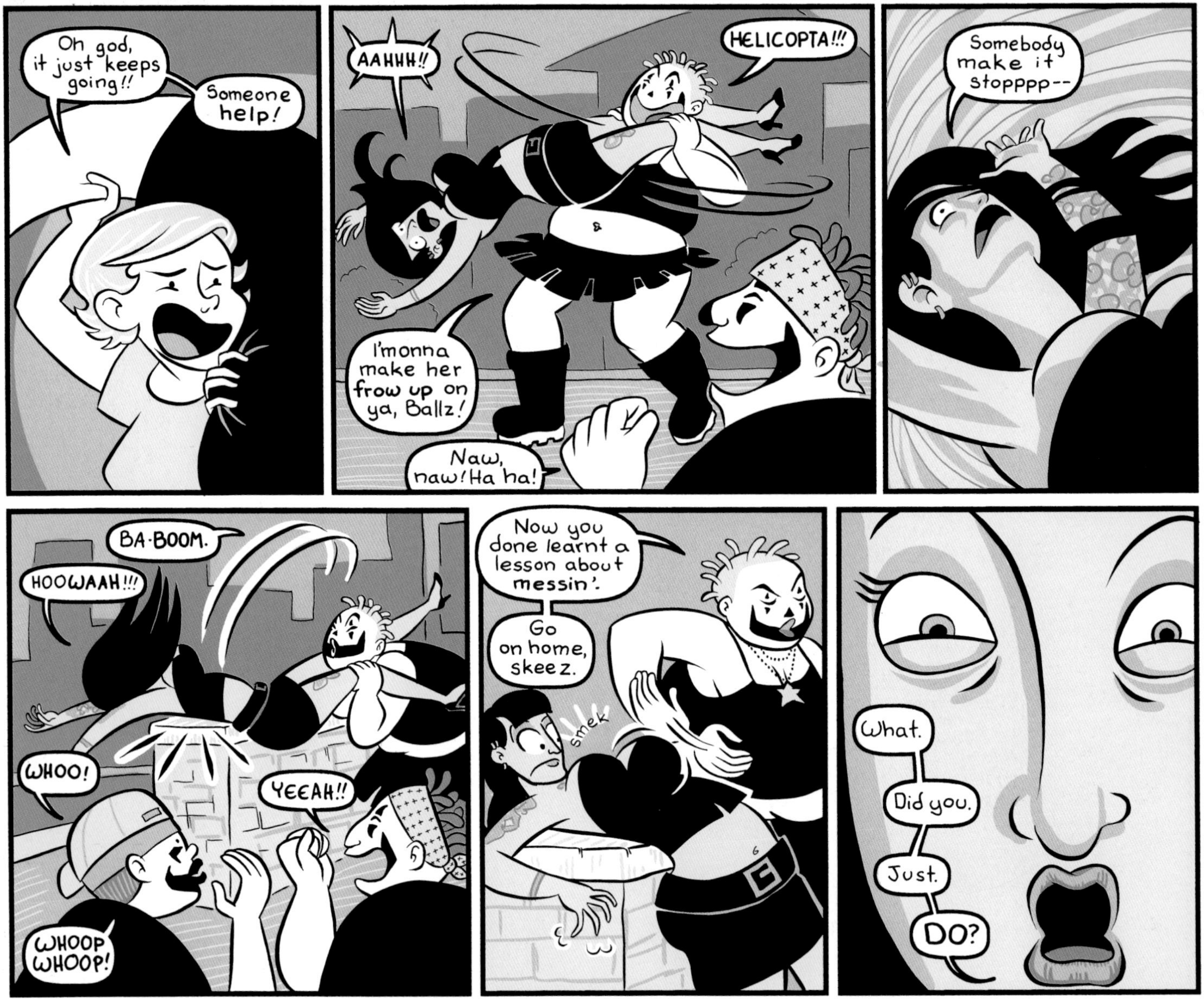
Oh god, it just keeps going!!
Someone help!
AAHHH!!
HELICOPTA!!!
I'monna make her frow up on ya, Ballz!
Naw, naw! Ha ha!
Somebody make it stopppp--
BA-BOOM.
HOOWAAH!!!
WHOO!
YEEAH!!
WHOOP WHOOP!
Now you done learnt a lesson about messin'.
Go on home, skeez.
smek
What.
Did you.
Just.
DO?

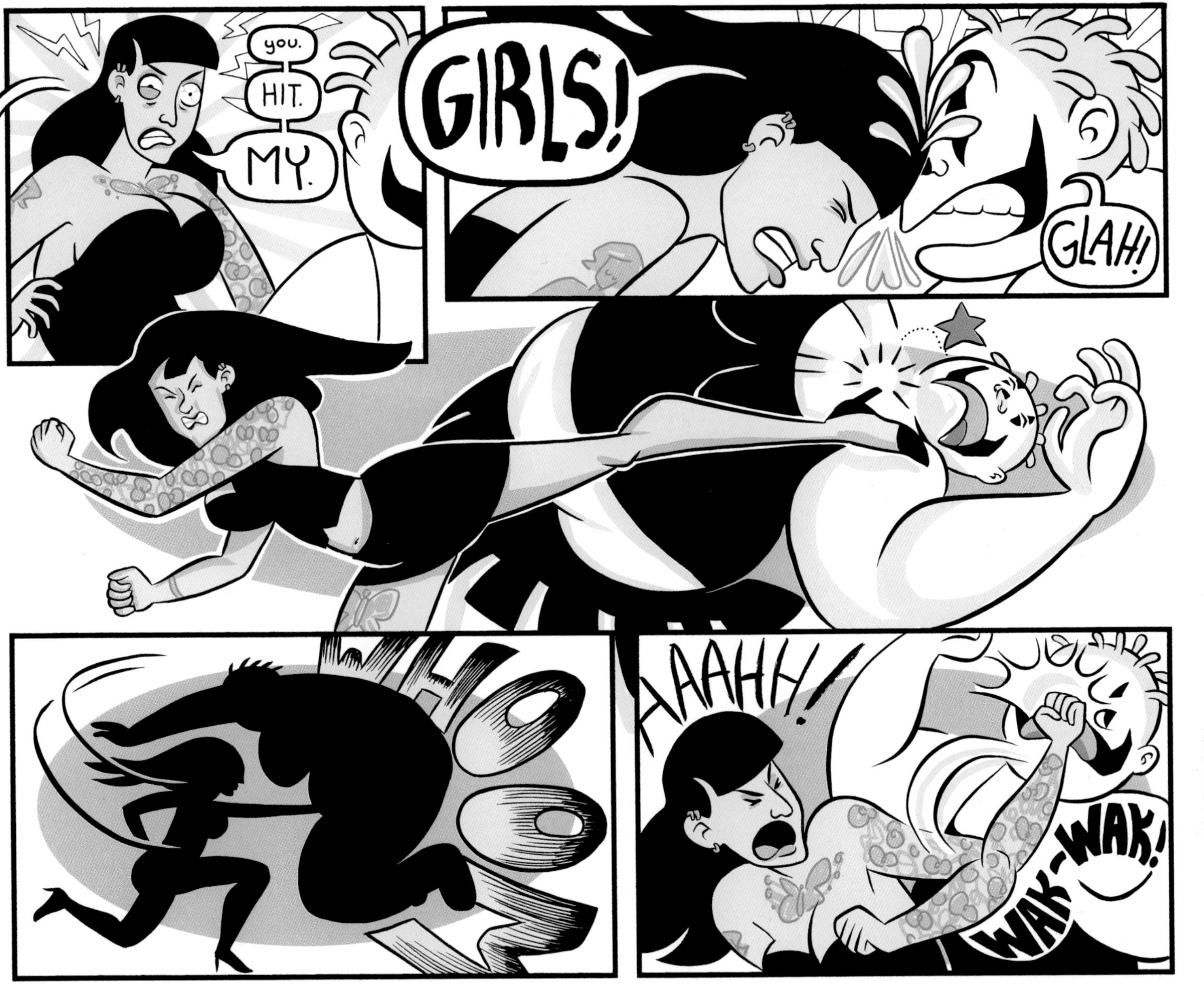

you.
HIT.
MY.
GIRLS!
GLAH!
AAAHH!!
WAK-WAK!

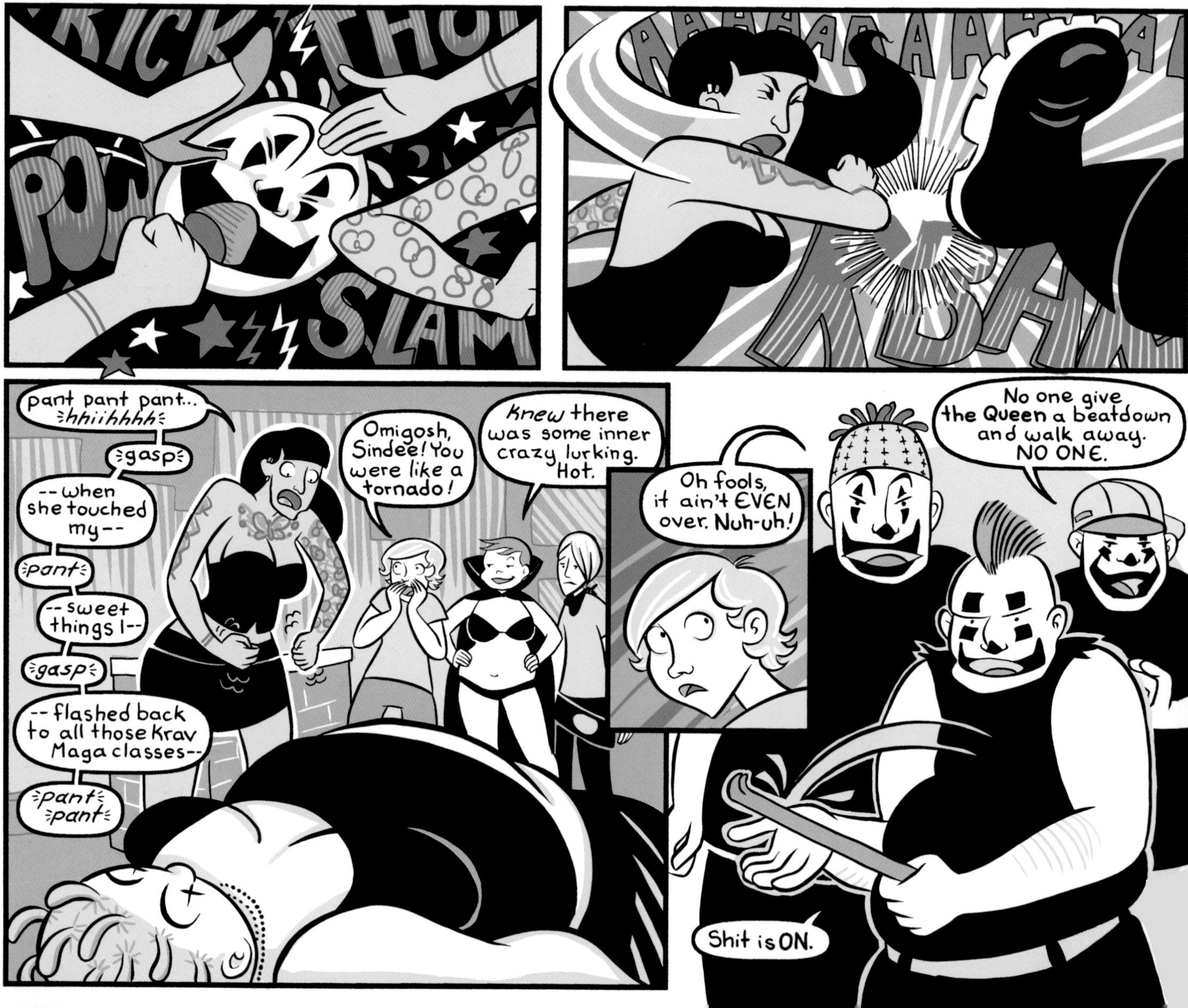
KICK
THO
POW
SLAM
AAAAAAAA
KBAM
pant pant pant... hhiihhhh
gasp
--when she touched my--
pant
--sweet things I--
gasp
--flashed back to all those Krav Maga classes--
pant pant
Omigosh, Sindee! You were like a tornado!
Knew there was some inner crazy lurking. Hot.
Oh fools, it ain't EVEN over. Nuh-uh!
No one give the Queen a beatdown and walk away. NO ONE.
Shit is ON.

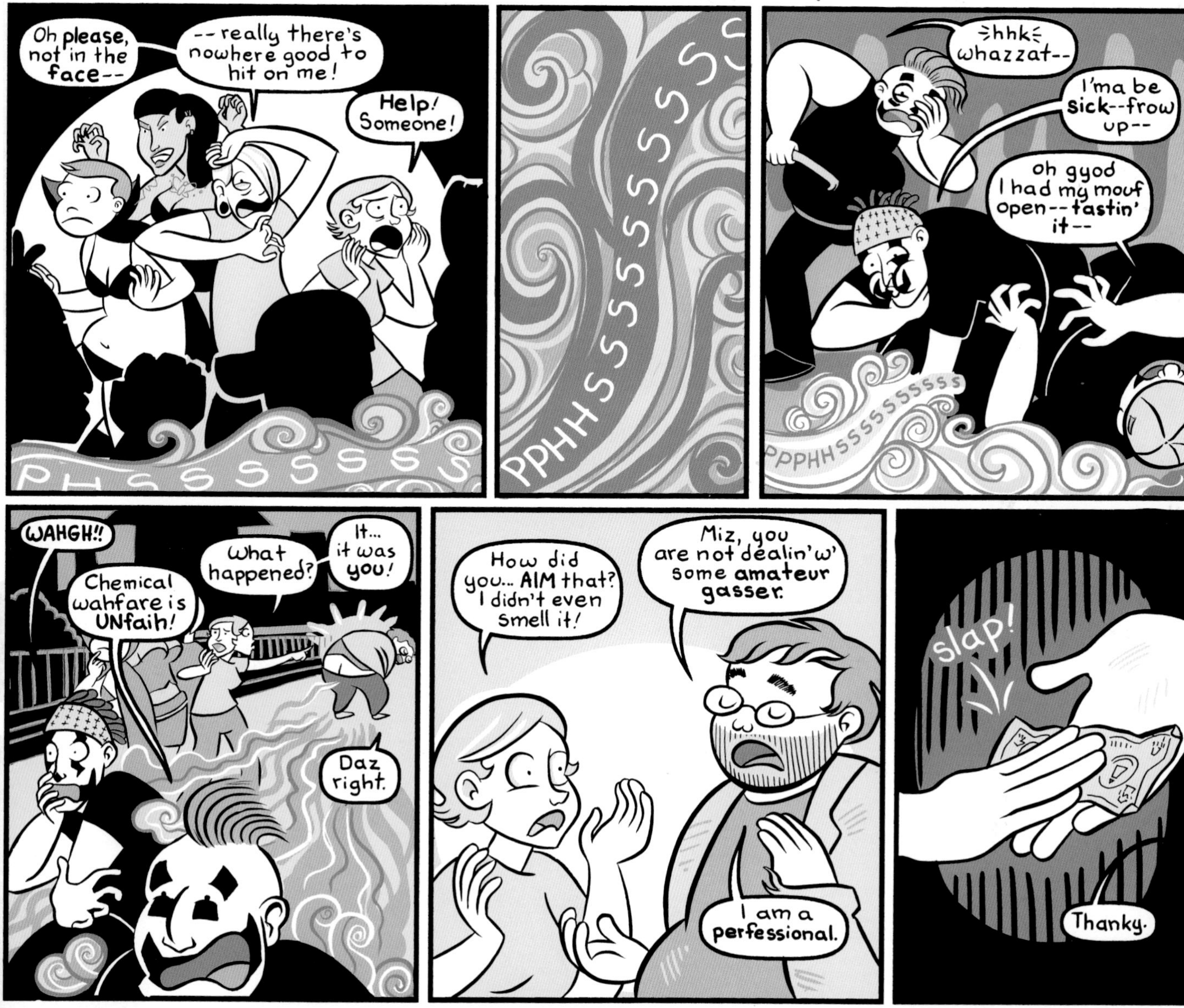
Oh please, not in the face--
--really there's nowhere good to hit on me!
Help! Someone!
PHSSSSSSS
PPHHSSSSSSSS
hhk whazzat--
I'ma be sick--frow up--
oh gyod I had my mouf open--tastin' it--
PPPHHSSSSSSSSSSS
WAHGH!!
Chemical wahfare is UNfaih!
What happened?
It... it was you!
Daz right.
How did you... AIM that? I didn't even smell it!
Miz, you are not dealin' w' some amateur gasser.
I am a perfessional.
slap!
Thanky.

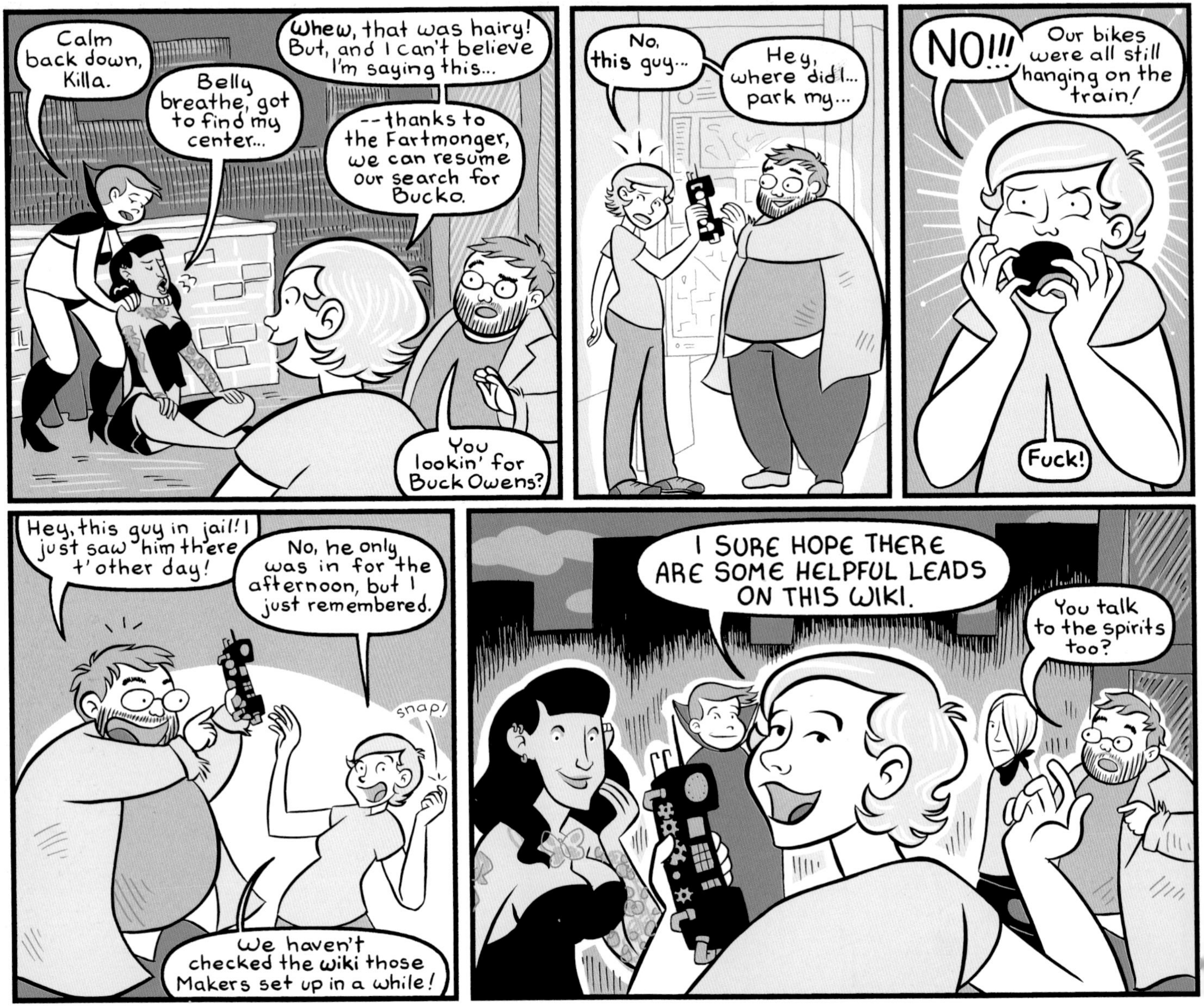

Calm back down, Killa.
Belly breathe, got to find my center...
Whew, that was hairy! But, and I can't believe I'm saying this...
--thanks to the Fartmonger, we can resume our search for Bucko.
You lookin' for Buck Owens?
No, this guy...
Hey, where did I... park my...
NO!!!...
Our bikes were all still hanging on the train!
Fuck!
Hey, this guy in jail! I just saw him there t'other day!
No, he only was in for the afternoon, but I just remembered.
snap!
We haven't checked the wiki those Makers set up in a while!
I SURE HOPE THERE ARE SOME HELPFUL LEADS ON THIS WIKI.
You talk to the spirits too?

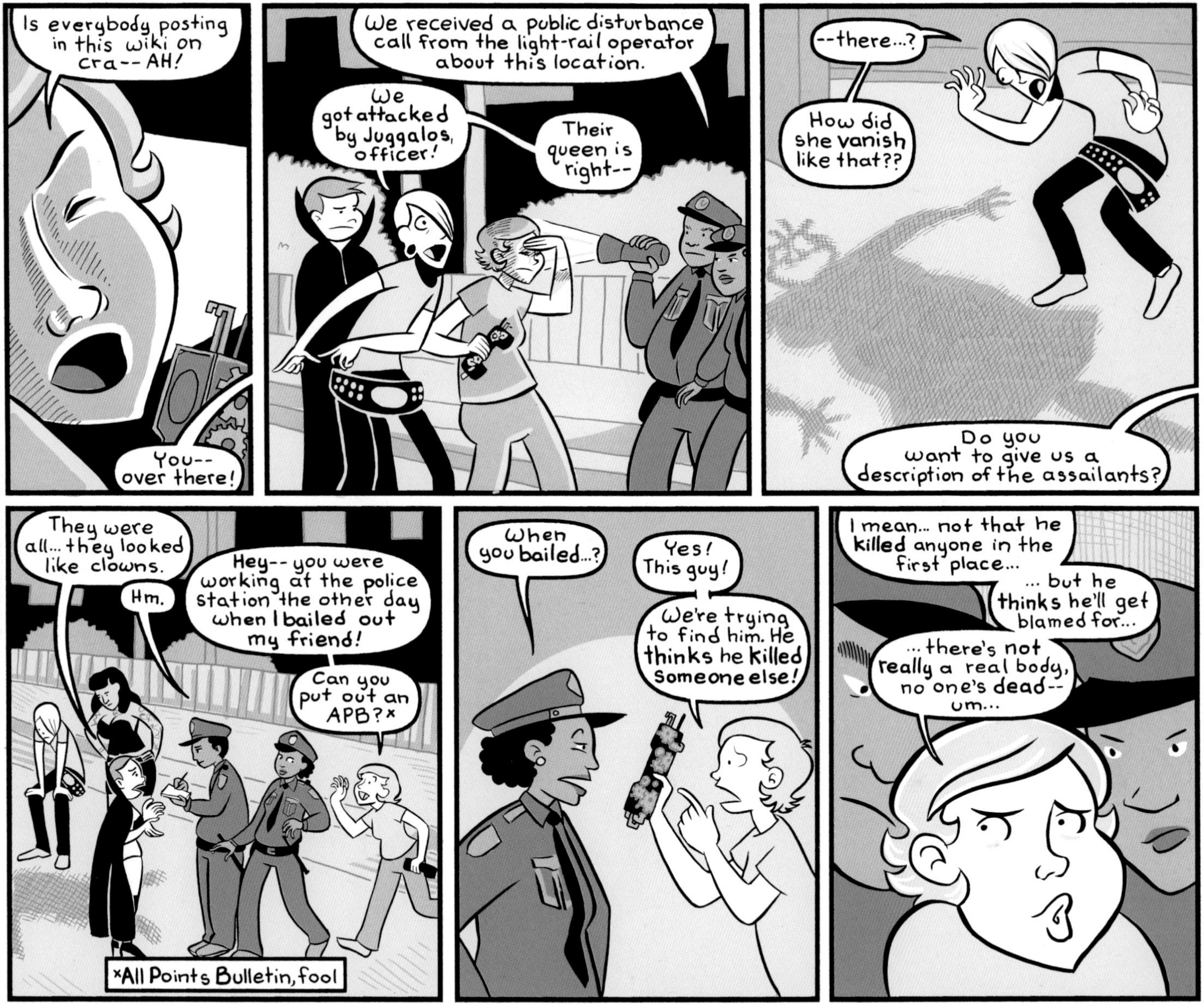
Is everybody posting in this wiki on cra-- AH!
You-- over there!
We received a public disturbance call from the light-rail operator about this location.
We got attacked by Juggalos, officer!
Their queen is right--
--there...?
How did she vanish like that??
Do you want to give us a description of the assailants?
They were all... they looked like clowns.
Hm.
Hey-- you were working at the police station the other day when I bailed out my friend!
Can you put out an APB?*
*All Points Bulletin, fool
When you bailed...?
Yes! This guy!
We're trying to find him. He thinks he killed someone else!
I mean... not that he killed anyone in the first place...
... but he thinks he'll get blamed for...
... there's not really a real body, no one's dead-- um...

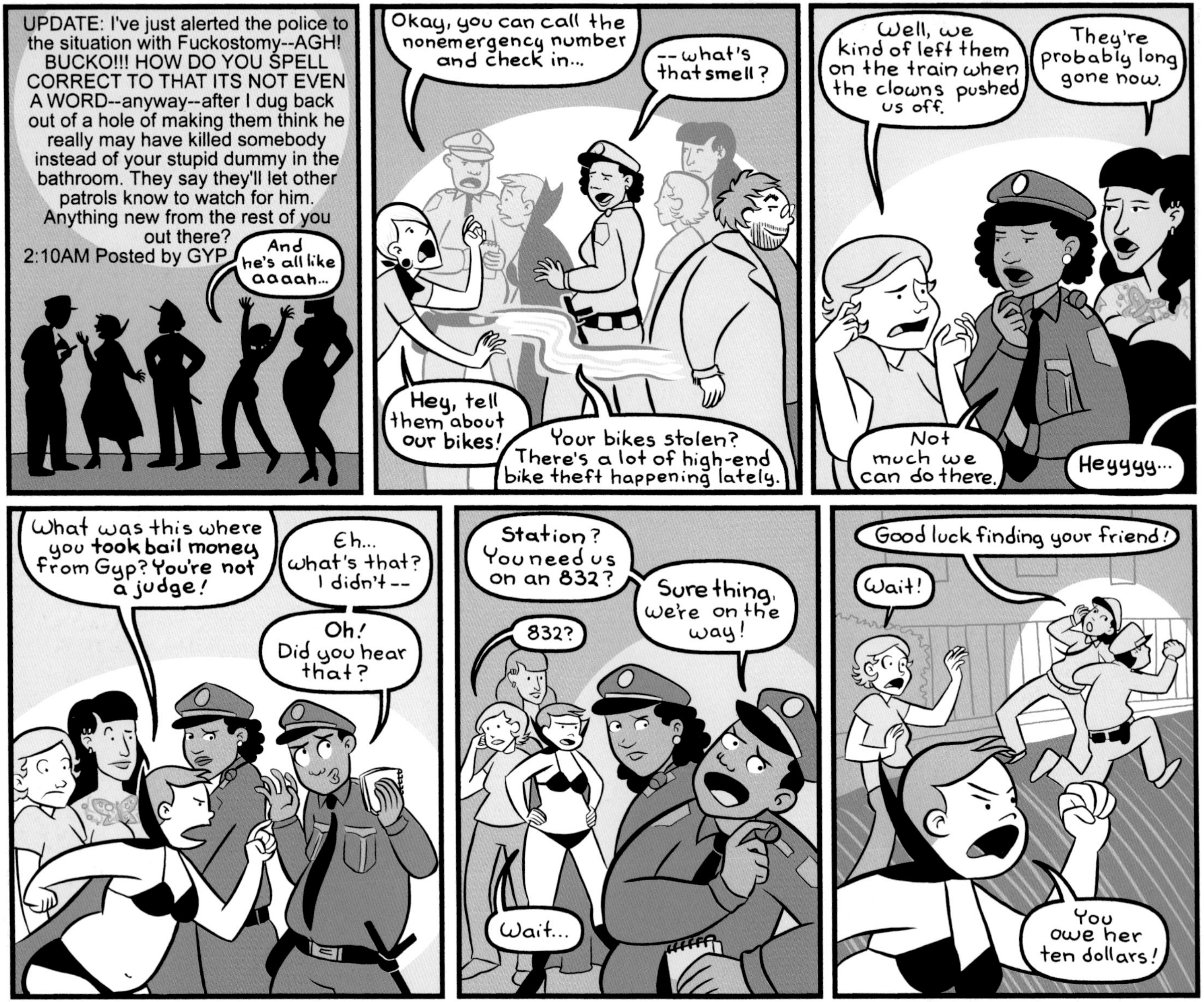
UPDATE: I've just alerted the police to the situation with Fuckostomy--AGH! BUCKO!!! HOW DO YOU SPELL CORRECT TO THAT ITS NOT EVEN A WORD--anyway--after I dug back out of a hole of making them think he really may have killed somebody instead of your stupid dummy in the bathroom. They say they'll let other patrols know to watch for him. Anything new from the rest of you out there?
2:10AM Posted by GYP
And he's all like aaaah...
Okay, you can call the nonemergency number and check in...
--what's that smell?
Hey, tell them about our bikes!
Your bikes stolen? There's a lot of high-end bike theft happening lately.
Well, we kind of left them on the train when the clowns pushed us off.
They're probably long gone now.
Not much we can do there.
Heyyyy...
What was this where you took bail money from Gyp? You're not a judge!
Eh... what's that? I didn't--
Oh! Did you hear that?
Station? You need us on an 832?
Sure thing, we're on the way!
832?
Wait...
Good luck finding your friend!
Wait!
You owe her ten dollars!

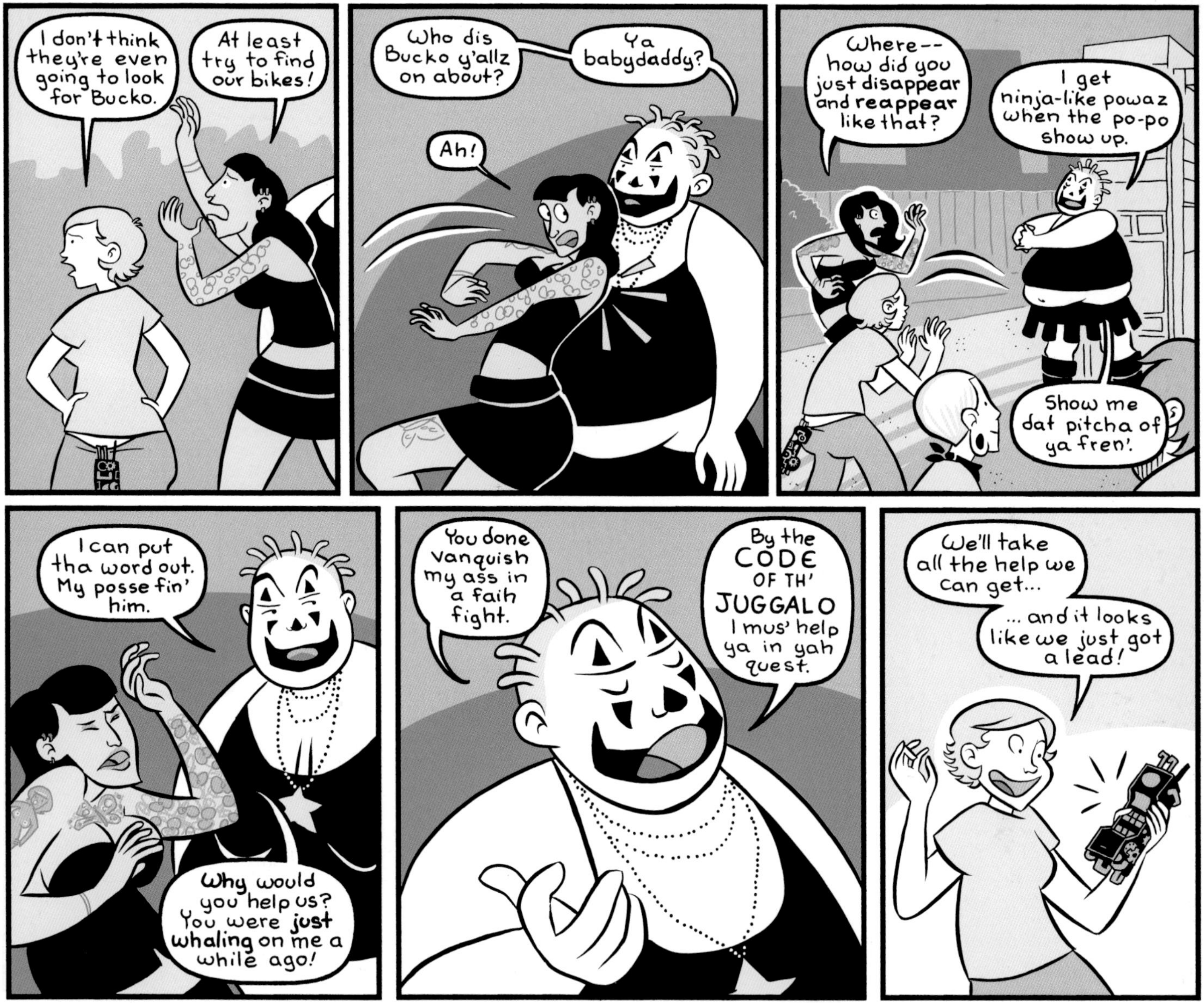
I don't think they're even going to look for Bucko.
At least try to find our bikes!
Who dis Bucko y'allz on about?
Ya babydaddy?
Ah!
Where-- how did you just disappear and reappear like that?
I get ninja-like powaz when the po-po show up.
Show me dat pitcha of ya fren'.
I can put tha word out. My posse fin' him.
Why would you help us? You were just whaling on me a while ago!
You done vanquish my ass in a faih fight.
By the CODE OF TH' JUGGALO I mus' help ya in yah quest.
We'll take all the help we can get...
...and it looks like we just got a lead!

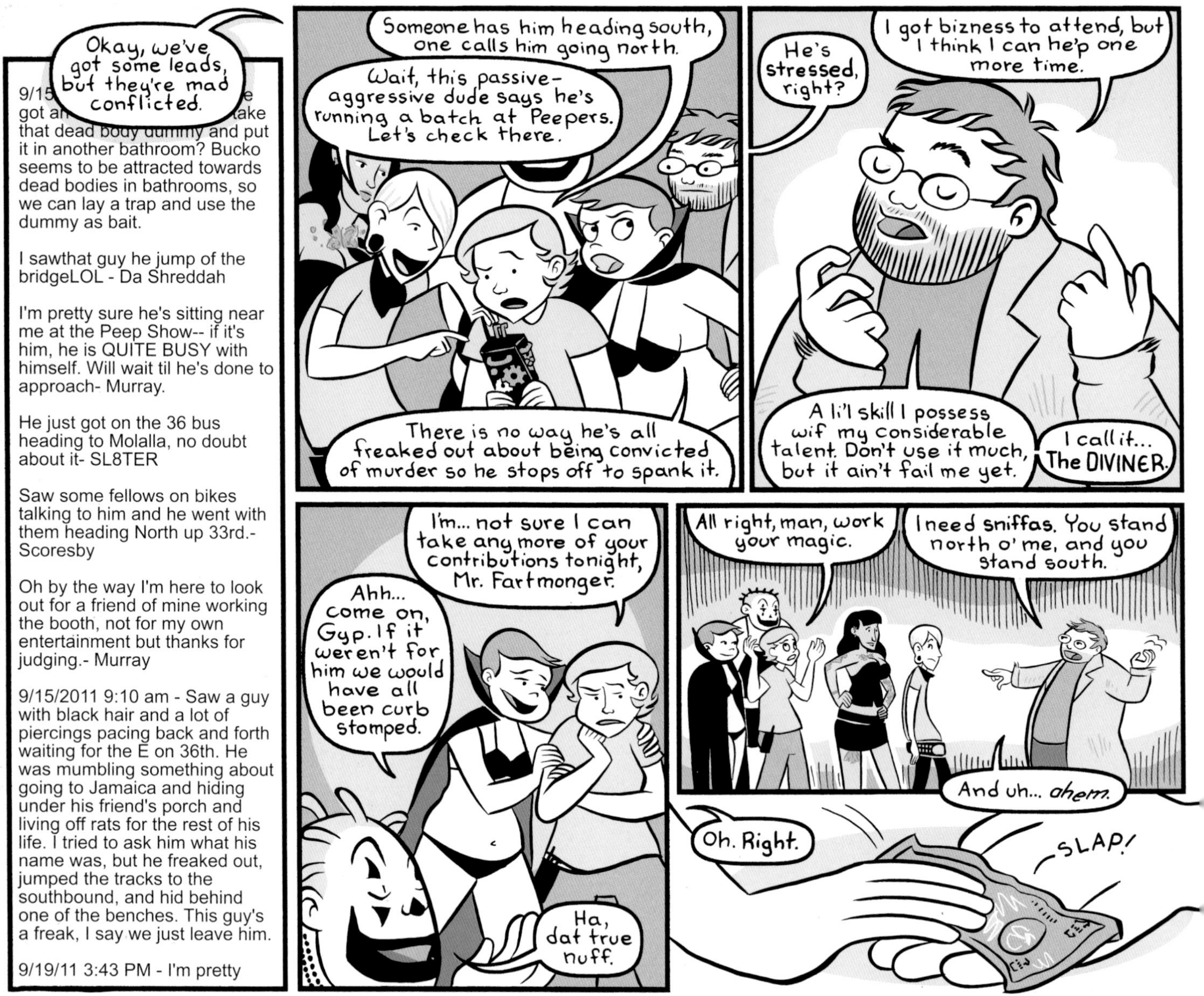
Okay, we've got some leads, but they're mad conflicted.
9/15 ... got an ... take that dead body dummy and put it in another bathroom? Bucko seems to be attracted towards dead bodies in bathrooms, so we can lay a trap and use the dummy as bait.
I sawthat guy he jump of the bridgeLOL - Da Shreddah
I'm pretty sure he's sitting near me at the Peep Show-- if it's him, he is QUITE BUSY with himself. Will wait til he's done to approach- Murray.
He just got on the 36 bus heading to Molalla, no doubt about it- SL8TER
Saw some fellows on bikes talking to him and he went with them heading North up 33rd.- Scoresby
Oh by the way I'm here to look out for a friend of mine working the booth, not for my own entertainment but thanks for judging.- Murray
9/15/2011 9:10 am - Saw a guy with black hair and a lot of piercings pacing back and forth waiting for the E on 36th. He was mumbling something about going to Jamaica and hiding under his friend's porch and living off rats for the rest of his life. I tried to ask him what his name was, but he freaked out, jumped the tracks to the southbound, and hid behind one of the benches. This guy's a freak, I say we just leave him.
9/19/11 3:43 PM - I'm pretty
Someone has him heading south, one calls him going north.
Wait, this passive-aggressive dude says he's running a batch at Peepers. Let's check there.
There is no way he's all freaked out about being convicted of murder so he stops off to spank it.
He's stressed, right?
I got bizness to attend, but I think I can he'p one more time.
A li'l skill I possess wif my considerable talent. Don't use it much, but it ain't fail me yet.
I call it... The DIVINER.
I'm... not sure I can take any more of your contributions tonight, Mr. Fartmonger.
Ahh... come on, Gyp. If it weren't for him we would have all been curb stomped.
Ha, dat true nuff.
All right, man, work your magic.
I need sniffas. You stand north o' me, and you stand south.
And uh... ahem.
Oh. Right.
SLAP!

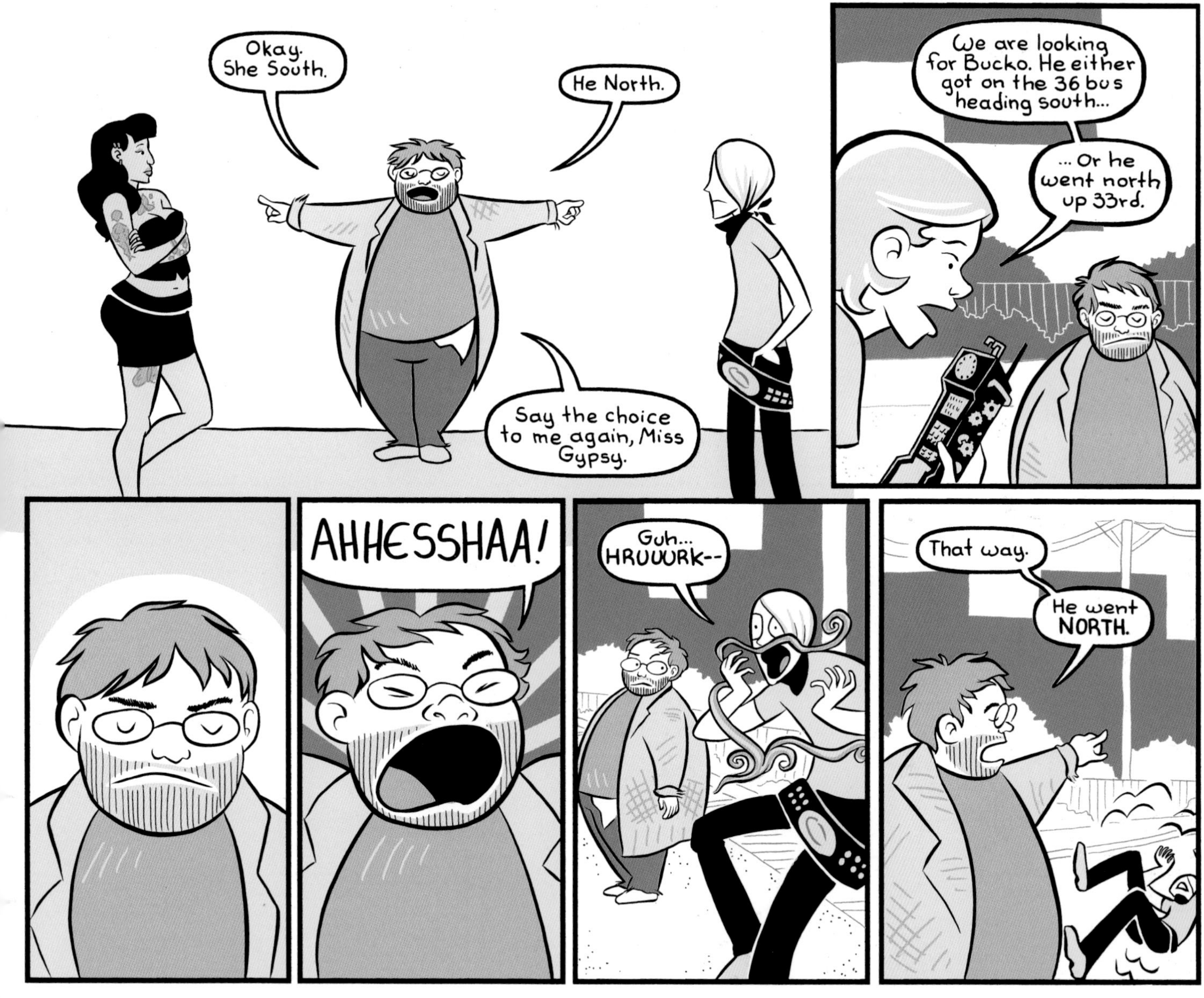
Okay. She South.
He North.
Say the choice to me again, Miss Gypsy.
We are looking for Bucko. He either got on the 36 bus heading south...
...Or he went north up 33rd.
AHHESSHAA!
Guh... HRUUURK--
That way.
He went NORTH.

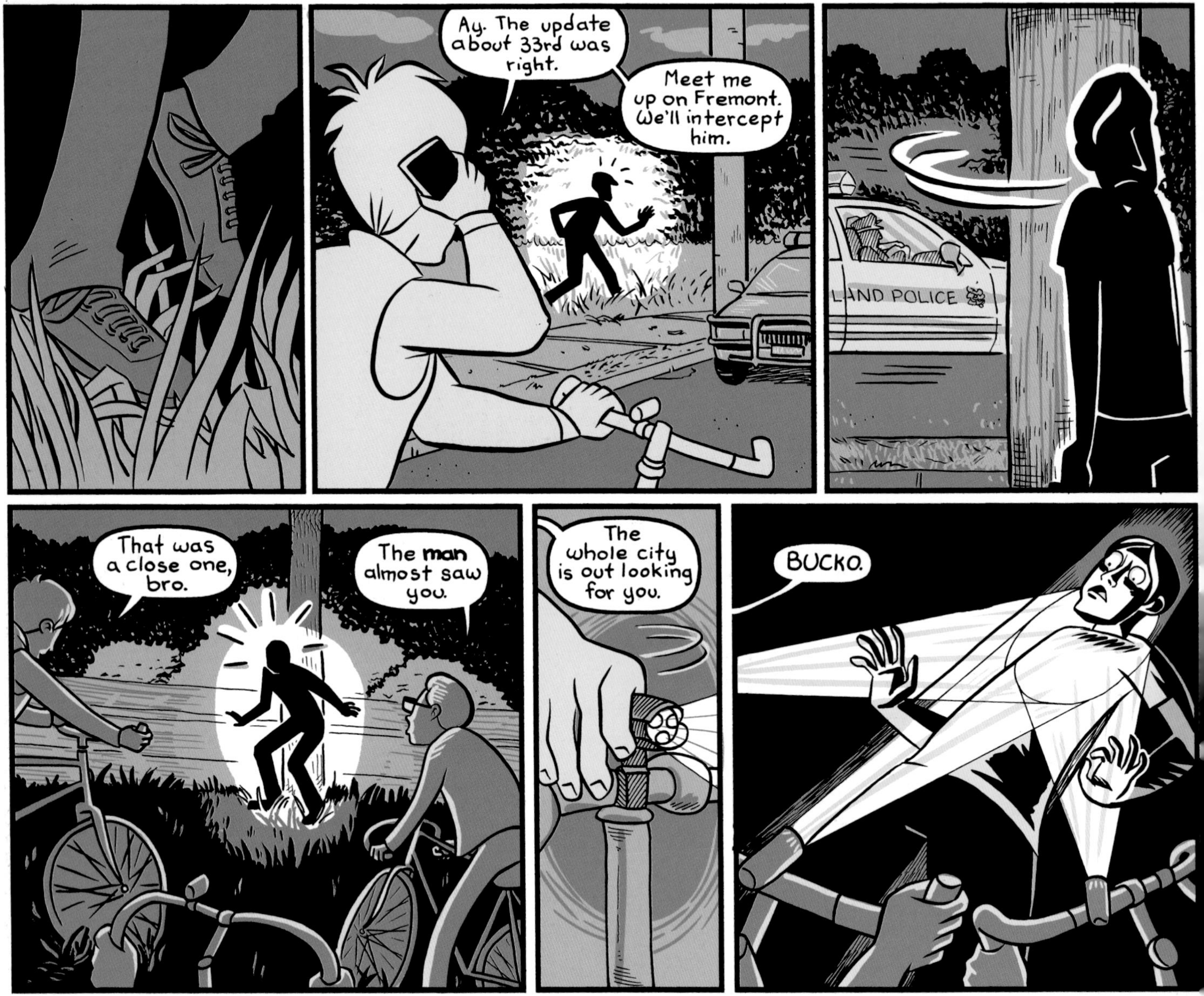
Ay. The update about 33rd was right.
Meet me up on Fremont. We'll intercept him.
LAND POLICE
That was a close one, bro.
The **man** almost saw you.
The whole city is out looking for you.
BUCKO.

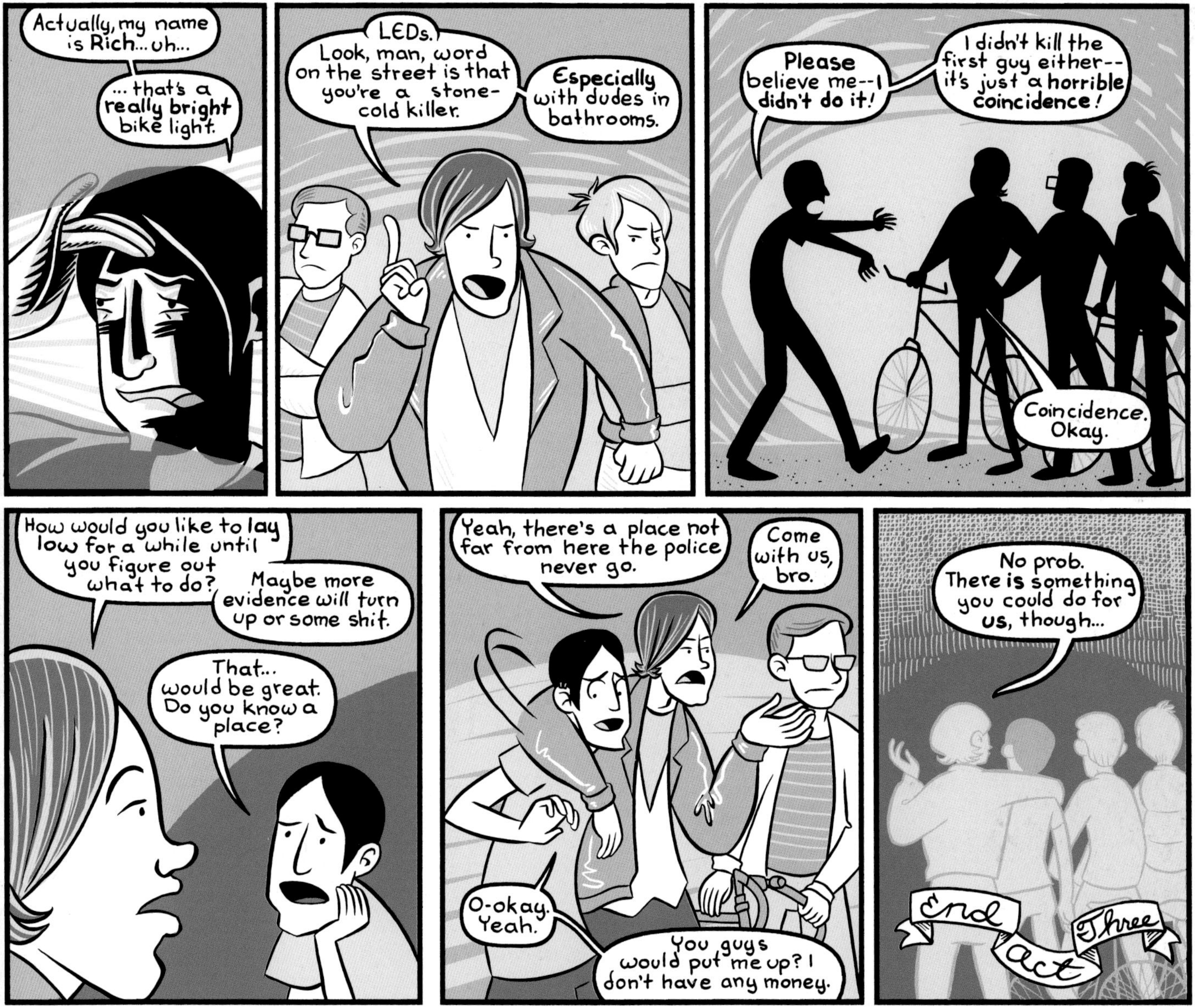
Actually, my name is Rich... uh...
... that's a really bright bike light.
LEDs.
Look, man, word on the street is that you're a stone-cold killer.
Especially with dudes in bathrooms.
Please believe me--I didn't do it!
I didn't kill the first guy either-- it's just a horrible coincidence!
Coincidence. Okay.
How would you like to lay low for a while until you figure out what to do?
Maybe more evidence will turn up or some shit.
That... would be great. Do you know a place?
Yeah, there's a place not far from here the police never go.
Come with us, bro.
O-okay. Yeah.
You guys would put me up? I don't have any money.
No prob. There is something you could do for us, though...
End act Three

fearless comedy

As we finish this book and look for more places to cram Funny in, I keep thinking about—of all things—one of the cable TV Comic Relief telethons, number eight from '98. When it came time for Whoopi Goldberg to reintroduce Bob Odenkirk and David Cross, their comedy bit from earlier in the show of selling the fundraising shirts like a late-night infomercial had clearly left her mystified. She even actually said, "I guess I'm old." But now she cited the uptick in donations after their piece and welcomed back the guys from "the Mr. Show."

Odenkirk and Cross had done a few seasons of *Mr. Show* at that point (at the latest, most secret time slot HBO could possibly give it) but were still clearly unknown to most of the audience, who had come for the comedy stylings of Ray Romano and Dennis Miller. With no reputation to coast on, all Bob and David could do was go out there and be funny, and show what they were willing to do for a joke (especially Bob). So they come out with a familiar approach for unknowns, bouncing around like a couple of comedy-sports improv guys, asking the crowd to think of a familiar phrase. Some of the attendees don't seem to get that it's a conceptual parody, even as Bob is escorted off so David and the audience can pick a phrase to guess. Bob's the gullible one being told by David, in the evil-jerk role, to take off all his clothes, reassured to just go along; it will all make sense.

Then Odenkirk walks back out through the aisles of Radio City Music Hall—*completely naked*, one hand cupped over his action, looking around, unsure and confused, in character. The audience howls, and the two continue with the guise of the improv skit, with David not acknowledging that Bob guessed the correct phrase, prolonging his torture. Bob finally "gets" it and screams, "You are not a friend! You are nothing but a stupid jerk-ass dick!" David cheers, "That's it, 'stupid jerk-ass dick' was the phrase!" and Bob clicks back to being happy for winning, and the two go offstage to a roaring audience. To Radio City season-ticket holders, it must have been a surreal bit to see.

It was hilarious, but to me the real moment came when Robin Williams and Billy Crystal walked back out. Williams manages to at least roll with it and try to riff off it all, but Crystal is noticeably stunned. Remember, he's one of those guys who like to talk the mechanics of comedy, that pontificating role Jerry Lewis and his lozenge would occupy in interviews. Stuff like how comedians don't laugh at something truly funny, they nod in acknowledgement, et cetera.

As I saw it, this was one of those points in time where everyone is forced to see their place in the universe. The two comedy vets try to recover their banter, but the stage has been nuked. They're left with played-out, ad-lib chum, like *Deliverance* jokes. The massive divide has just been clearly shown: You're willing to ham it up and "work blue," but you don't have it in you to go as far for a joke as Odenkirk just did. That guy is *the real deal*.

I don't know that we're that brave here (though Erika is working naked at her desk right now, if that counts for anything), but I think we aspire toward that. Something that goes beyond just hitting the marks of what's usually done

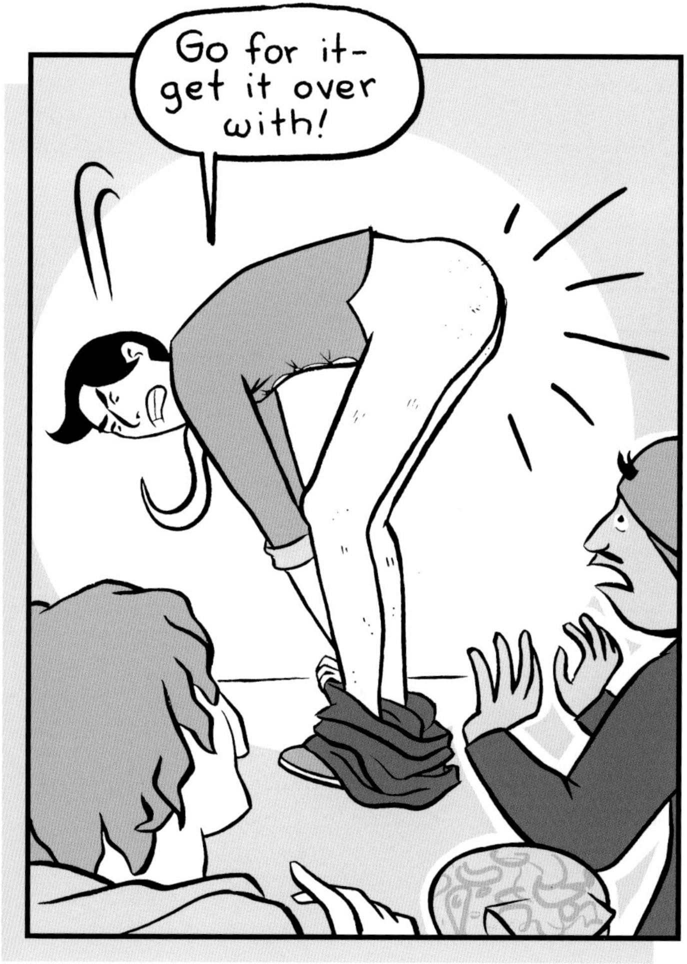
Go for it-
get it over
with!

in a comic strip—joke goes here, character makes bug eyes here, and so on—and explores areas you haven't necessarily spent a lot of head time on yourself, likely for good reason.

We are at least more than happy to make ourselves look horrible for a laugh. None of the characters, and by extension we the creators, are allowed to be cool or superior in this strip. We're not really lampooning anyone; the first and biggest butt of the joke is always us and our heroes. I generally despise "zing" humor, where one character busts on another, usually with the punishable-by-firing-squad smirk and raised eyebrow. I wanted us to go beyond that and create our own divide with strips that pluck those lame notes.

I'll admit, many of the bits I wrote came with an implied question—will Erika draw *this*? And repeatedly, without fail, she'd face me down and depict it. Funnier than I imagined. She had already set the tone way back in *DAR* with memorable bits like she and her roommates trying to solve the mystery of poo on the bathroom floor, Agatha Christie style. That let us pick up from there—tone is what lets you swing for that certain comic fence. Tone is everything, as is the willingness to follow a joke to its end and see what's really behind it.

Act Four

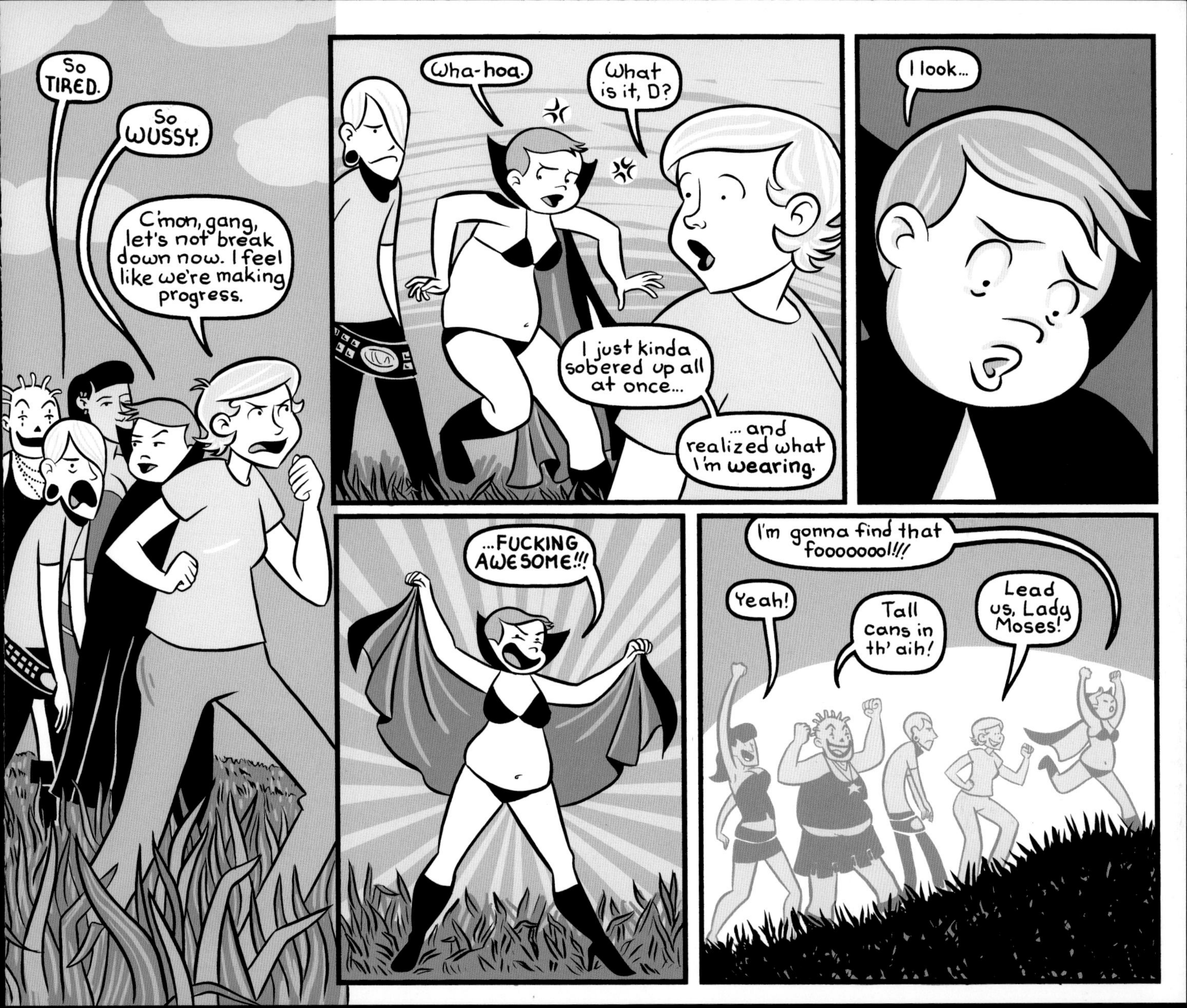
So TIRED.
So WUSSY.
C'mon, gang, let's not break down now. I feel like we're making progress.
Wha-hoa.
What is it, D?
I just kinda sobered up all at once...
... and realized what I'm wearing.
I look...
...FUCKING AWESOME!!!
I'm gonna find that foooooool!!!
Yeah!
Tall cans in th' aih!
Lead us, Lady Moses!

A subtle distinction, but now that we're supposed to like Juggalette, she goes from probably quoting Insane Clown Posse songs to quoting Transplants.

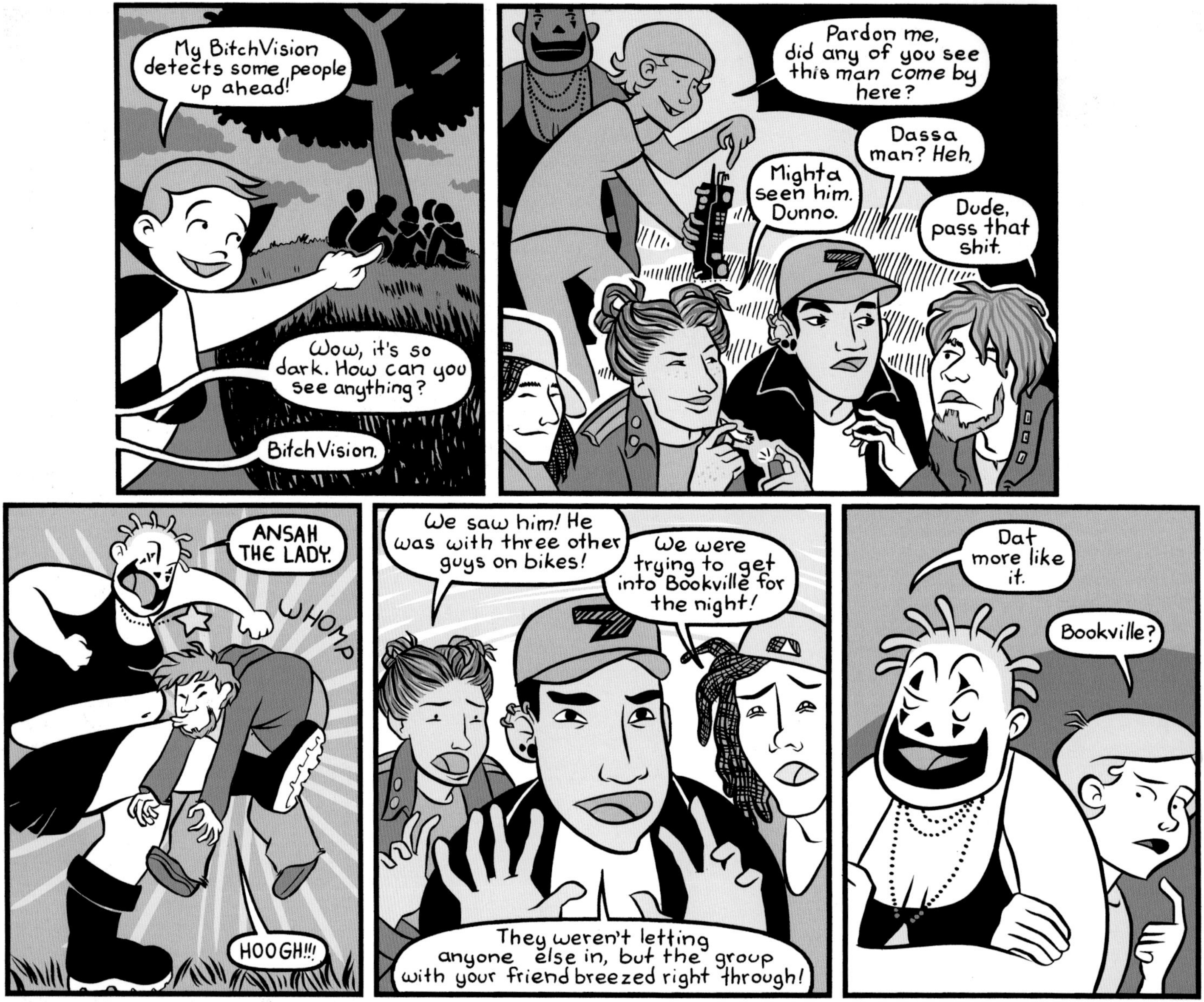
My BitchVision detects some people up ahead!
Wow, it's so dark. How can you see anything?
BitchVision.
Pardon me, did any of you see this man come by here?
Dassa man? Heh.
Mighta seen him. Dunno.
Dude, pass that shit.
ANSAH THE LADY.
WHOMP
HOOGH!!!
We saw him! He was with three other guys on bikes!
We were trying to get into Bookville for the night!
They weren't letting anyone else in, but the group with your friend breezed right through!
Dat more like it.
Bookville?

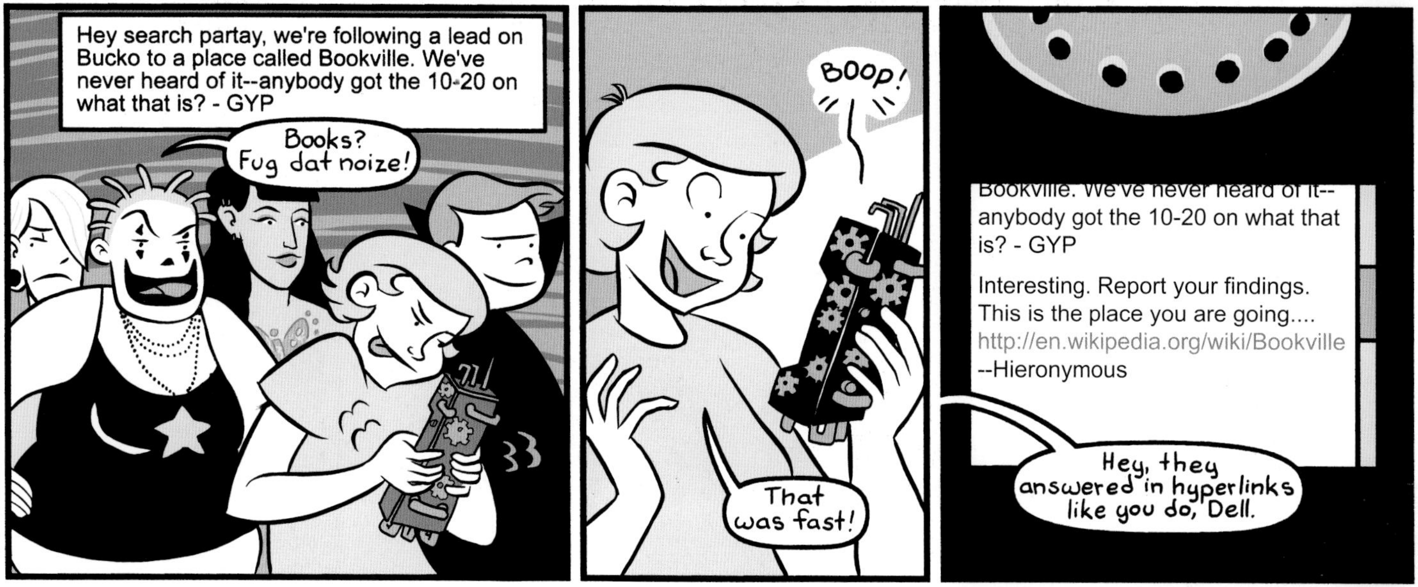
Hey search partay, we're following a lead on Bucko to a place called Bookville. We've never heard of it--anybody got the 10-20 on what that is? - GYP
Books? Fug dat noize!
BOOP!
That was fast!
Bookville. We've never heard of it--anybody got the 10-20 on what that is? - GYP
Interesting. Report your findings. This is the place you are going.... http://en.wikipedia.org/wiki/Bookville --Hieronymous
Hey, they answered in hyperlinks like you do, Dell.

Bookville

From Wikipedia, the free encyclopedia

Bookville (also redirects from Book Village, as well as HoBooken)is a city-recognized encampment of an estimated 60 homeless people in Multnomah County.

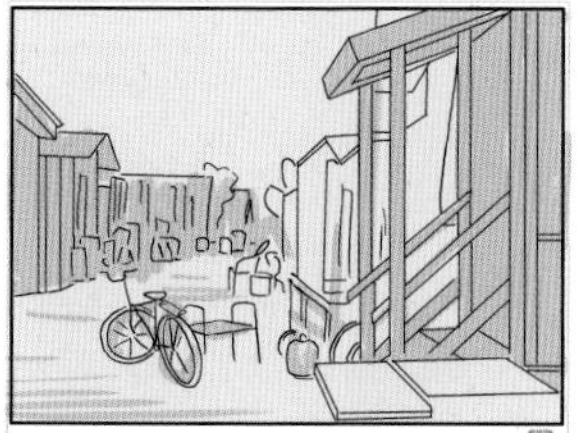

There are dozens of structures measuring up to 10 by 15 feet. As shelters wear, their materials are recycled to fashion new structures.

In the days before Christmas of 2000, a group of local indigents and drifters succeeded in establishing a tent city which garnered a great deal of both opposition and support, and quickly evolved from a group of self-described "outsiders" who practiced civil disobedience, to a self-regulating, city-recognized "campground" as defined by city code.

Now featuring dedicated land near PDX Airport, elected community officials and crude but functional cooking, social, electric, and sanitary facilities,[1]

Bookville gained its defining characteristics when local bookstore chain Village Of Books donated the entirety of a warehouse of new and used backstock that had been damaged by a rainstorm collapsing the roof. "They're a little warpy, but good enough for hobos," explained owner Milo Howell. "They'll learn valuable skills and we get a giant charity write-off. Everybody wins!"[3]

Roughly 27 tons of books were delivered to the location, though it was explained to Howell that the shanty town had nowhere to house the tomes. At this point some industrious dwellers began to use the books themselves to build the structures of the encampment. "You use the oversized books, the heavy stuff for the foundations," explained a local craftsman known as Itchy Walter, "and you surface the outer walls with glossy magazines, the slick stuff- it really repels the rain!" [4]

Social and political

Bookville is an intentional community which endorses or practices many socialist/communal principles.[5]

Within the area, an unusual organizational structure has been adopted allowing

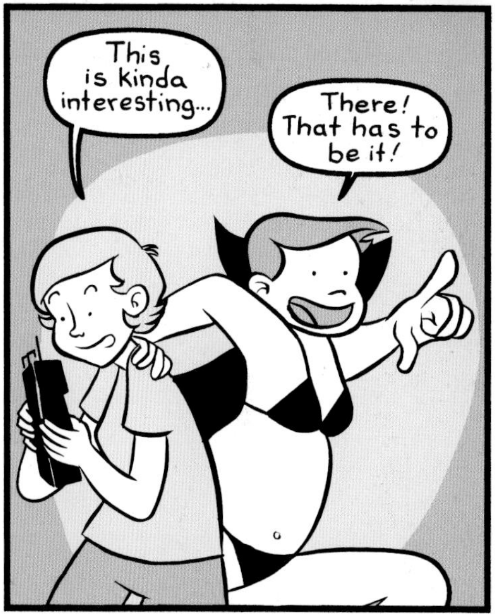
This is kinda interesting...
There! That has to be it!

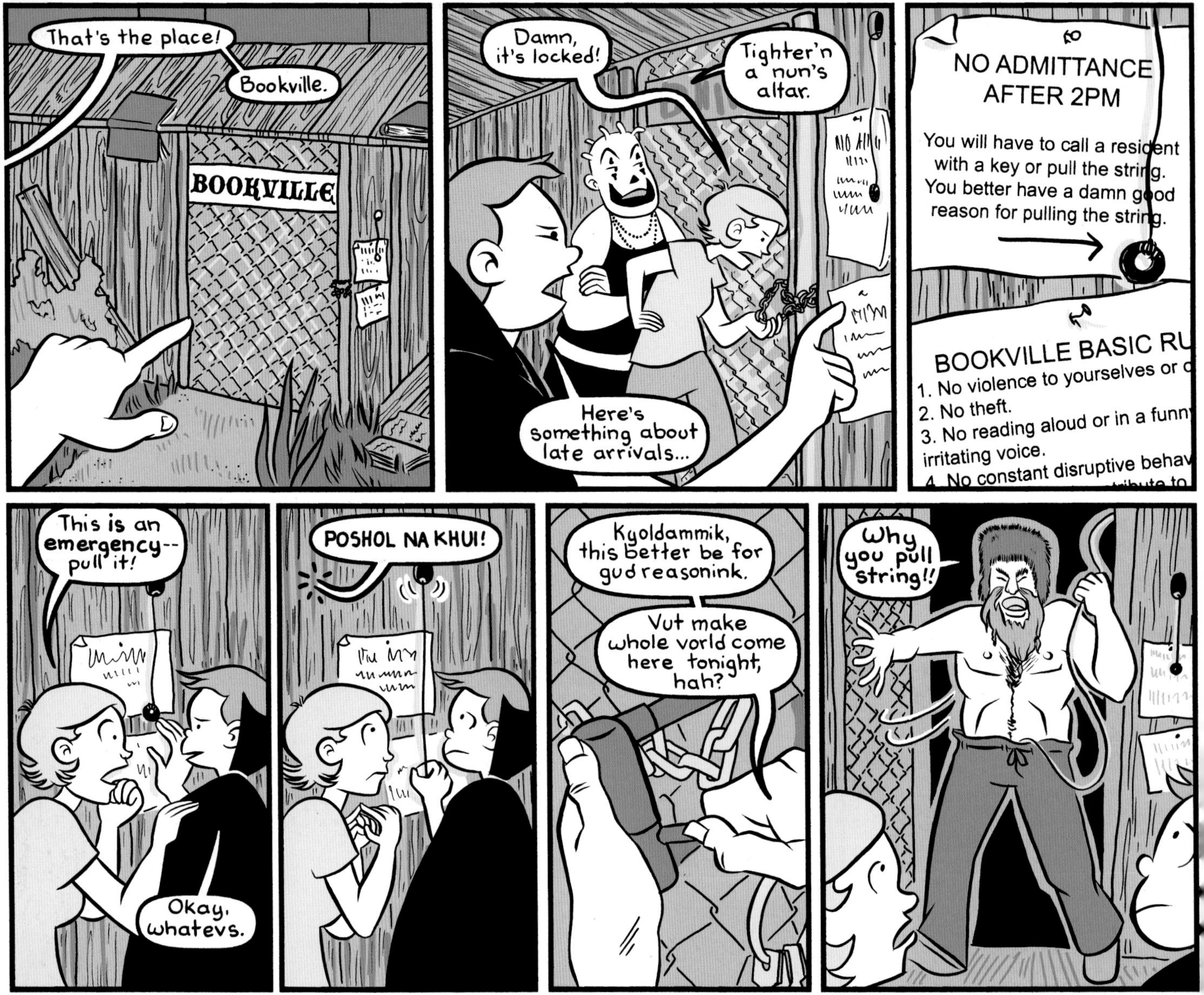
That's the place!
Bookville.
BOOKVILLE
Damn, it's locked!
Tighter'n a nun's altar.
Here's something about late arrivals...
NO ADMITTANCE AFTER 2PM
You will have to call a resident with a key or pull the string. You better have a damn good reason for pulling the string.
BOOKVILLE BASIC RU
1. No violence to yourselves or o
2. No theft.
3. No reading aloud or in a funny irritating voice.
4. No constant disruptive behav
This is an emergency-- pull it!
Okay, whatevs.
POSHOL NA KHUI!
Kyoldammik, this better be for gud reasonink.
Vut make whole vorld come here tonight, hah?
Why you pull string!!

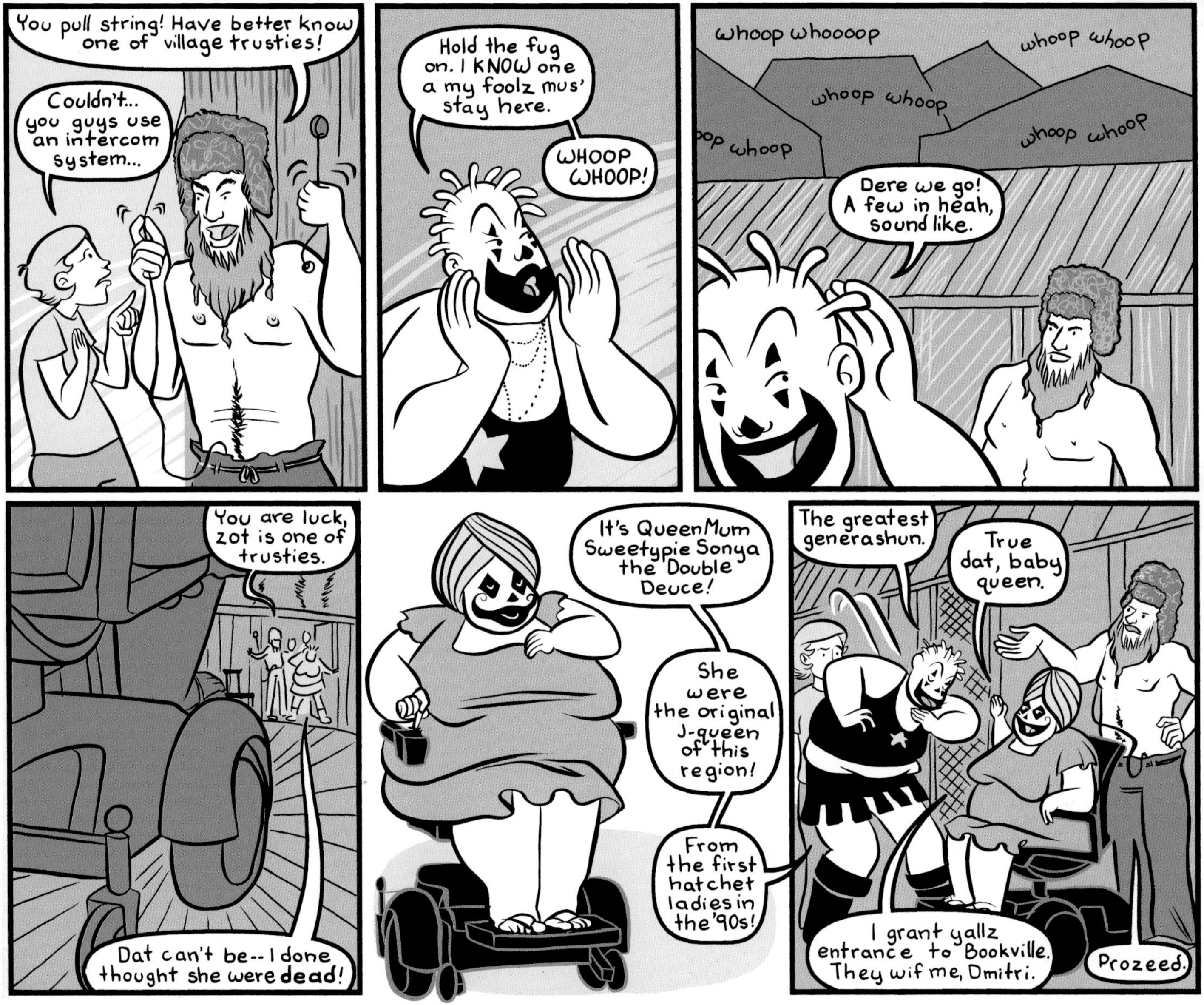
You pull string! Have better know one of village trusties!
Couldn't... you guys use an intercom system...
Hold the fug on. I KNOW one a my foolz mus' stay here.
WHOOP WHOOP!
whoop whoooop
whoop whoop
whoop whoop
op whoop
whoop whoop
Dere we go! A few in heah, sound like.
You are luck, zot is one of trusties.
Dat can't be-- I done thought she were **dead**!
It's QueenMum Sweetypie Sonya the Double Deuce!
She were the original J-queen of this region!
From the first hatchet ladies in the '90s!
The greatest generashun.
True dat, baby queen.
I grant yallz entrance to Bookville. They wif me, Dmitri.
Prozeed.

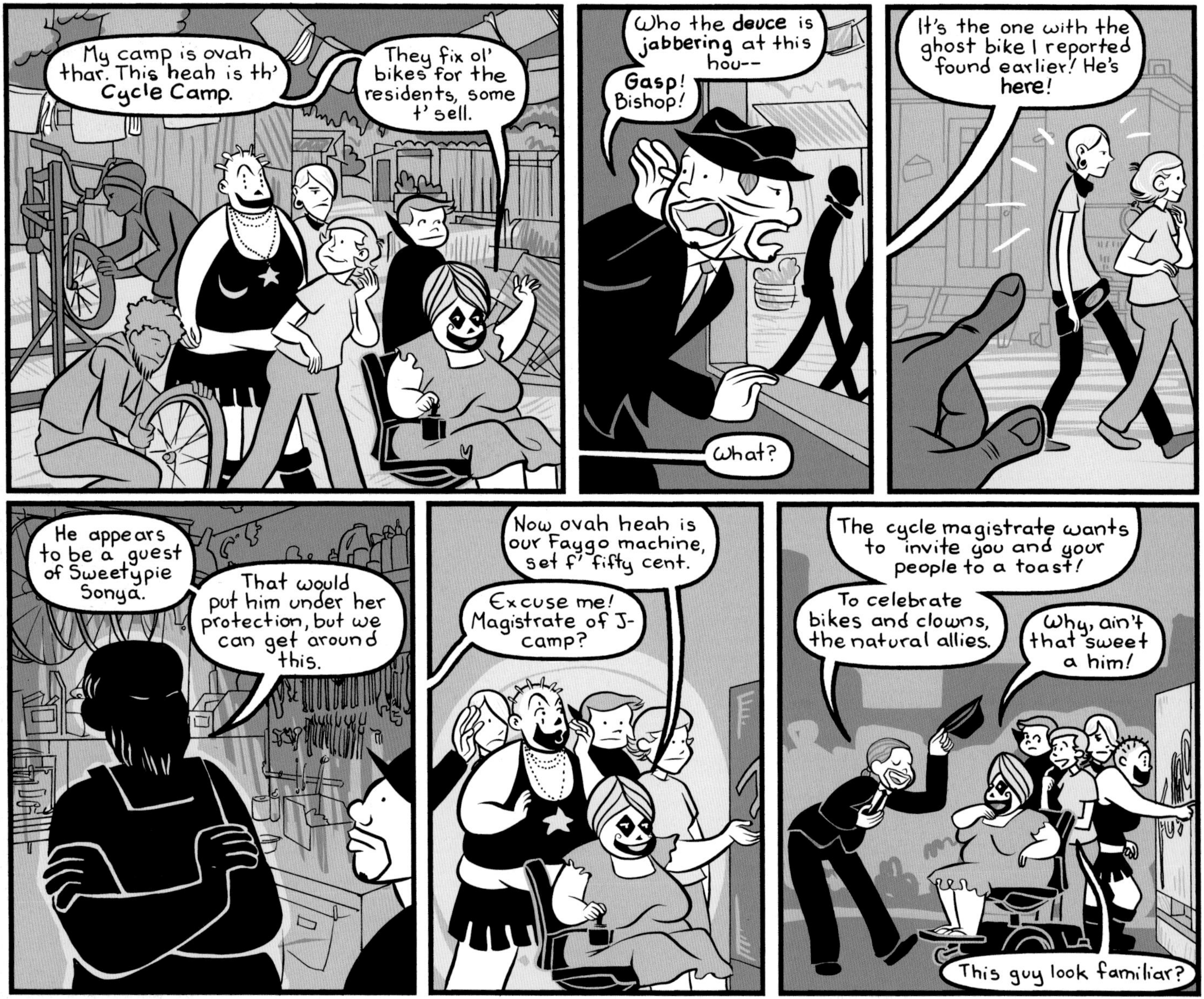
My camp is ovah thar. This heah is th' Cycle Camp.
They fix ol' bikes for the residents, some t' sell.
Who the deuce is jabbering at this hou--
Gasp! Bishop!
What?
It's the one with the ghost bike I reported found earlier! He's here!
He appears to be a guest of Sweetypie Sonya.
That would put him under her protection, but we can get around this.
Now ovah heah is our Faygo machine, set f' fifty cent.
Excuse me! Magistrate of J-camp?
The cycle magistrate wants to invite you and your people to a toast!
To celebrate bikes and clowns, the natural allies.
Why, ain't that sweet a him!
This guy look familiar?

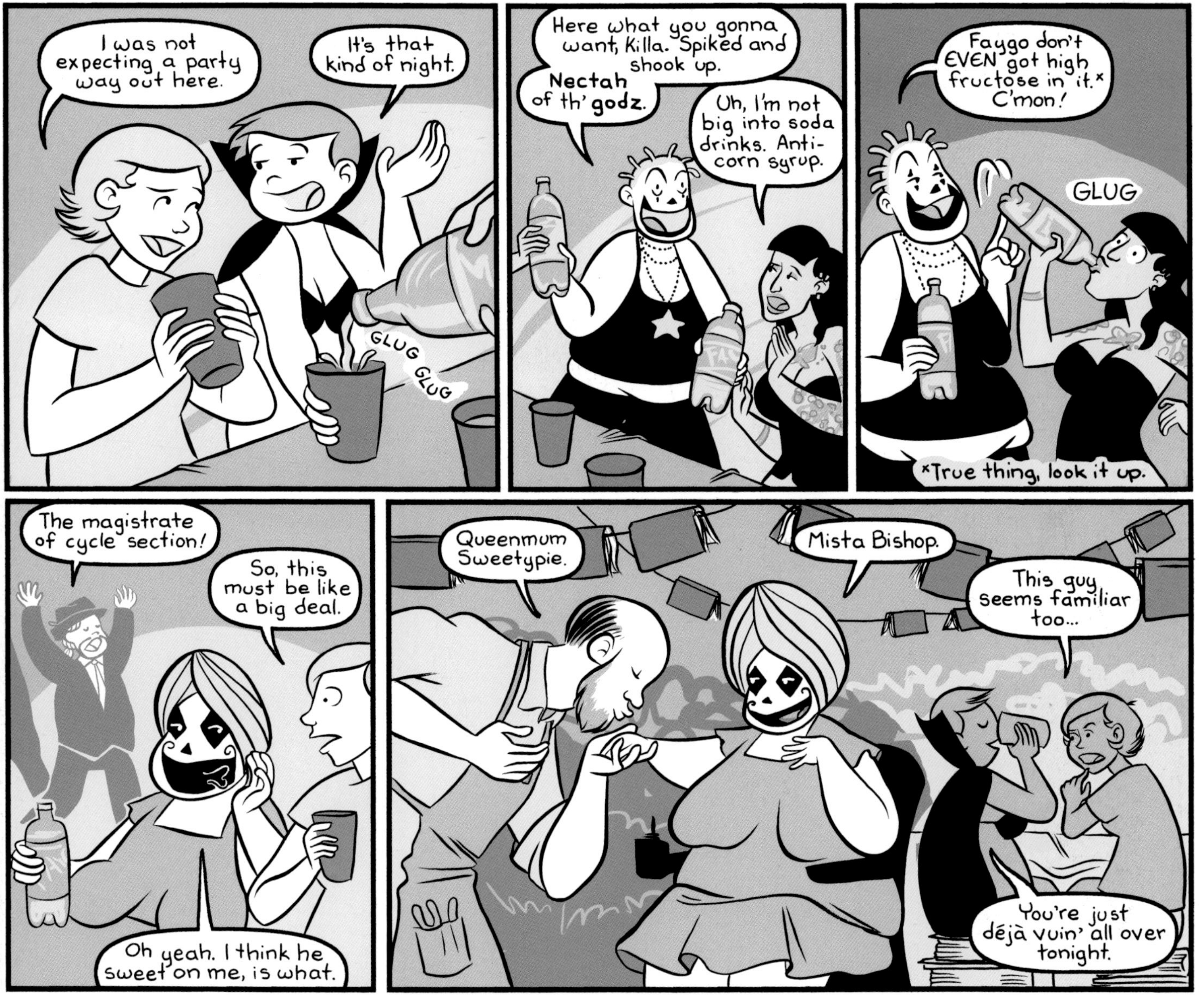
I was not expecting a party way out here.
It's that kind of night.
GLUG GLUG GLUG
Here what you gonna want, Killa. Spiked and shook up.
Nectah of th' godz.
Uh, I'm not big into soda drinks. Anti-corn syrup.
Faygo don't EVEN got high fructose in it.* C'mon!
GLUG
*True thing, look it up.
The magistrate of cycle section!
So, this must be like a big deal.
Oh yeah. I think he sweet on me, is what.
Queenmum Sweetypie.
Mista Bishop.
This guy seems familiar too...
You're just déjà vuin' all over tonight.

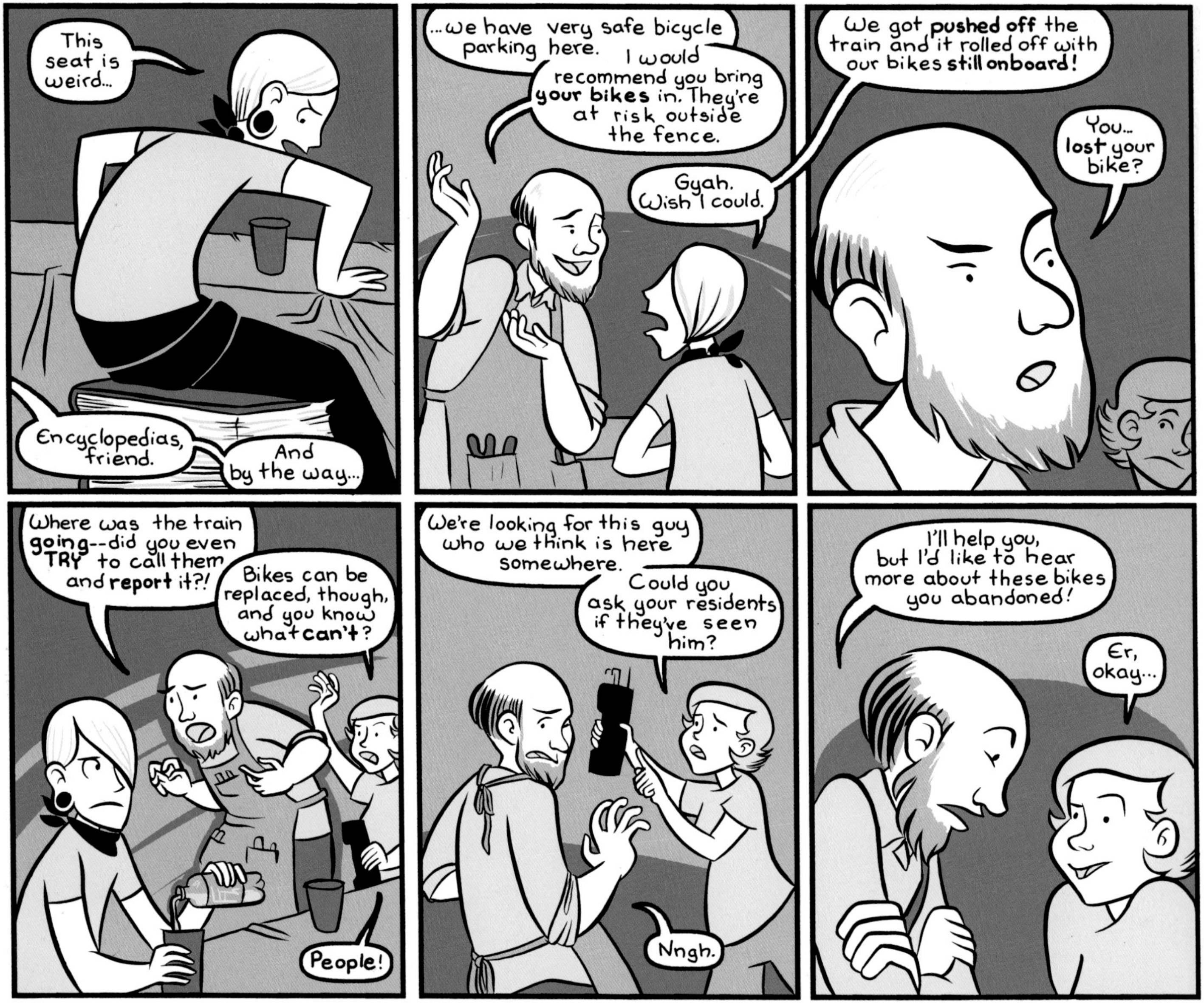
This seat is weird...
Encyclopedias, friend.
And by the way...
...we have very safe bicycle parking here.
I would recommend you bring **your bikes** in. They're at risk outside the fence.
Gyah. Wish I could.
We got **pushed off** the train and it rolled off with our bikes **still onboard!**
You... **lost** your bike?
Where was the train **going**--did you even **TRY** to call them and **report** it?!
Bikes can be replaced, though, and you know what **can't**?
People!
We're looking for this guy who we think is here somewhere.
Could you ask your residents if they've seen him?
Nngh.
I'll help you, but I'd like to hear more about these bikes you abandoned!
Er, okay...

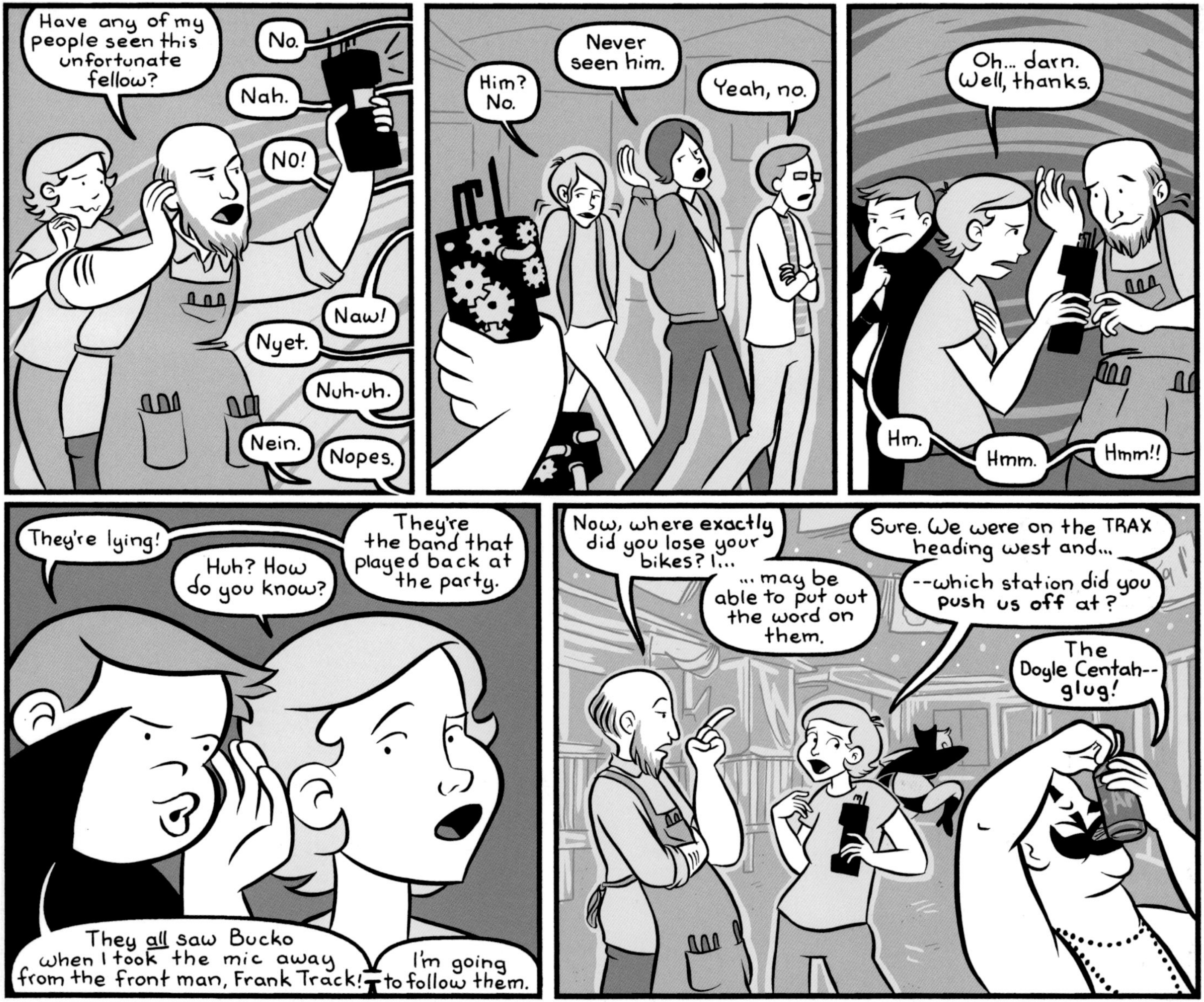

Have any of my people seen this unfortunate fellow?
No.
Nah.
NO!
Naw!
Nyet.
Nuh-uh.
Nein.
Nopes.
Him? No.
Never seen him.
Yeah, no.
Oh... darn. Well, thanks.
Hm.
Hmm.
Hmm!!
They're lying!
Huh? How do you know?
They're the band that played back at the party.
They all saw Bucko when I took the mic away from the front man, Frank Track!
I'm going to follow them.
Now, where exactly did you lose your bikes? I...
... may be able to put out the word on them.
Sure. We were on the TRAX heading west and...
--which station did you push us off at?
The Doyle Centah--glug!

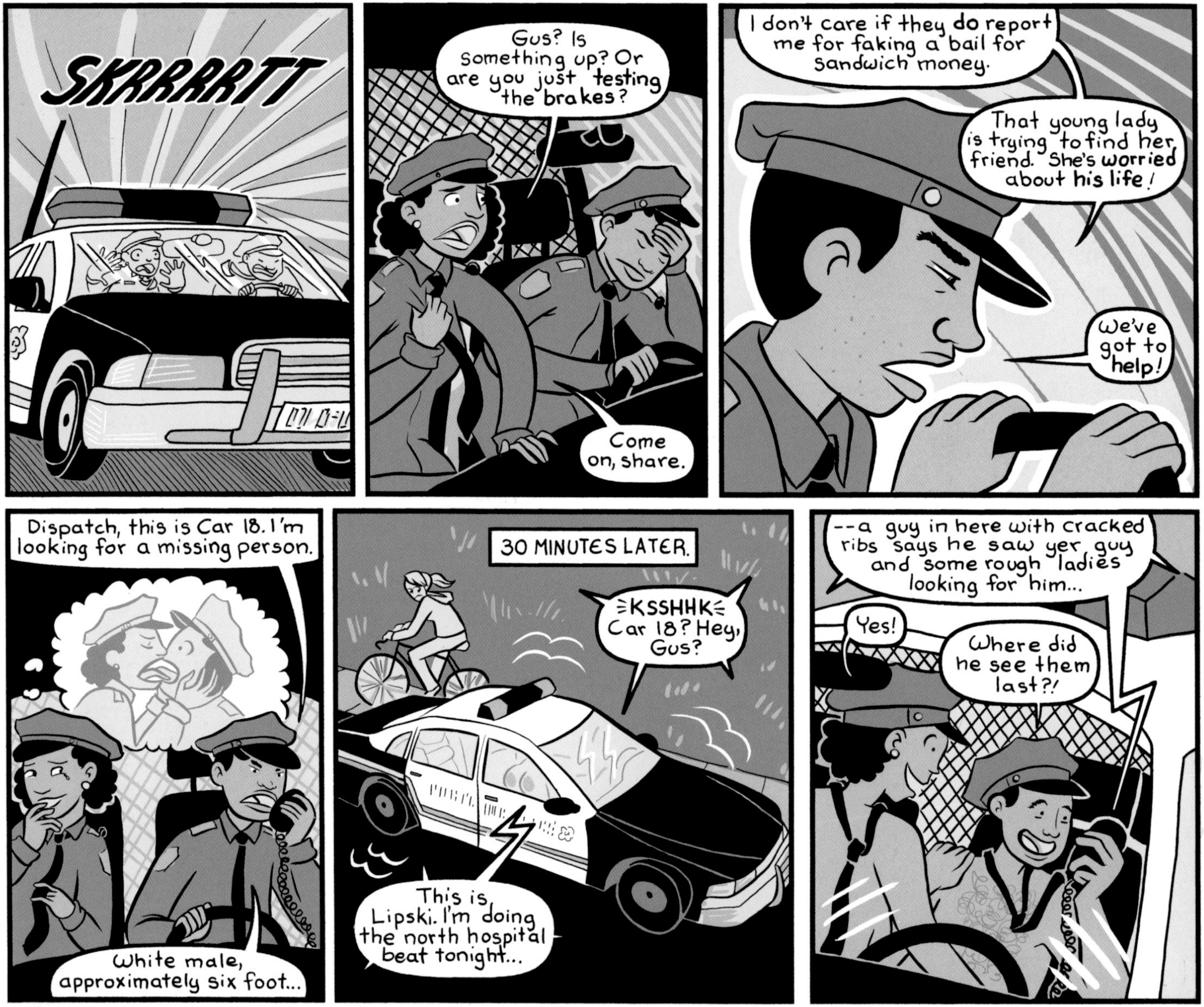
SKRRRRTT
Gus? Is something up? Or are you just testing the brakes?
Come on, share.
I don't care if they do report me for faking a bail for sandwich money.
That young lady is trying to find her friend. She's worried about his life!
We've got to help!
Dispatch, this is Car 18. I'm looking for a missing person.
White male, approximately six foot...
30 MINUTES LATER.
KSSHHK Car 18? Hey, Gus?
This is Lipski. I'm doing the north hospital beat tonight...
--a guy in here with cracked ribs says he saw yer guy and some rough ladies looking for him...
Yes!
Where did he see them last?!

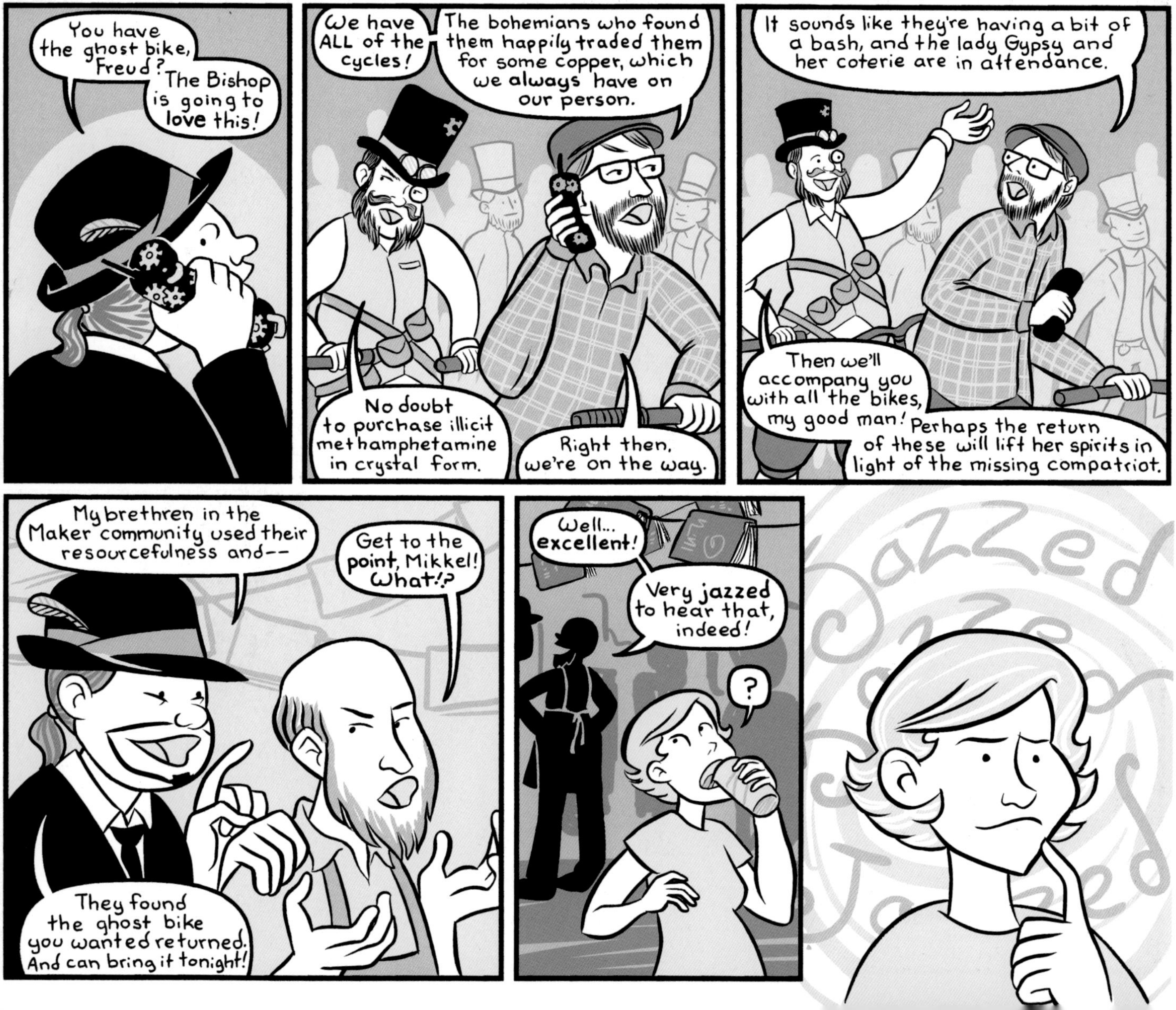
You have the ghost bike, Freud?
The Bishop is going to **love** this!
We have ALL of the cycles!
The bohemians who found them happily traded them for some copper, which we **always** have on our person.
No doubt to purchase illicit methamphetamine in crystal form.
Right then, we're on the way.
It sounds like they're having a bit of a bash, and the lady Gypsy and her coterie are in attendance.
Then we'll accompany you with all the bikes, my good man!
Perhaps the return of these will lift her spirits in light of the missing compatriot.
My brethren in the Maker community used their resourcefulness and--
Get to the **point, Mikkel! What!?**
They found the ghost bike you wanted returned. And can bring it tonight!
Well... **excellent!**
Very **jazzed** to hear that, indeed!
?

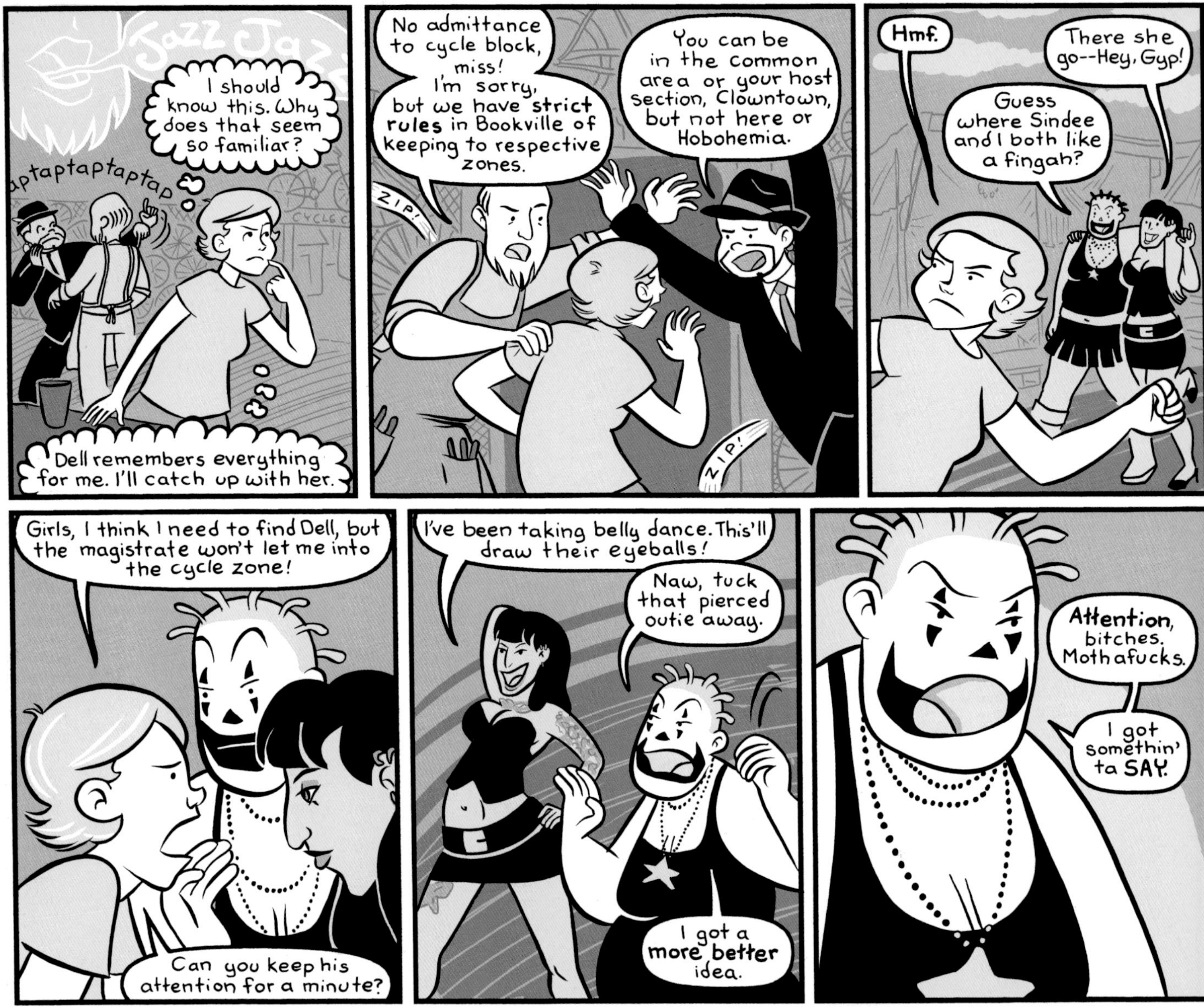
Jazz Jazz
I should know this. Why does that seem so familiar?
aptaptaptaptaptap
Dell remembers everything for me. I'll catch up with her.
No admittance to cycle block, miss! I'm sorry, but we have **strict rules** in Bookville of keeping to respective zones.
ZIP!
You can be in the common area or your host section, Clowntown, but not here or Hobohemia.
ZIP!
Hmf.
There she go--Hey, Gyp!
Guess where Sindee and I both like a fingah?
Girls, I think I need to find Dell, but the magistrate won't let me into the cycle zone!
Can you keep his attention for a minute?
I've been taking belly dance. This'll draw their eyeballs!
Naw, tuck that pierced outie away.
I got a **more better** idea.
Attention, bitches. Mothafucks.
I got somethin' ta **SAY**.

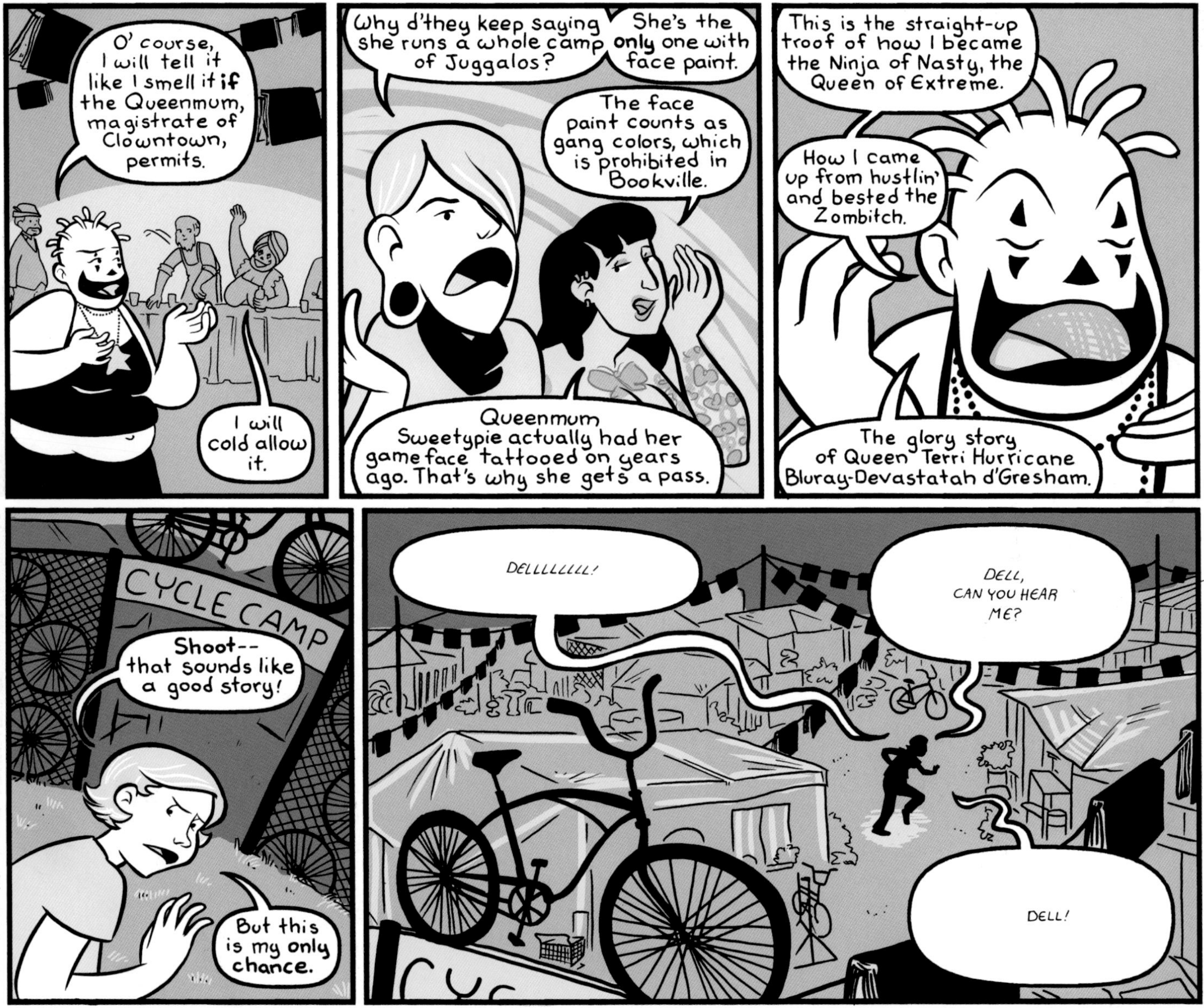
O' course, I will tell it like I smell it **if** the Queenmum, magistrate of Clowntown, permits.
I will cold allow it.
Why d'they keep saying she runs a whole camp of Juggalos?
She's the **only** one with face paint.
The face paint counts as gang colors, which is prohibited in Bookville.
Queenmum Sweetypie actually had her game face tattooed on years ago. That's why she gets a pass.
This is the straight-up troof of how I became the Ninja of Nasty, the Queen of Extreme.
How I came up from hustlin' and bested the Zombitch.
The glory story of Queen Terri Hurricane Bluray-Devastatah d'Gresham.
CYCLE CAMP
Shoot-- that sounds like a good story!
But this is my **only** chance.
DELLLLLLLL!
DELL, CAN YOU HEAR ME?
DELL!

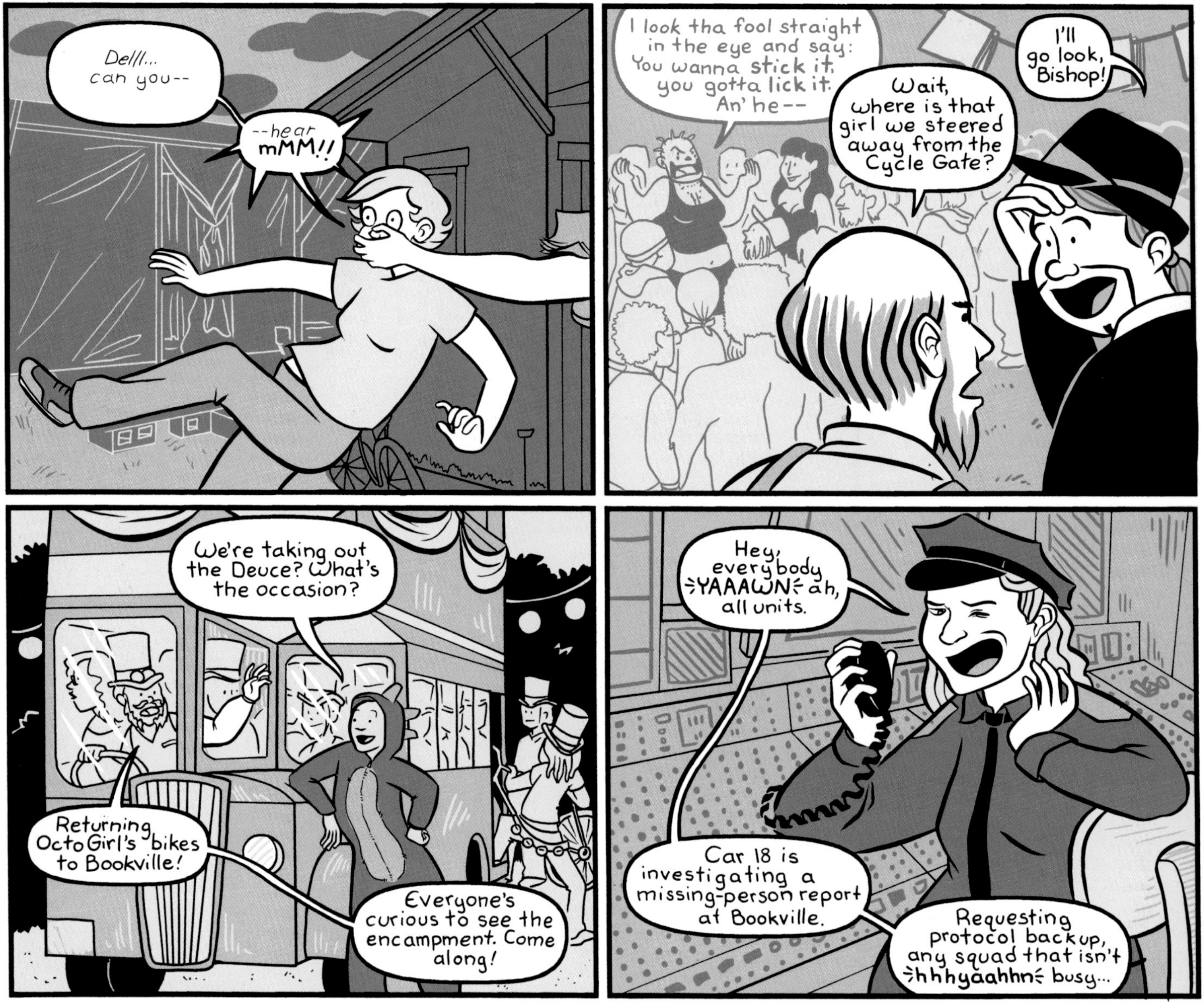
Delll... can you--
--hear mMM!!
I look tha fool straight in the eye and say: You wanna stick it, you gotta lick it. An' he--
Wait, where is that girl we steered away from the Cycle Gate?
I'll go look, Bishop!
We're taking out the Deuce? What's the occasion?
Returning OctoGirl's bikes to Bookville!
Everyone's curious to see the encampment. Come along!
Hey, everybody ⋛YAAAWN⋚ ah, all units.
Car 18 is investigating a missing-person report at Bookville.
Requesting protocol backup, any squad that isn't ⋛hhhyaahhn⋚ busy...

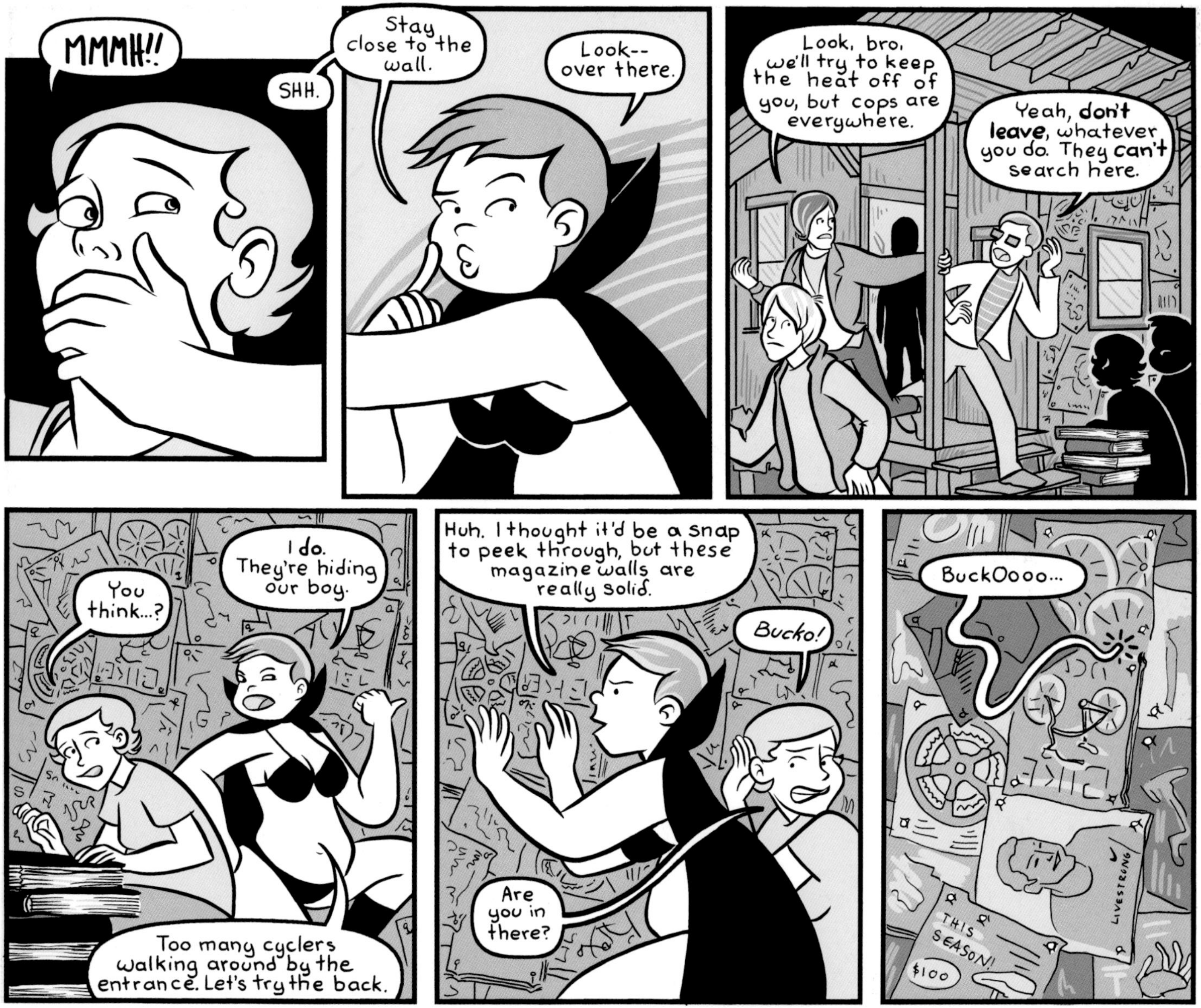
MMMH!!
SHH.
Stay close to the wall.
Look-- over there.
Look, bro, we'll try to keep the heat off of you, but cops are everywhere.
Yeah, **don't leave**, whatever you do. They **can't** search here.
You think...?
I **do**. They're hiding our boy.
Too many cyclers walking around by the entrance. Let's try the back.
Huh. I thought it'd be a snap to peek through, but these magazine walls are really solid.
Bucko!
Are you in there?
BuckOooo...
LIVESTRONG
THIS SEASON!
$100

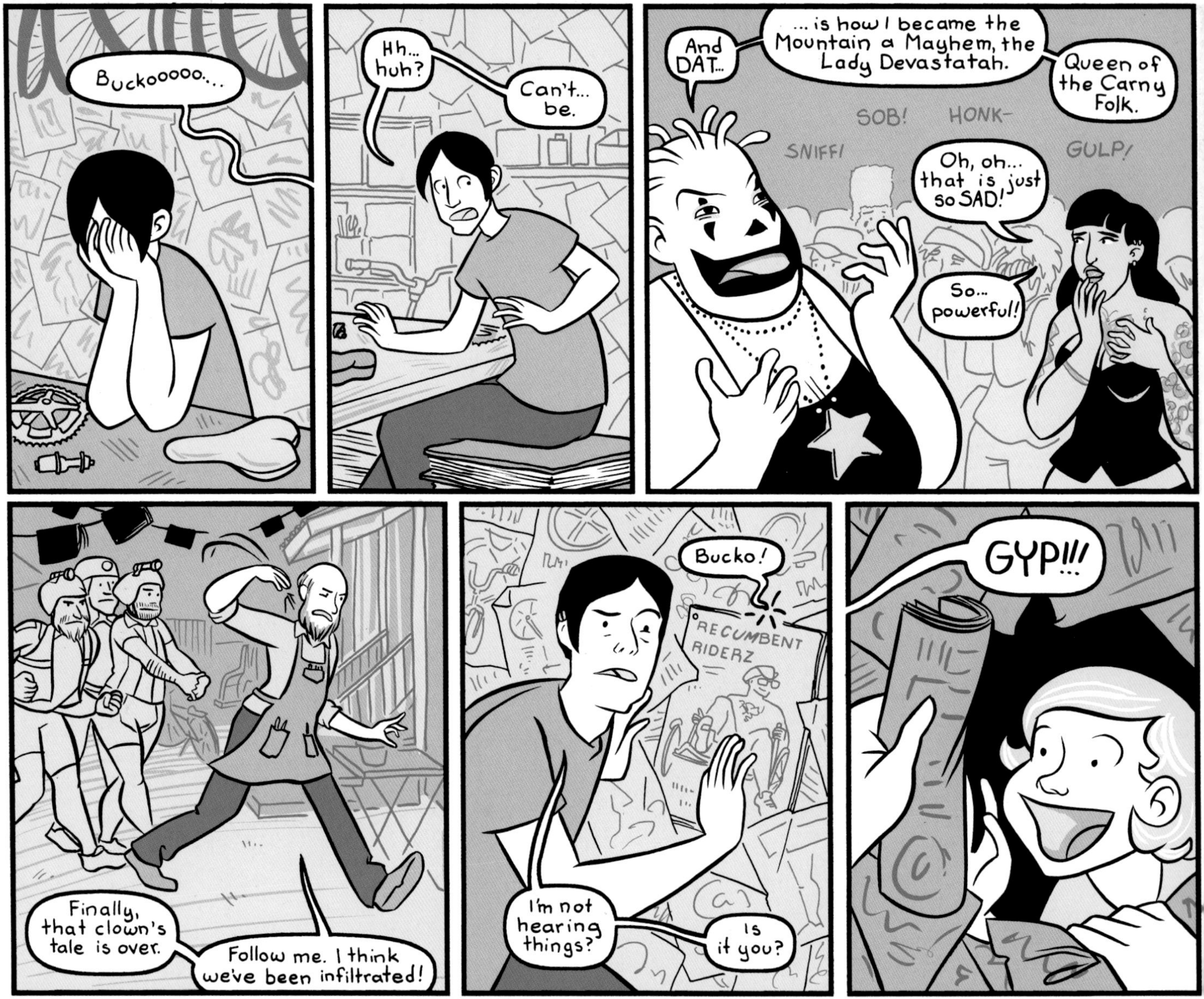
Buckooooo...
Hh... huh?
Can't... be.
And DAT...
... is how I became the Mountain a Mayhem, the Lady Devastatah.
Queen of the Carny Folk.
SOB!
HONK-
SNIFF!
GULP!
Oh, oh... that is just so SAD!
So... powerful!
Finally, that clown's tale is over.
Follow me. I think we've been infiltrated!
Bucko!
RECUMBENT RIDERZ
I'm not hearing things?
Is it you?
GYP!!!...

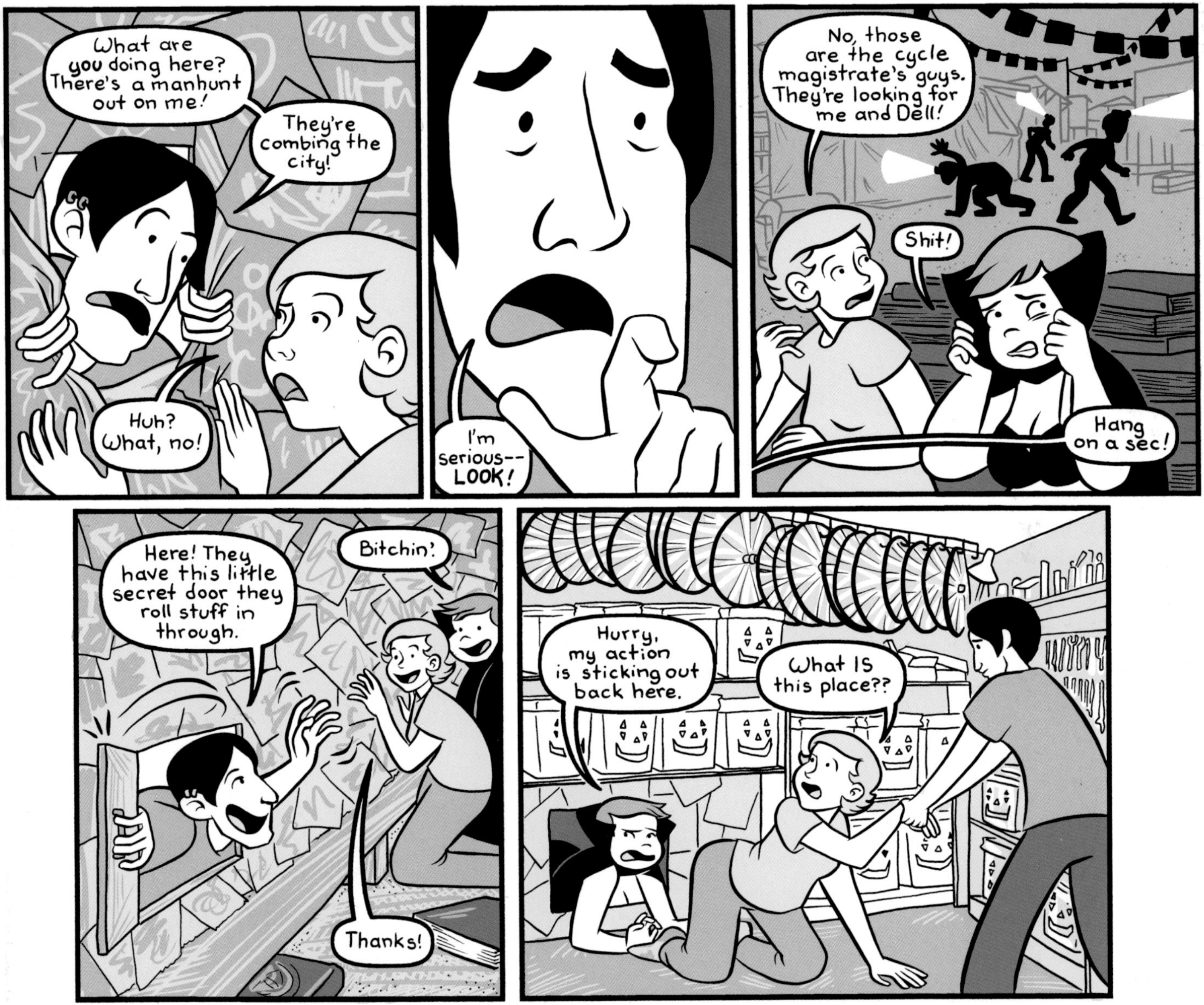
What are you doing here? There's a manhunt out on me!
They're combing the city!
Huh? What, no!
I'm serious-- LOOK!
No, those are the cycle magistrate's guys. They're looking for me and Dell!
Shit!
Hang on a sec!
Here! They have this little secret door they roll stuff in through.
Bitchin'.
Thanks!
Hurry, my action is sticking out back here.
What IS this place??

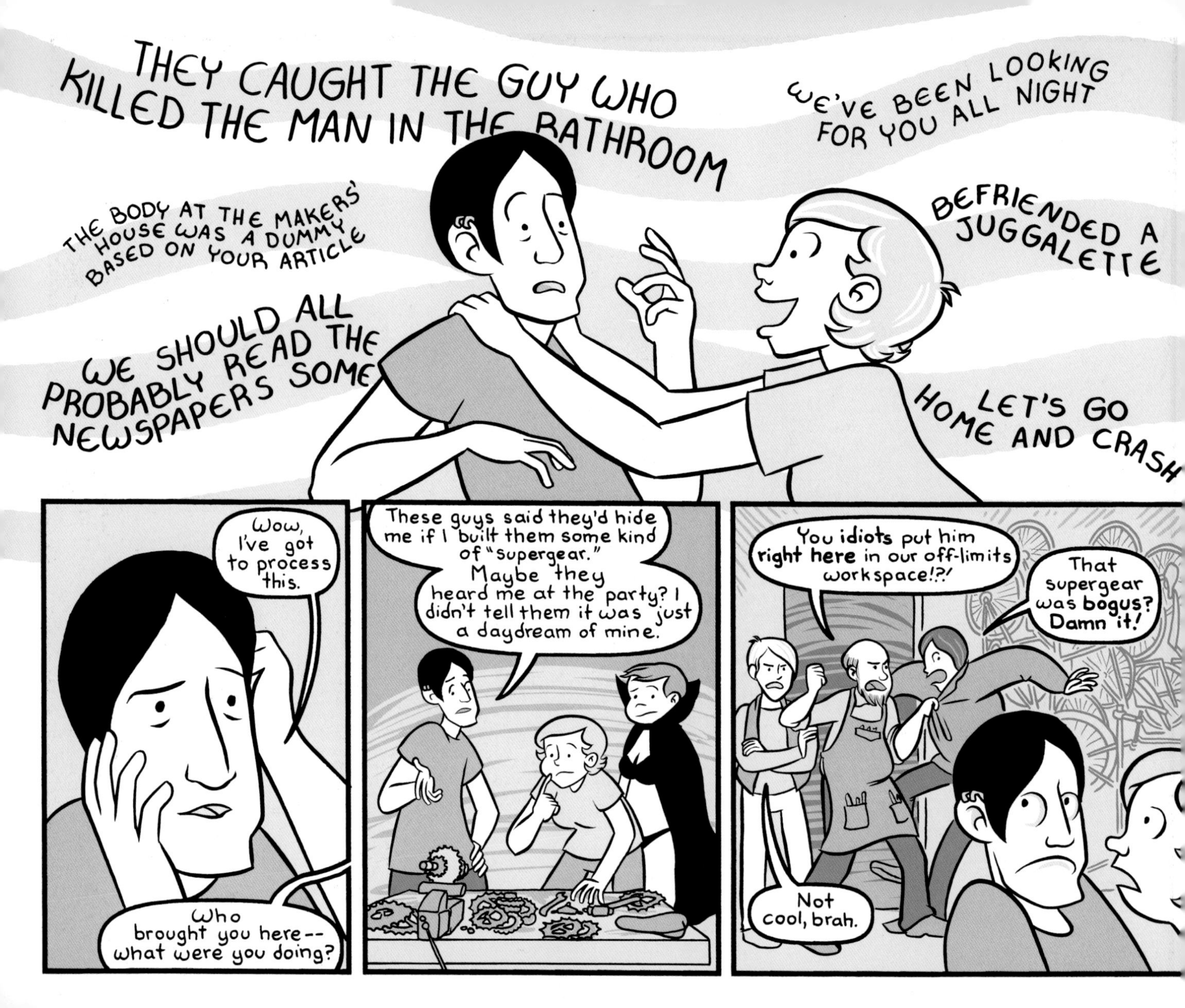
THEY CAUGHT THE GUY WHO KILLED THE MAN IN THE BATHROOM
WE'VE BEEN LOOKING FOR YOU ALL NIGHT
THE BODY AT THE MAKERS' HOUSE WAS A DUMMY BASED ON YOUR ARTICLE
BEFRIENDED A JUGGALETTE
WE SHOULD ALL PROBABLY READ THE NEWSPAPERS SOME
LET'S GO HOME AND CRASH
Wow, I've got to process this.
Who brought you here-- what were you doing?
These guys said they'd hide me if I built them some kind of "supergear." Maybe they heard me at the party? I didn't tell them it was just a daydream of mine.
You **idiots** put him **right here** in our off-limits workspace!?!
That supergear was **bogus**? Damn it!
Not cool, brah.

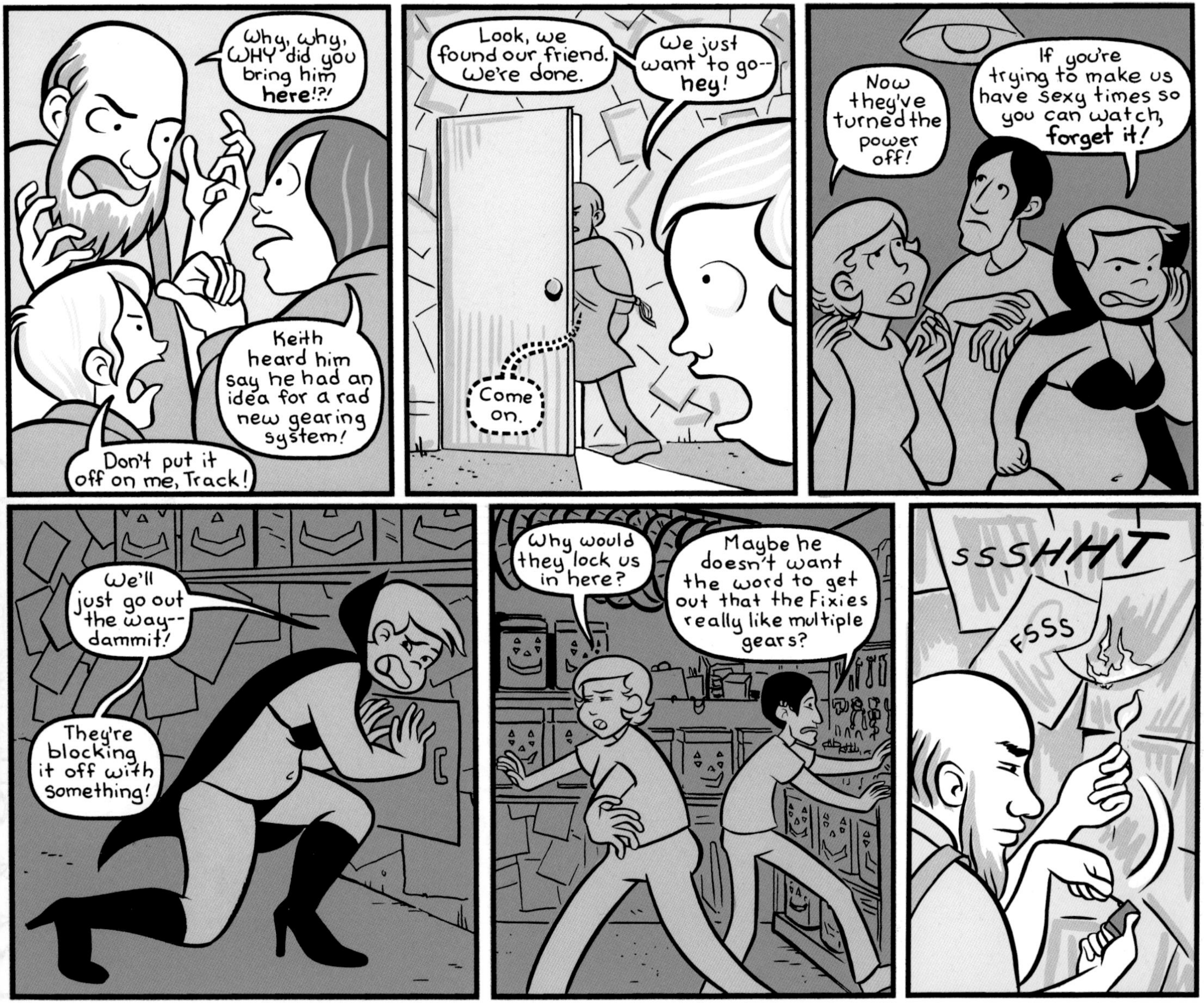
Why, why, WHY did you bring him here!?!
Keith heard him say he had an idea for a rad new gearing system!
Don't put it off on me, Track!
Look, we found our friend. We're done.
We just want to go-- hey!
Come on.
Now they've turned the power off!
If you're trying to make us have sexy times so you can watch, forget it!
We'll just go out the way-- dammit!
They're blocking it off with something!
Why would they lock us in here?
Maybe he doesn't want the word to get out that the Fixies really like multiple gears?
SSSHHT
FSSS

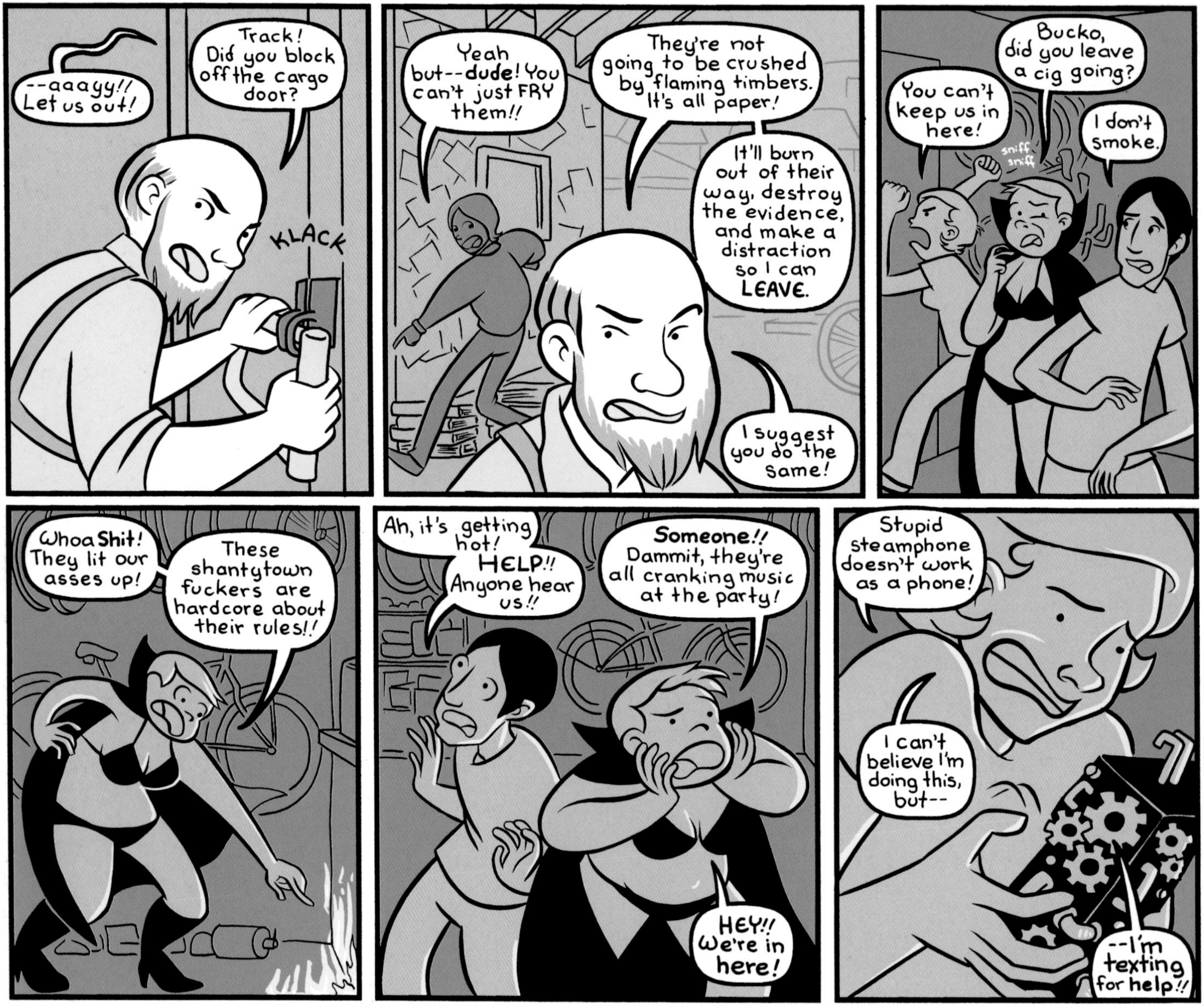
--aaayy!! Let us out!
Track! Did you block off the cargo door?
KLACK
Yeah but--**dude**! You can't just FRY them!!
They're not going to be crushed by flaming timbers. It's all paper!
It'll burn out of their way, destroy the evidence, and make a distraction so I can **LEAVE**.
I suggest you do the same!
Bucko, did you leave a cig going?
You can't keep us in here!
sniff sniff
I don't smoke.
Whoa **Shit**! They lit our asses up!
These shantytown fuckers are hardcore about their rules!!
Ah, it's getting hot! **HELP**!! Anyone hear us!!
Someone!! Dammit, they're all cranking music at the party!
HEY!! We're in here!
Stupid steamphone doesn't work as a phone!
I can't believe I'm doing this, but--
--I'm **texting for help**!!

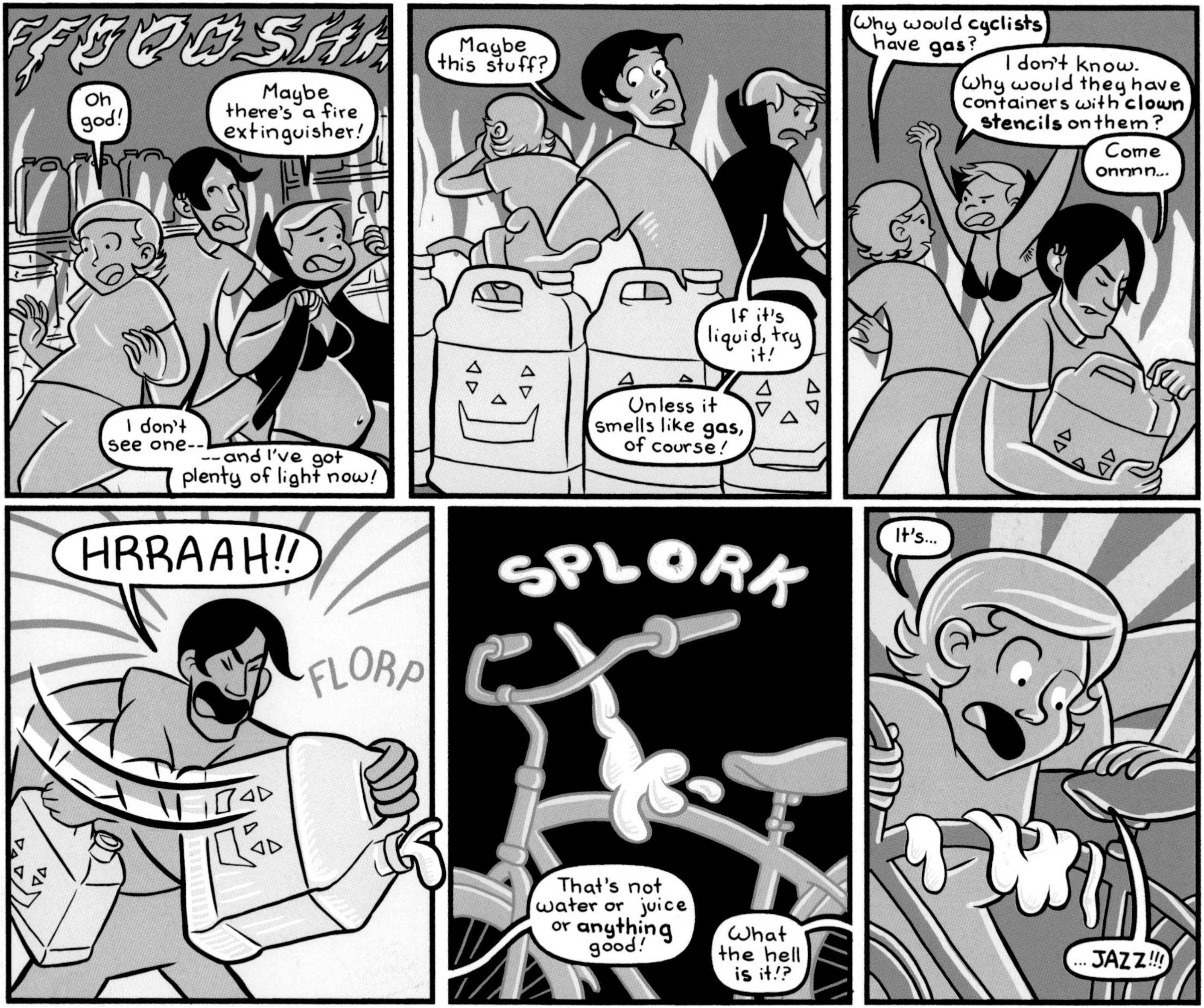
FFOOOSHH
Oh god!
Maybe there's a fire extinguisher!
I don't see one--
--and I've got plenty of light now!
Maybe this stuff?
If it's liquid, try it!
Unless it smells like gas, of course!
Why would cyclists have gas?
I don't know. Why would they have containers with clown stencils on them?
Come onnnn...
HRRAAH!!
FLORP
SPLORK
That's not water or juice or anything good!
What the hell is it!?
It's...
...JAZZ!!!

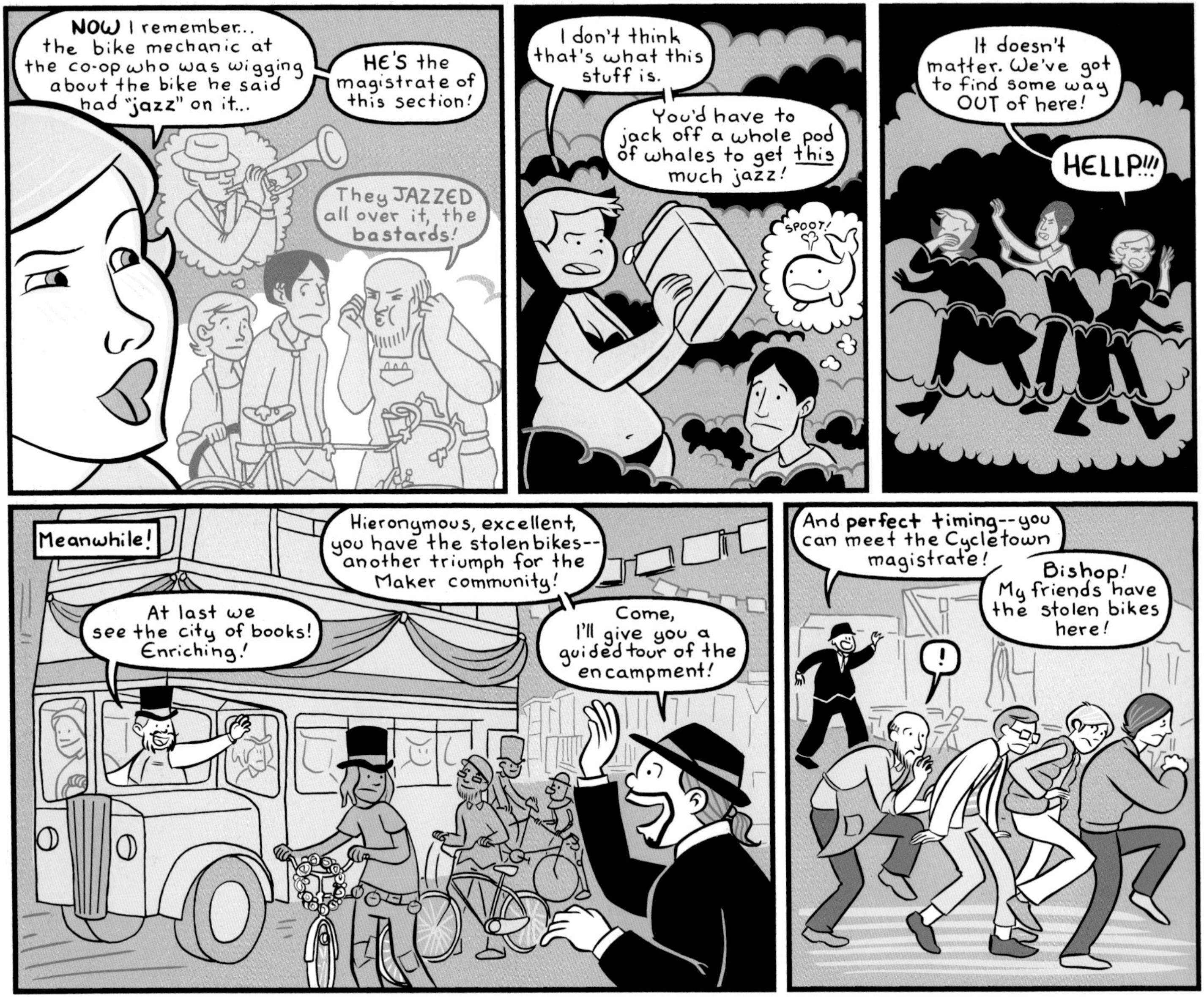
NOW I remember... the bike mechanic at the co-op who was wigging about the bike he said had "jazz" on it...
HE'S the magistrate of this section!
They JAZZED all over it, the bastards!
I don't think that's what this stuff is.
You'd have to jack off a whole pod of whales to get this much jazz!
SPOOT!
It doesn't matter. We've got to find some way OUT of here!
HELLP!!!
Meanwhile!
At last we see the city of books! Enriching!
Hieronymous, excellent, you have the stolen bikes-- another triumph for the Maker community!
Come, I'll give you a guided tour of the encampment!
And perfect timing--you can meet the Cycletown magistrate!
Bishop! My friends have the stolen bikes here!
!

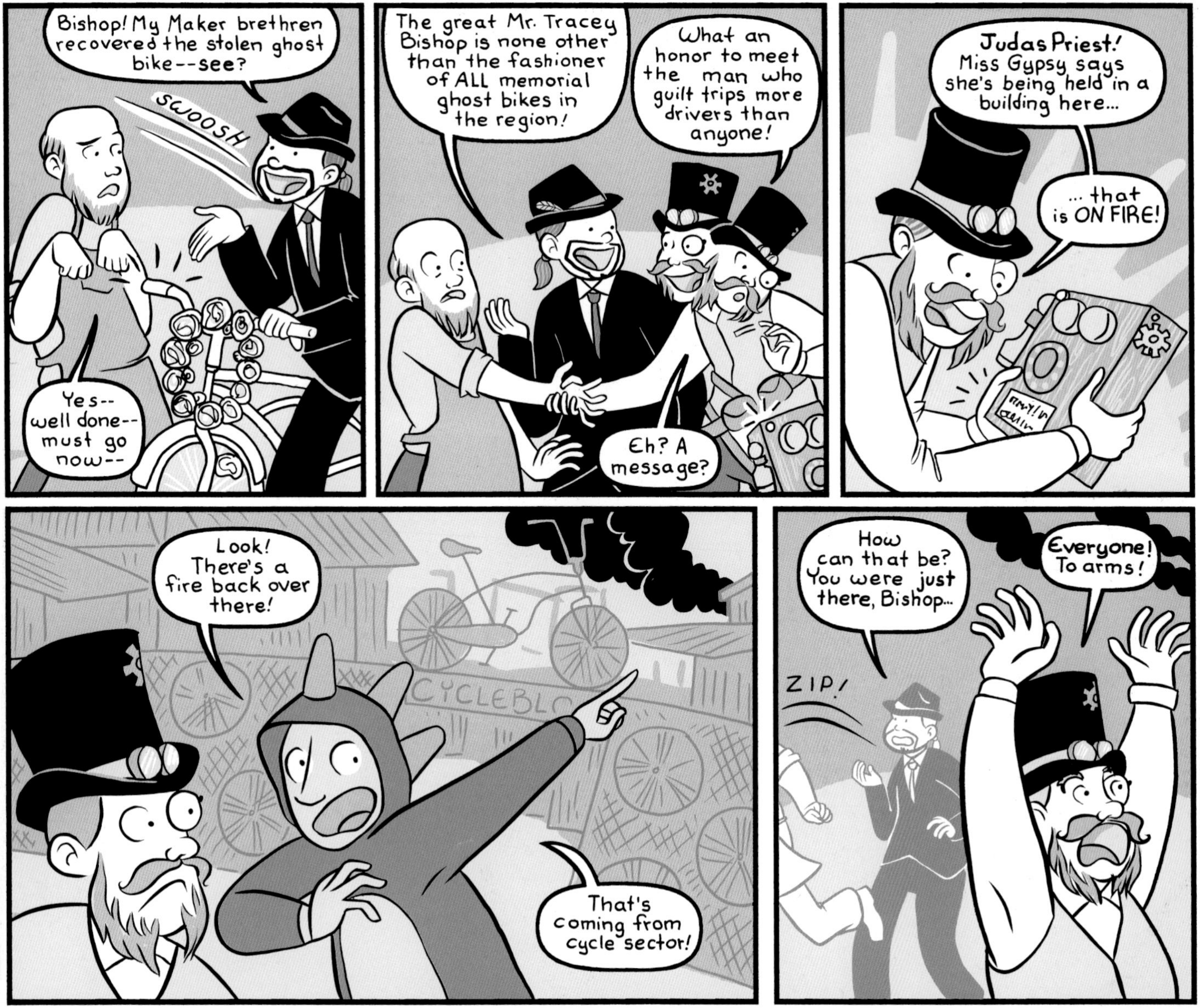
Bishop! My Maker brethren recovered the stolen ghost bike--see?
SWOOSH
Yes--well done--must go now--
The great Mr. Tracey Bishop is none other than the fashioner of ALL memorial ghost bikes in the region!
What an honor to meet the man who guilt trips more drivers than anyone!
Eh? A message?
Judas Priest! Miss Gypsy says she's being held in a building here...
... that is ON FIRE!
Look! There's a fire back over there!
CYCLEBLO
That's coming from cycle sector!
How can that be? You were just there, Bishop...
ZIP!
Everyone! To arms!

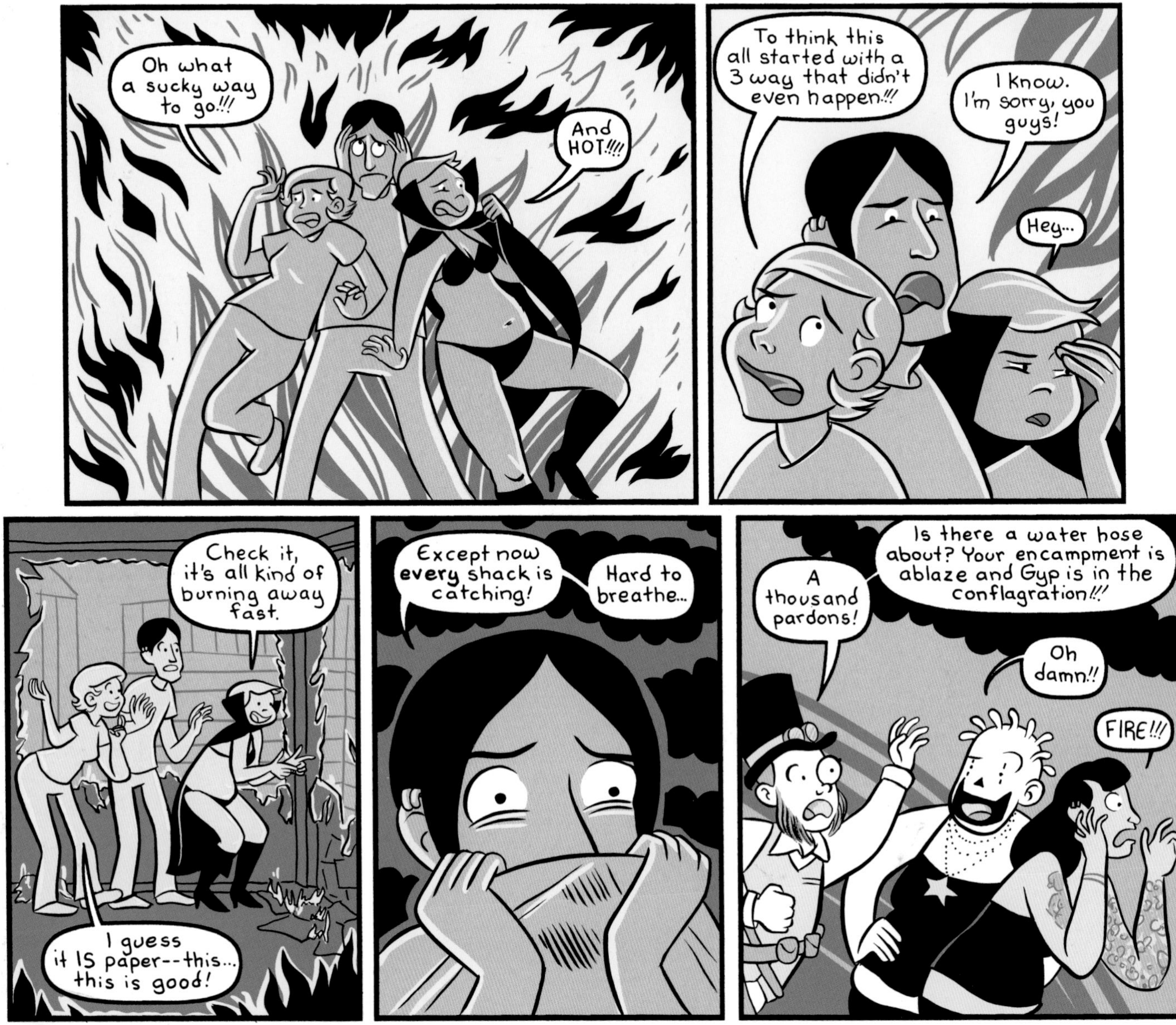
Oh what a sucky way to go!!!
And HOT!!!!
To think this all started with a 3 way that didn't even happen!!!
I know. I'm sorry, you guys!
Hey...
Check it, it's all kind of burning away fast.
I guess it IS paper--this... this is good!
Except now every shack is catching!
Hard to breathe...
A thousand pardons!
Is there a water hose about? Your encampment is ablaze and Gyp is in the conflagration!!!
Oh damn!!
FIRE!!!

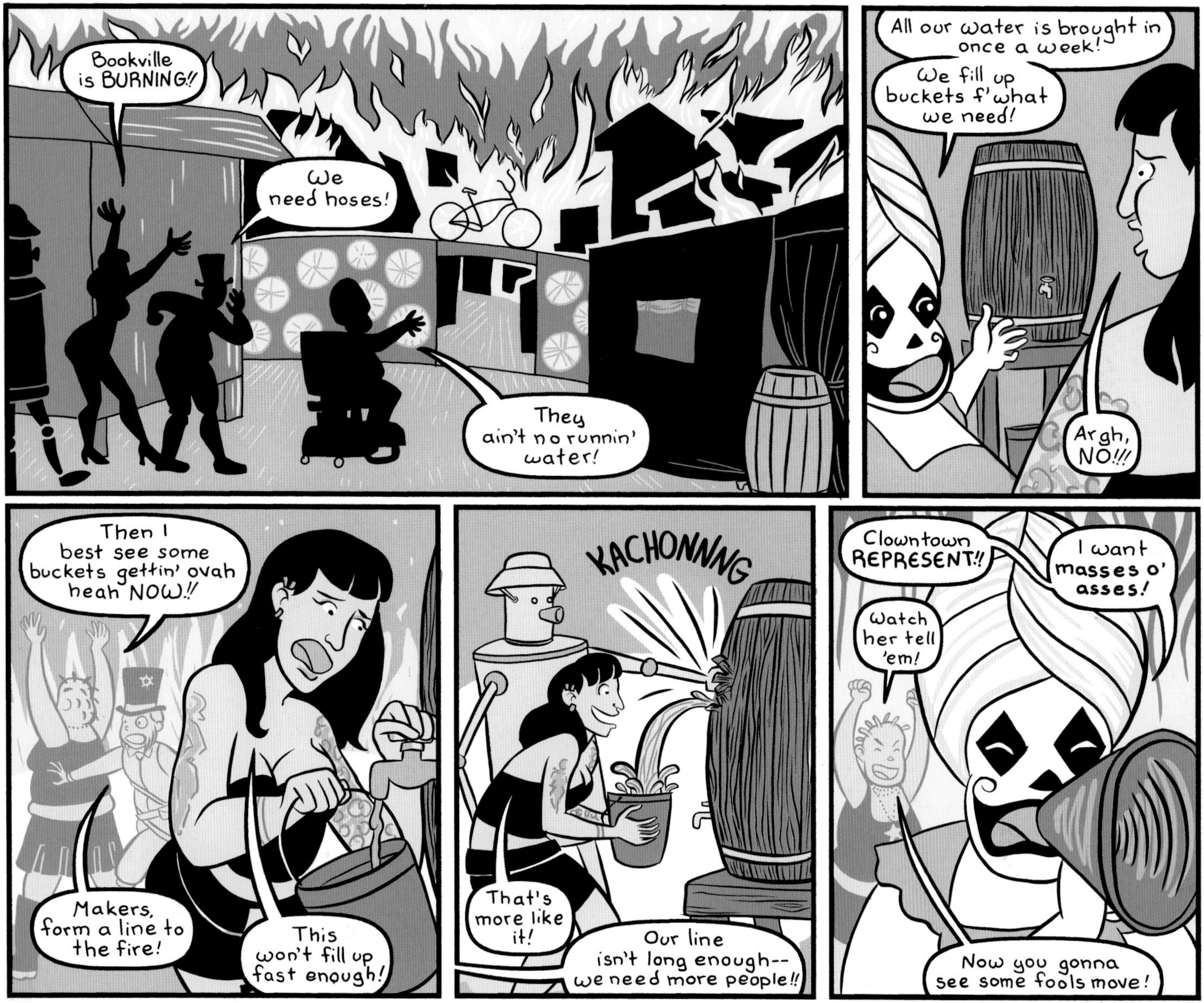
Bookville is BURNING!!
We need hoses!
They ain't no runnin' water!
All our water is brought in once a week!
We fill up buckets f'what we need!
Argh, NO!!!
Then I best see some buckets gettin' ovah heah NOW!!
Makers, form a line to the fire!
This won't fill up fast enough!
KACHONNNG
That's more like it!
Our line isn't long enough-- we need more people!!
Clowntown REPRESENT!!
I want masses o' asses!
Watch her tell 'em!
Now you gonna see some fools move!

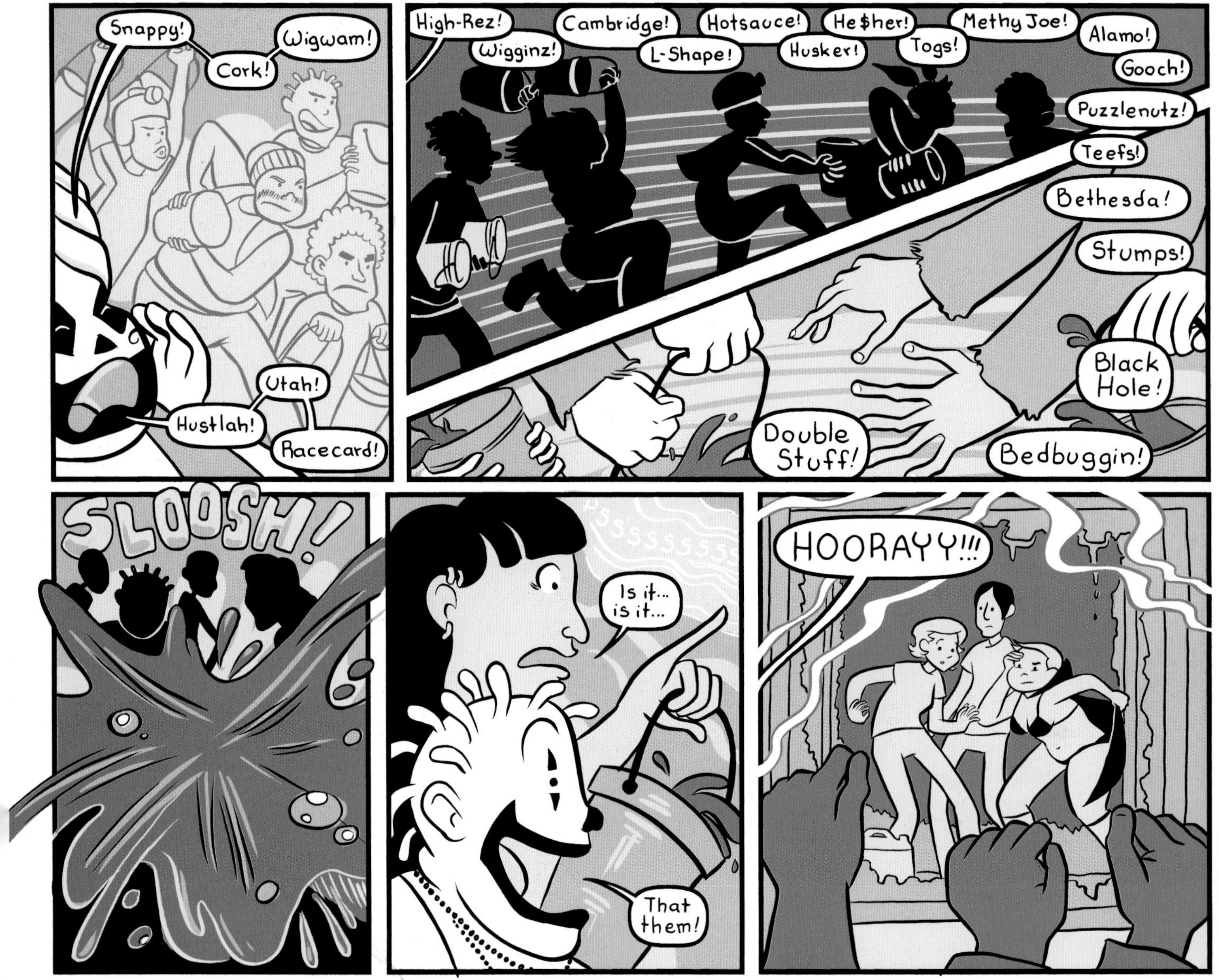
Snappy!
Cork!
Wigwam!
Utah!
Hustlah!
Racecard!
High-Rez!
Wigginz!
Cambridge!
L-Shape!
Hotsauce!
Husker!
He$her!
Togs!
Methy Joe!
Alamo!
Gooch!
Puzzlenutz!
Teefs!
Bethesda!
Stumps!
Black Hole!
Double Stuff!
Bedbuggin!
SLOOSH!
Is it... is it...
That them!
HOORAYY!!!

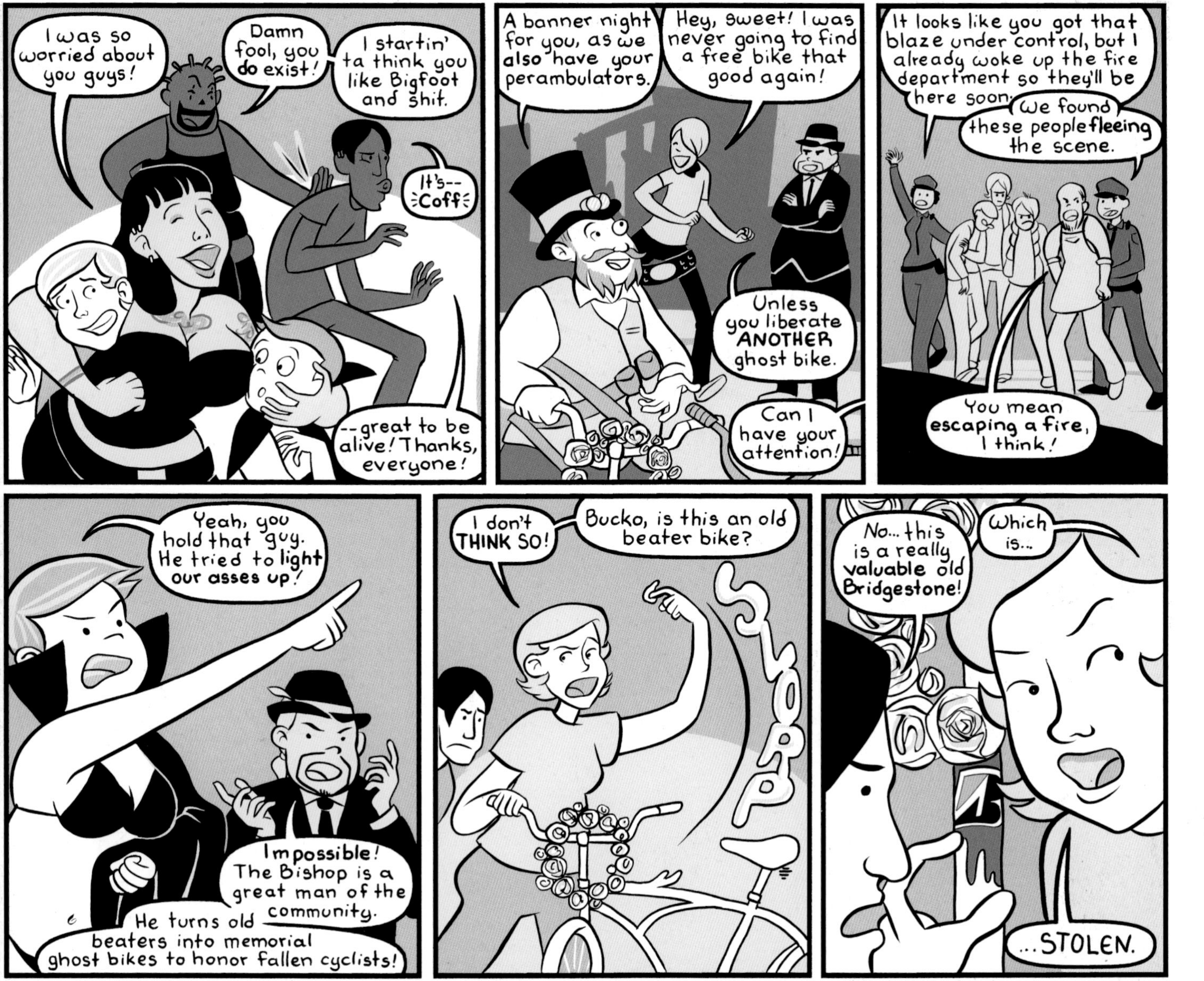

I was so worried about you guys!
Damn fool, you do exist!
I startin' ta think you like Bigfoot and shit.
It's-- Coff
--great to be alive! Thanks, everyone!
A banner night for you, as we also have your perambulators.
Hey, sweet! I was never going to find a free bike that good again!
Unless you liberate ANOTHER ghost bike.
Can I have your attention!
It looks like you got that blaze under control, but I already woke up the fire department so they'll be here soon.
We found these people fleeing the scene.
You mean escaping a fire, I think!
Yeah, you hold that guy. He tried to light our asses up!
Impossible! The Bishop is a great man of the community.
He turns old beaters into memorial ghost bikes to honor fallen cyclists!
I don't THINK SO!
Bucko, is this an old beater bike?
SHLORP
No... this is a really valuable old Bridgestone!
Which is...
...STOLEN.

Here's what Mr. Bishop wanted destroyed-- evidence!

Ay! Thas Clowntown's grease paint, for when we go out Juggaloin'!

A whole truckload done went missin' way back!

Which can be quickly applied to any stolen cycle to make a "ghost bike."

He then locks the bike to a phone pole and his accomplices--

A shitty gimmick cover band.

--later pick up the good bike and replace it with a white-painted beater!

slorp!

Which... no one notices because who pays close attention to ghost bikes.

A fine drunken theory, miss, but there's no way you can prove that!

Oh, yes I can...

...in just a few hours.

LATER, AT THE PEDALPHILE...

You see, Bishop tried to fake a robbery that got ruined by one of the employees coming in before he could coat this Raleigh and lock it outside.

So he had to invent a ludicrous story about someone "jazzing" on it.

Tracey, I can't believe you'd steal from us!

Damned co-op shop!

You better get another mechanic, sir.

This won't look good on the review, man.

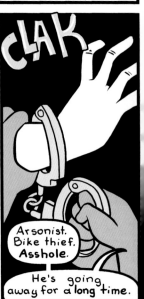

CLAK

Arsonist. Bike thief. Asshole.

He's going away for a long time.

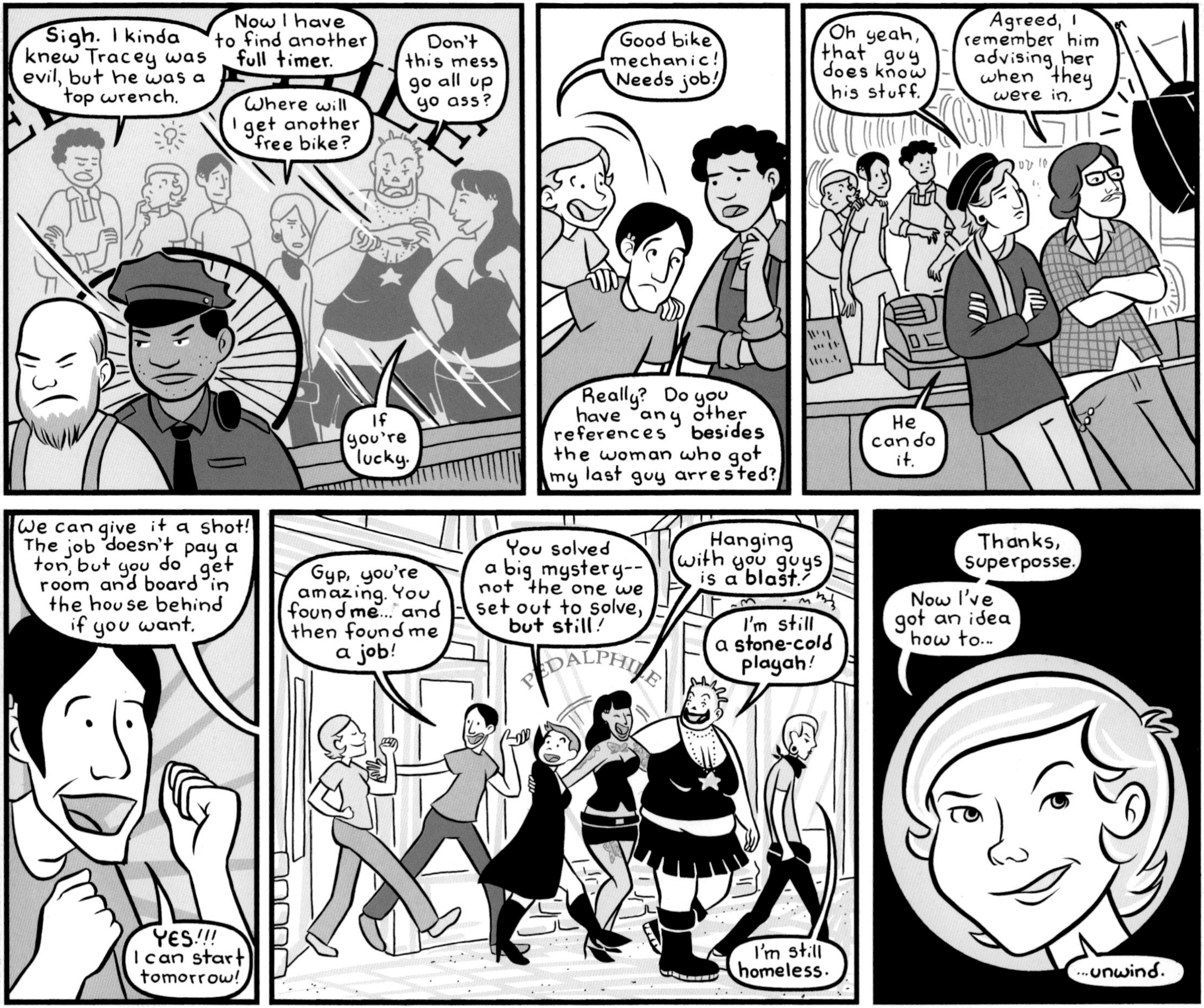
Sigh. I kinda knew Tracey was evil, but he was a top wrench.
Now I have to find another full timer.
Where will I get another free bike?
Don't this mess go all up yo ass?
If you're lucky.
Good bike mechanic! Needs job!
Really? Do you have any other references besides the woman who got my last guy arrested?
Oh yeah, that guy does know his stuff.
Agreed, I remember him advising her when they were in.
He can do it.
We can give it a shot! The job doesn't pay a ton, but you do get room and board in the house behind if you want.
YES!!! I can start tomorrow!
Gyp, you're amazing. You found me... and then found me a job!
You solved a big mystery-- not the one we set out to solve, but still!
Hanging with you guys is a blast!
I'm still a stone-cold playah!
PEDALPHILE
I'm still homeless.
Thanks, superposse.
Now I've got an idea how to...
...unwind.

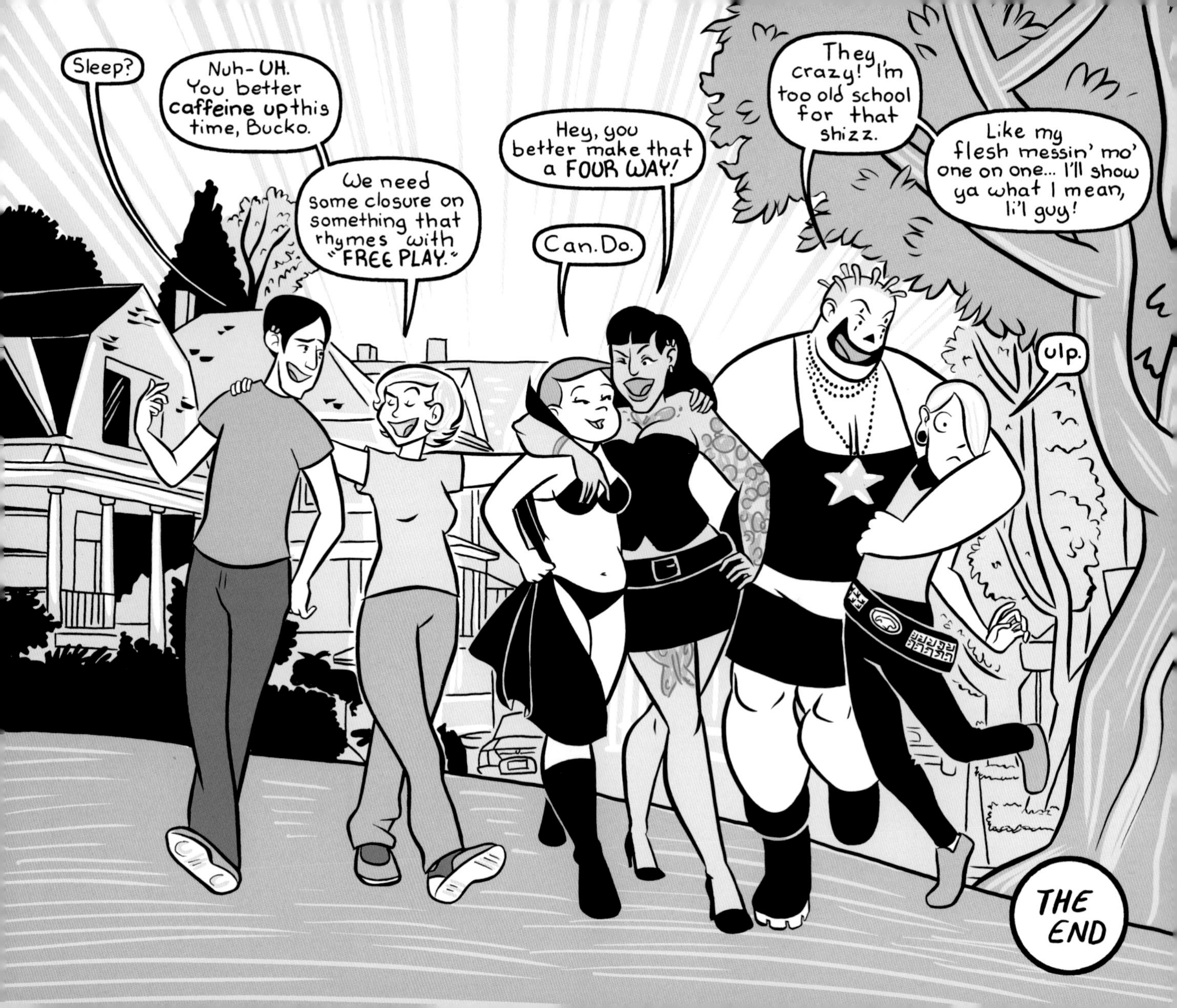
Sleep?
Nuh-UH. You better caffeine up this time, Bucko.
We need some closure on something that rhymes with "FREE PLAY."
Hey, you better make that a FOUR WAY!
Can. Do.
They crazy! I'm too old school for that shizz.
Like my flesh messin' mo' one on one... I'll show ya what I mean, li'l guy!
ulp.
THE END

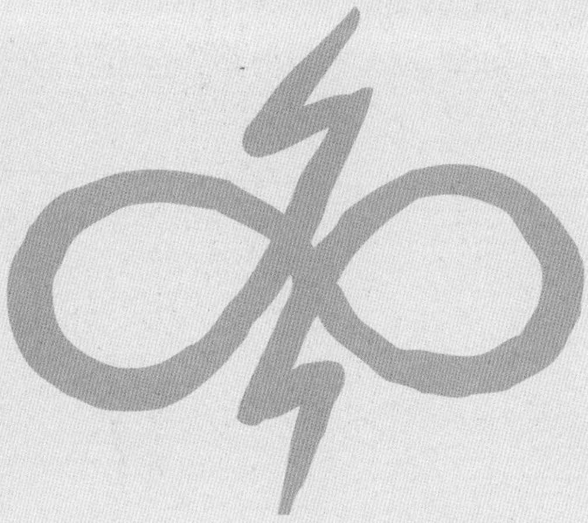

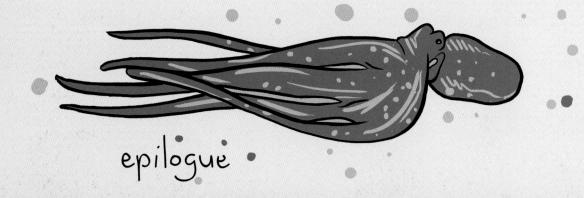

epilogue

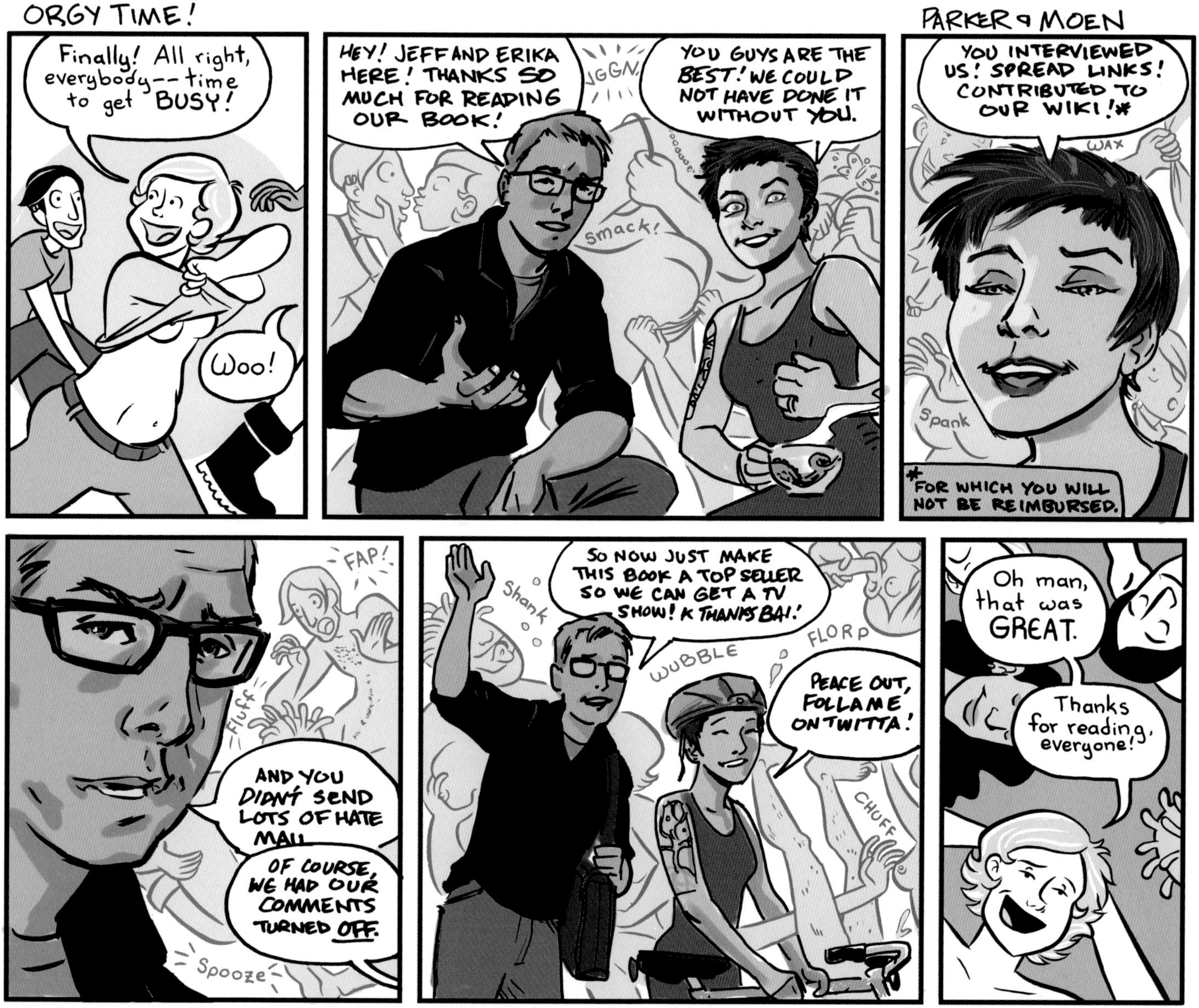
ORGY TIME!
PARKER & MOEN
Finally! All right, everybody-- time to get BUSY!
Woo!
HEY! JEFF AND ERIKA HERE! THANKS SO MUCH FOR READING OUR BOOK!
YOU GUYS ARE THE BEST! WE COULD NOT HAVE DONE IT WITHOUT YOU.
JGGN
Smack!
YOU INTERVIEWED US! SPREAD LINKS! CONTRIBUTED TO OUR WIKI!*
WAX
Spank
*FOR WHICH YOU WILL NOT BE REIMBURSED.
FAP!
Fluff
AND YOU DIDN'T SEND LOTS OF HATE MAIL
OF COURSE, WE HAD OUR COMMENTS TURNED OFF.
Spooze
SO NOW JUST MAKE THIS BOOK A TOP SELLER SO WE CAN GET A TV SHOW! K THANKS BAI!
Shank
WUBBLE
FLORP
PEACE OUT, FOLLA ME ON TWITTA!
CHUFF
Oh man, that was GREAT.
Thanks for reading, everyone!

EXTRA STUFF

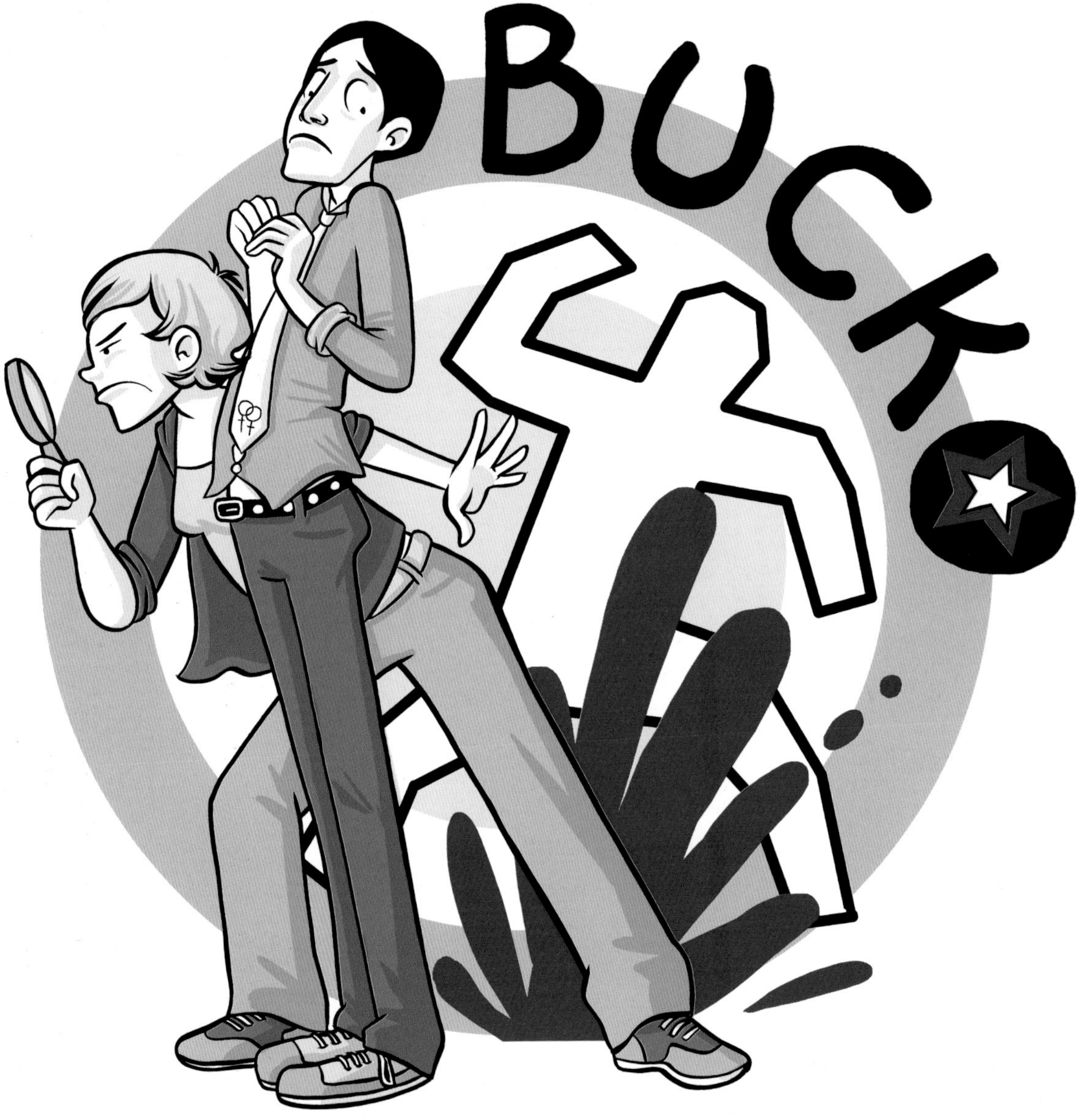
BUCKO

The original promo image for BuckoComic.com and the inspiration for the cover of the book.

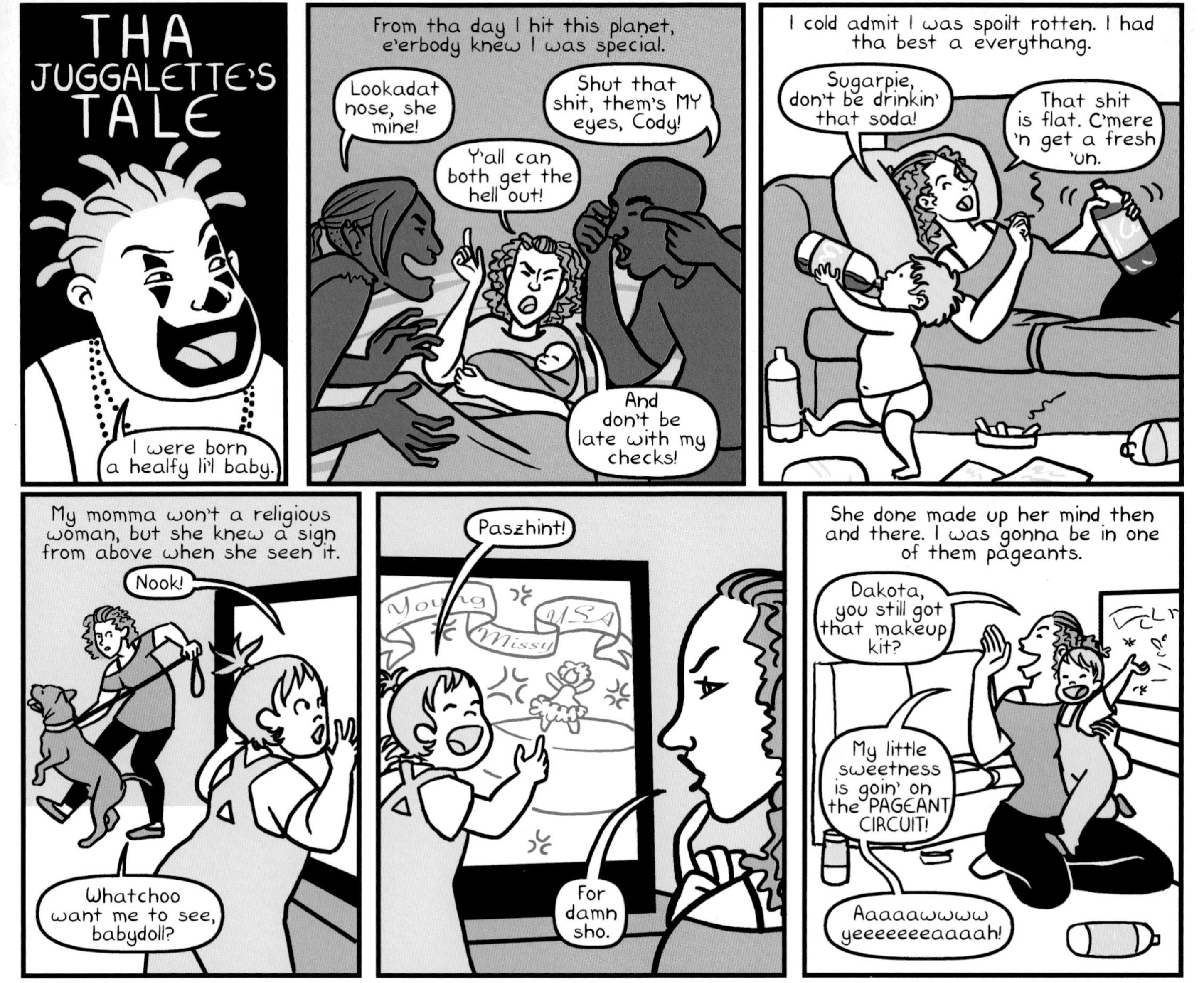
THA JUGGALETTE'S TALE
I were born a healfy li'l baby.
From tha day I hit this planet, e'erbody knew I was special.
Lookadat nose, she mine!
Shut that shit, them's MY eyes, Cody!
Y'all can both get the hell out!
And don't be late with my checks!
I cold admit I was spoilt rotten. I had tha best a everythang.
Sugarpie, don't be drinkin' that soda!
That shit is flat. C'mere 'n get a fresh 'un.
My momma won't a religious woman, but she knew a sign from above when she seen it.
Nook!
Whatchoo want me to see, babydoll?
Paszhint!
Young Missy USA
For damn sho.
She done made up her mind then and there. I was gonna be in one of them pageants.
Dakota, you still got that makeup kit?
My little sweetness is goin' on the PAGEANT CIRCUIT!
Aaaaawwww yeeeeeeeaaaah!

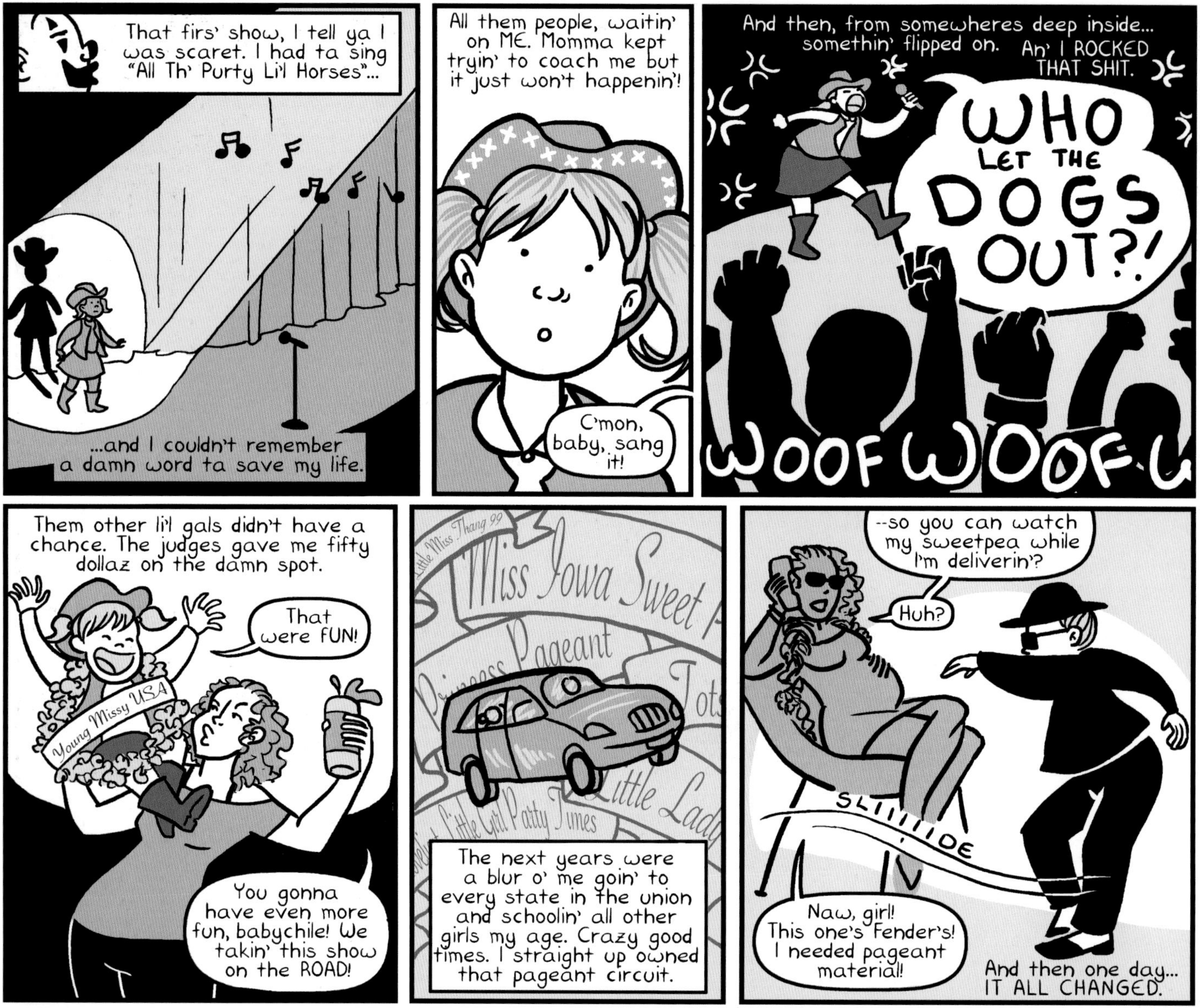

That firs' show, I tell ya I was scaret. I had ta sing "All Th' Purty Li'l Horses"...
...and I couldn't remember a damn word ta save my life.
All them people, waitin' on ME. Momma kept tryin' to coach me but it just won't happenin'!
C'mon, baby, sang it!
And then, from somewheres deep inside... somethin' flipped on.
An' I ROCKED THAT SHIT.
WHO LET THE DOGS OUT?!
WOOF WOOF
Them other li'l gals didn't have a chance. The judges gave me fifty dollaz on the damn spot.
That were FUN!
Young Missy USA
You gonna have even more fun, babychile! We takin' this show on the ROAD!
Little Miss Thang 99
Miss Iowa Sweet
Pageant
Princess
Tots
Little Lady
Little Girl Party Times
The next years were a blur o' me goin' to every state in the union and schoolin' all other girls my age. Crazy good times. I straight up owned that pageant circuit.
--so you can watch my sweetpea while I'm deliverin'?
Huh?
SLIIIIIDE
Naw, girl! This one's Fender's! I needed pageant material!
And then one day... IT ALL CHANGED.

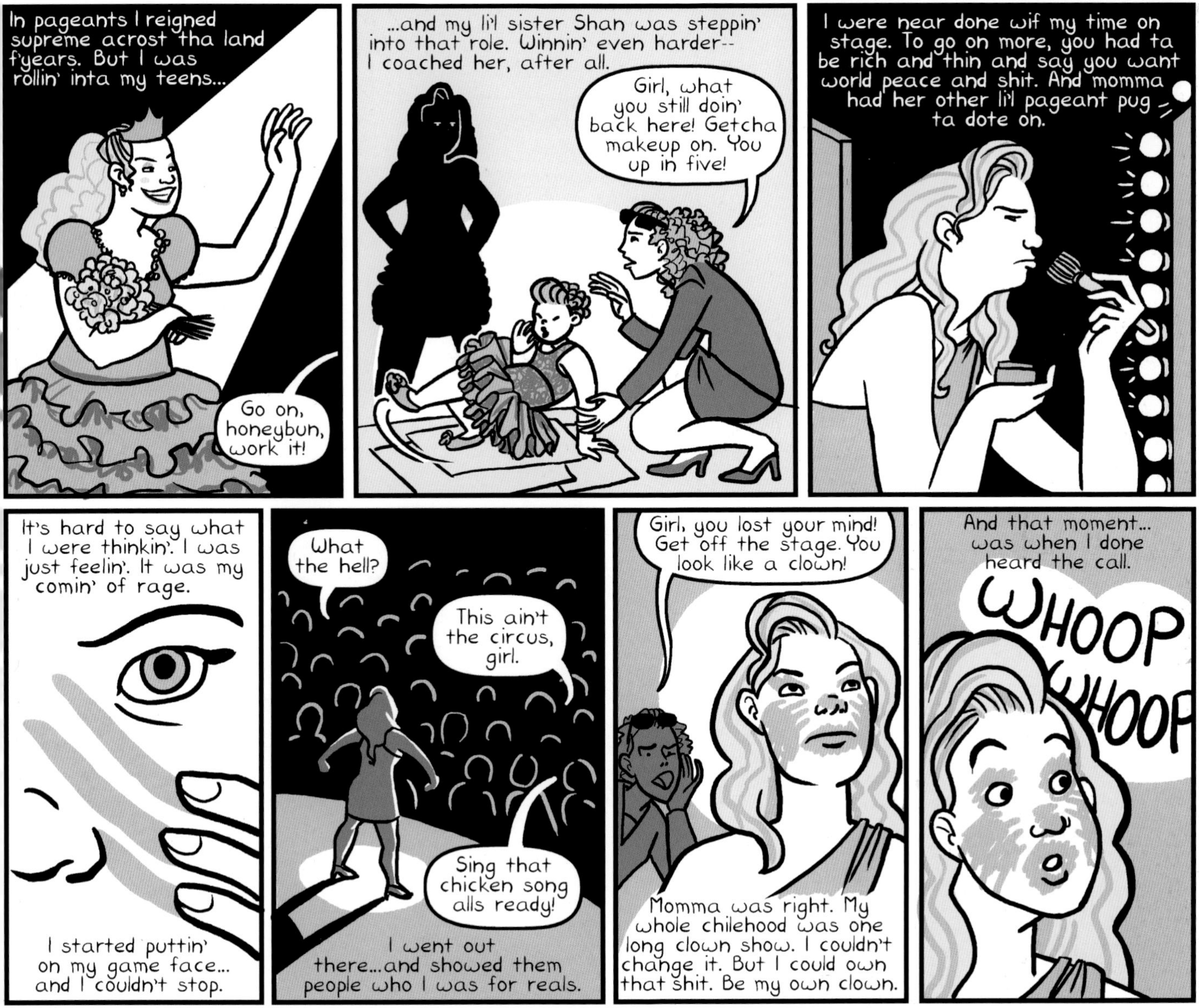
In pageants I reigned supreme acrost tha land f'years. But I was rollin' inta my teens...
Go on, honeybun, work it!
...and my li'l sister Shan was steppin' into that role. Winnin' even harder-- I coached her, after all.
Girl, what you still doin' back here! Getcha makeup on. You up in five!
I were near done wif my time on stage. To go on more, you had ta be rich and thin and say you want world peace and shit. And momma had her other li'l pageant pug ta dote on.
It's hard to say what I were thinkin'. I was just feelin'. It was my comin' of rage.
I started puttin' on my game face... and I couldn't stop.
What the hell?
This ain't the circus, girl.
Sing that chicken song alls ready!
I went out there...and showed them people who I was for reals.
Girl, you lost your mind! Get off the stage. You look like a clown!
Momma was right. My whole chilehood was one long clown show. I couldn't change it. But I could own that shit. Be my own clown.
And that moment... was when I done heard the call.
WHOOP
WHOOP

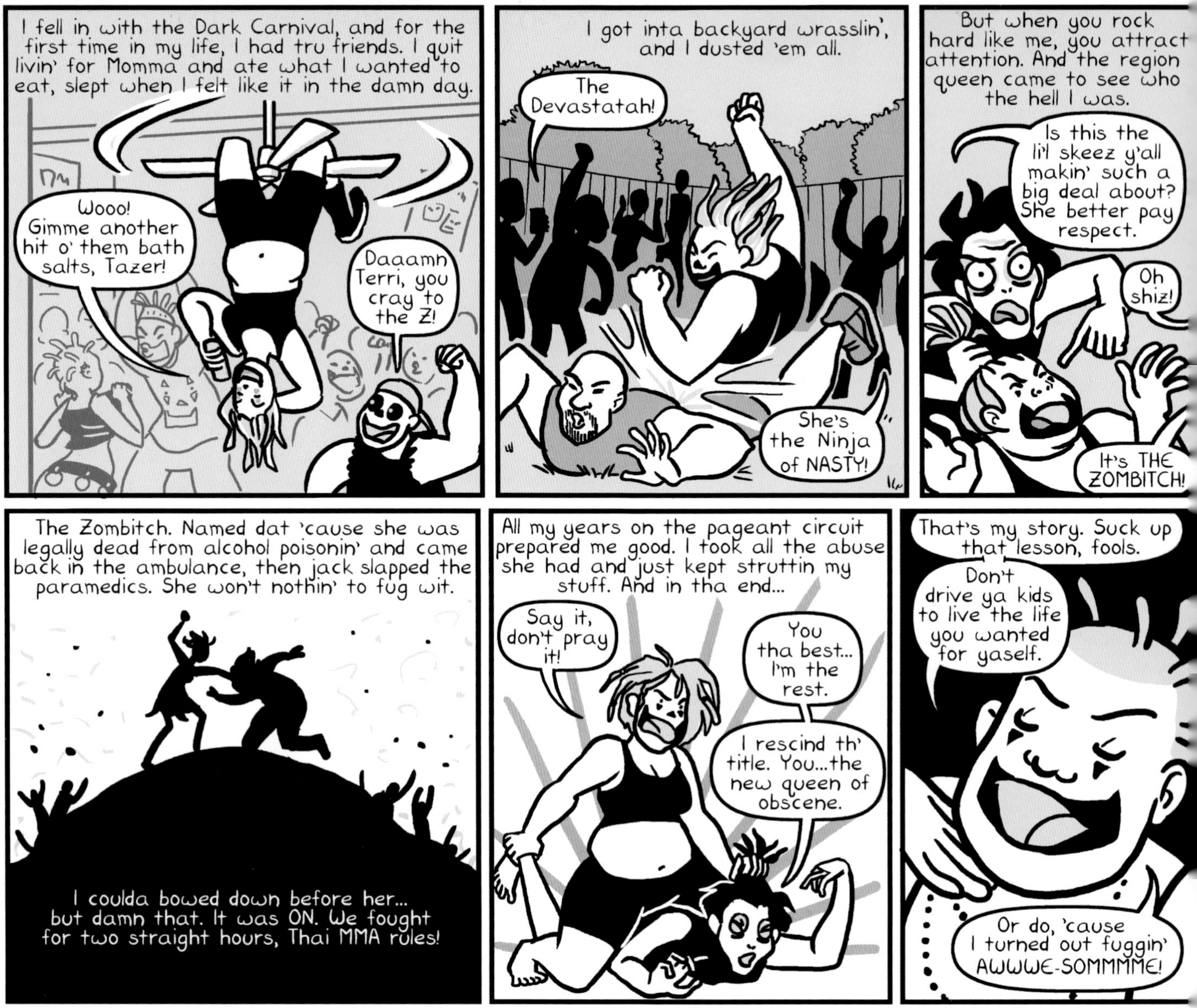
I fell in with the Dark Carnival, and for the first time in my life, I had tru friends. I quit livin' for Momma and ate what I wanted to eat, slept when I felt like it in the damn day.
Wooo! Gimme another hit o' them bath salts, Tazer!
Daaamn Terri, you cray to the Z!
I got inta backyard wrasslin', and I dusted 'em all.
The Devastatah!
She's the Ninja of NASTY!
But when you rock hard like me, you attract attention. And the region queen came to see who the hell I was.
Is this the li'l skeez y'all makin' such a big deal about? She better pay respect.
Oh shiz!
It's THE ZOMBITCH!
The Zombitch. Named dat 'cause she was legally dead from alcohol poisonin' and came back in the ambulance, then jack slapped the paramedics. She won't nothin' to fug wit.
I coulda bowed down before her... but damn that. It was ON. We fought for two straight hours, Thai MMA rules!
All my years on the pageant circuit prepared me good. I took all the abuse she had and just kept struttin my stuff. And in tha end...
Say it, don't pray it!
You tha best... I'm the rest.
I rescind th' title. You...the new queen of obscene.
That's my story. Suck up that lesson, fools.
Don't drive ya kids to live the life you wanted for yaself.
Or do, 'cause I turned out fuggin' AWWWE-SOMMMME!

Hey folks, Erika here!

Personally, I love behind-the-scenes sections in comics and movies, so here is my little peek into how I put together a page of *Bucko*!

With this new strip, I was eager to push myself stylistically as far away from my previous one as I could, so I really tried to play with new (to me) page layouts and balloon positioning, and with breaking free from panel borders.

Parker wanted me to be as surprised as the story unfolded as our audience would be, so he only sent one page of script at a time, to keep me in the dark about what would be coming up. I mean, there were some overall elements I knew to expect, but aside from Bucko and Gyp, I had no idea which characters would stay in the background or become key players, or what specifically was going to happen to them all next.

When I finished drawing each page I'd e-mail Parker to let him know I was ready for the script of the next one. To illustrate, here's the e-mail chain that started after I told him I was ready for page 62's script (page 77 in this book).

8/15/11

From: Jeff Parker
To: Erika Moen
RE: page 62!

It's pure fight, so I'd rather just draw it all out. I was thinking for effect we could stack two so that day it reads like once Sindee cut loose it just blew all up! Not a lot of speaking beyond "YOU... HIT... MY..."

And then I can't think of any word good enough that she would call her breasts. Help! Maybe we keep slipping in a shot of them after she says MY a few times, like she can't even reach the thought that her breasts could be harmed.

JP

From: Erika Moen
To: Jeff Parker
RE: page 62!

I've always been fond of calling breasts "boys" or "girls", as in, "the girls/the boys" or "my girls/my boys"

Are you coming into the studio today? Do you want me to just start drawing what pops into my head, or did you wanna do a thumbnail for me?

From: Jeff Parker
To: Erika Moen
RE: page 62!

I'll be by in a little while and we'll GET IT DONE yo

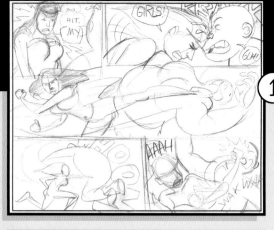

YOU,
HIT.
MY.
GIRLS!
GLAH!
AAAH
WAK WAK

1

Normally I'd go ahead and thumbnail out a script myself, but since Parker had a specific idea of how he wanted this page laid out, he provided me with his own thumbnail. That was fiiiiiine with me, because it makes my job go a lot faster when I can just draw on top of Parker's sweet lines.

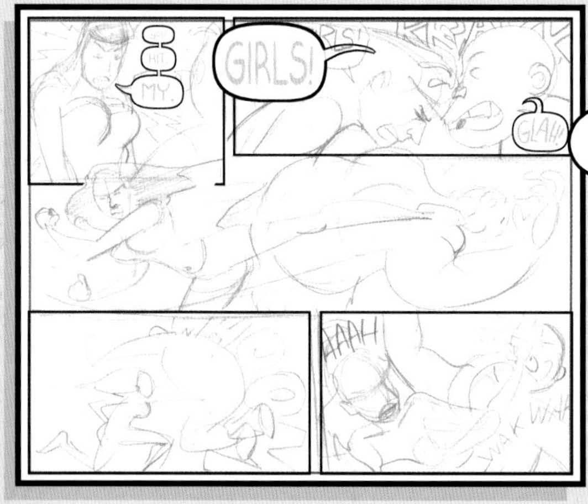

HIT
MY
GIRLS!
GLAH
AAAH
WAK

2

After scanning in his layout, I opened it up in my totally legitimately acquired copy of Photoshop and dropped in panel borders and word balloons using my Cintiq. I like to start with borders and word balloons so I can draw with them in mind, so everything always fits together, you know? The font is based on my handwriting.

HIT
MY
GIRLS!
GLAH
AAAHH!!
WAK WAK!

3

Penciling (digitally—I guess I should put "penciling" in quote marks, since there are no actual pencils involved when I'm drawing with my Cintiq) this page was super easy, because I was just going over Parker's lines. Normally my "penciling" stage would be a lot messier.

After my (usually much rougher) "pencils," I create a new layer where I retrace my best lines, to leave a crisp, clear drawing. You'll notice that my borders and word balloons are in black and my lettering and line work is in blue. That is because I print out my digital pages onto Bristol board to physically ink them with a brush. Printing out the borders and balloons in black means I don't have to ink them by hand, which is great because I am crap at making straight, even lines.

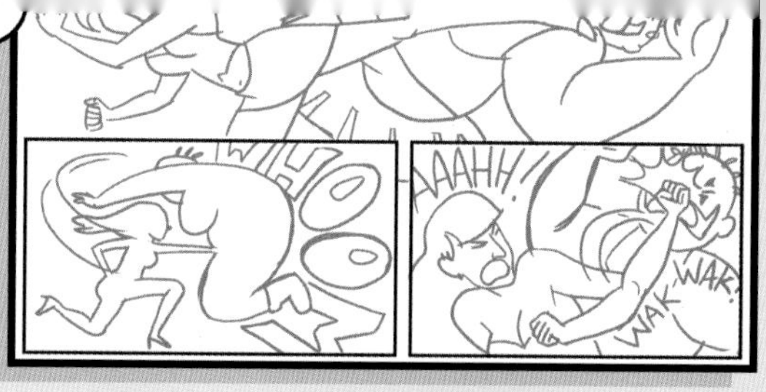

AAAHH!
WAK-WAK!

5

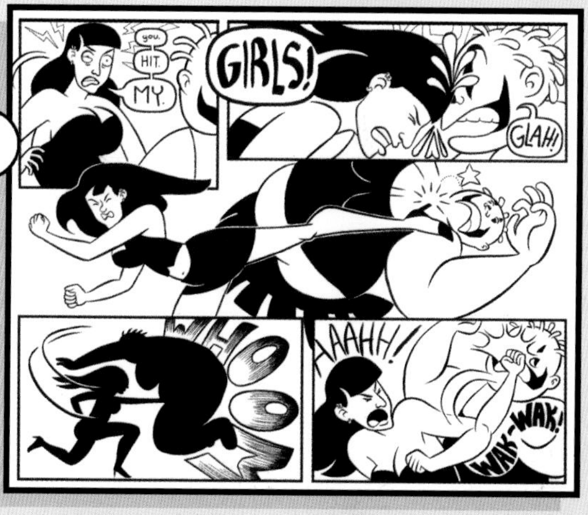

you.
HIT.
MY.
GIRLS!
GLAH!
AAAHH!
WAK-WAK!

Woo! This is my favorite part of making comics, *inking*! I use a Winsor & Newton Series 7 #2 brush and black India ink of the same brand.

6

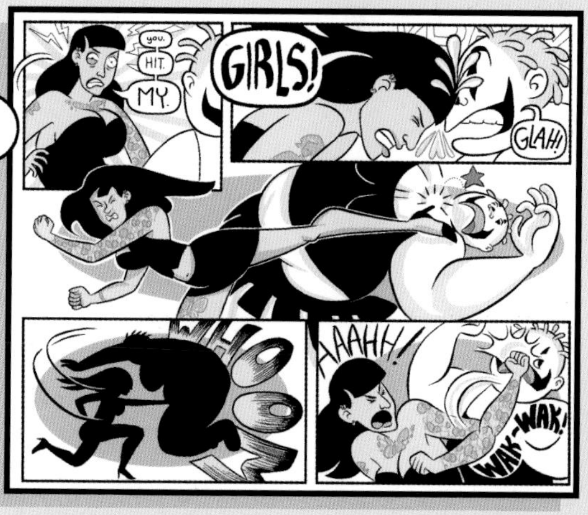

you.
HIT.
MY.
GIRLS!
GLAH!
AAAHH!
WAK-WAK!

Once the ink is dry, I scan the artwork back in and then add the blue tones in Photoshop.

BAM! There you have it!

Bucko

Bucko's design is secretly based on the way one of our studiomates looked when he was still interning for us. He has no idea.

Gyp

Parker said Gyp should look like a hybrid of our studiomate Dylan Meconis and me, but I also pretty heavily based this design on the *Batman: The Animated Series* role-playing character I made up and drew obsessively when I was fourteen to sixteen years old. She was the daughter of Harley Quinn and the Joker, and her name was Marionette. I didn't have many real-life friends then.

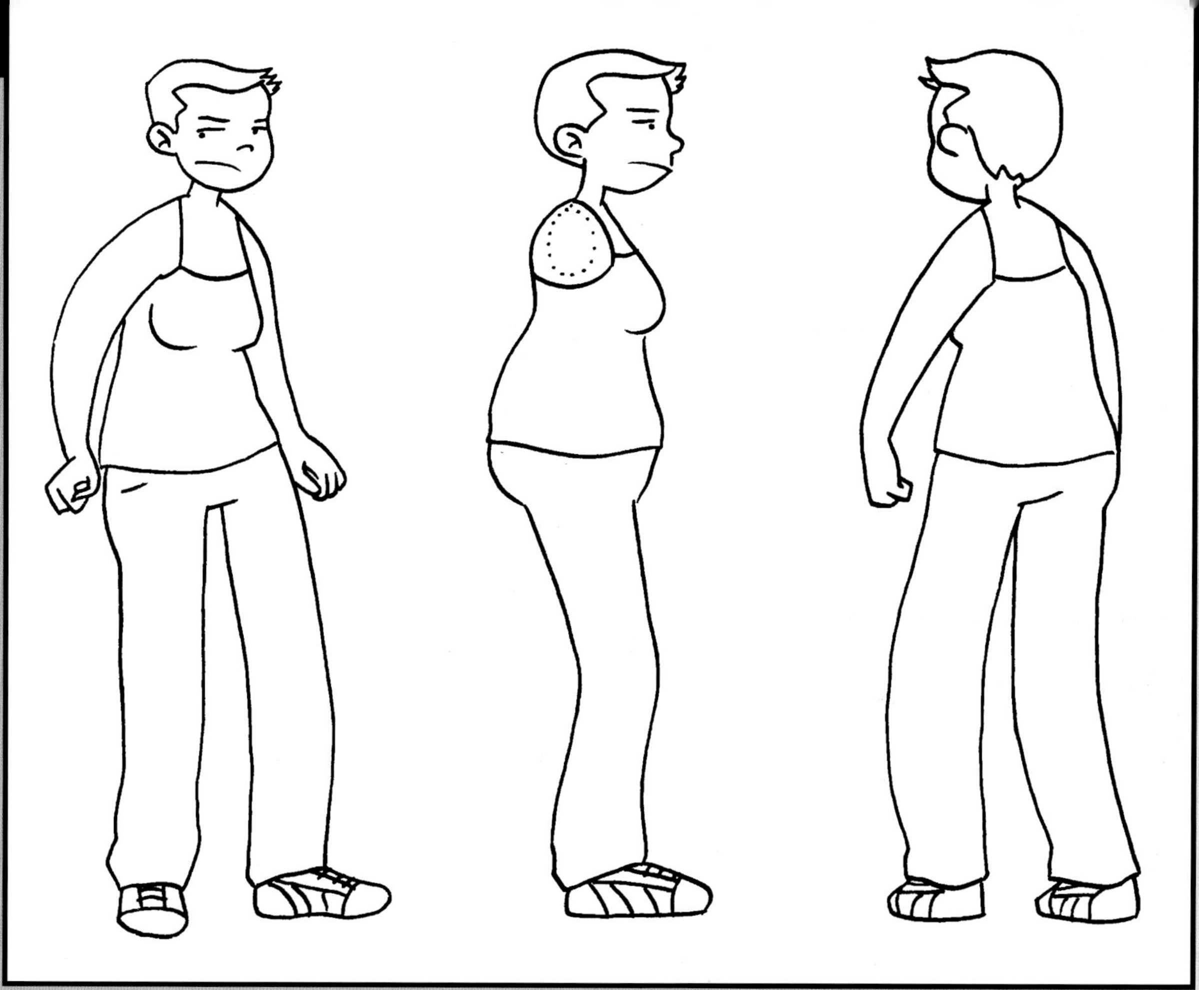

Dell

Dell actually kind of wound up being the closest to a self-portrait. I kept expecting someone to mention I was basically drawing my avatar from *DAR*, but no one ever did.

photo reference

In the process of drawing, I often refer to photo reference for poses and backgrounds that I have trouble envisioning in my own mind. Here are a few samples! All guest models are my studiomates here at Periscope Studio.

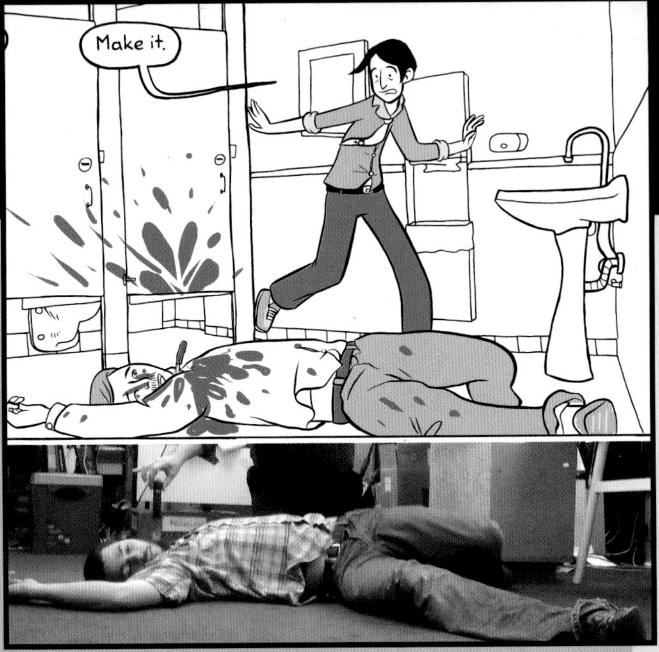

Make it.

Panel from page 15. That is Benjamin Dewey, being my murdered body. Wotta guy.

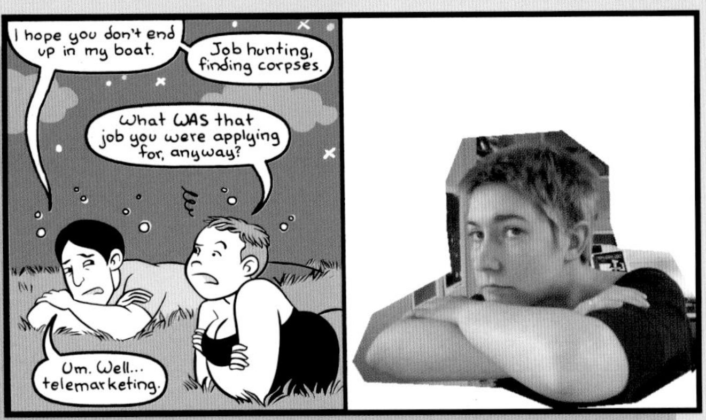

I hope you don't end up in my boat.
Job hunting, finding corpses.
What WAS that job you were applying for, anyway?
Um. Well... telemarketing.

Panel from page 49. Haha, I forgot I was blond for a while.

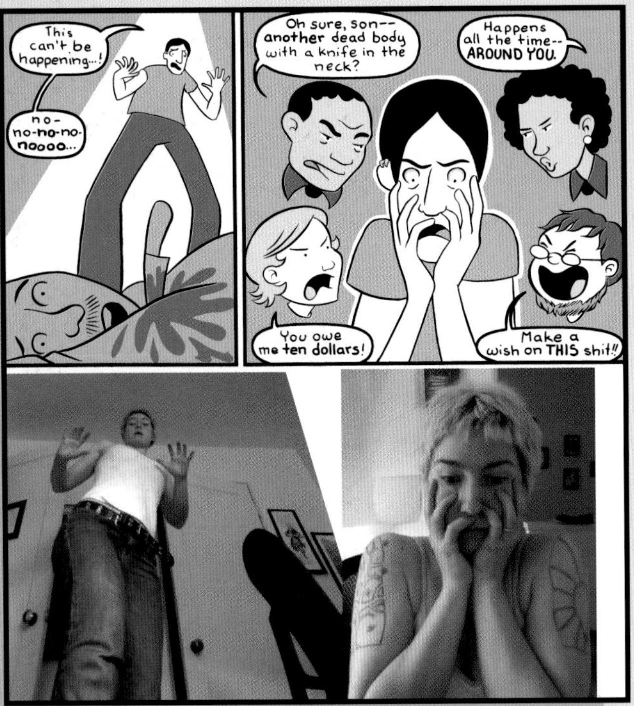

This can't be happening...!
no-no-no-no-no-noooo...
Oh sure, son-- another dead body with a knife in the neck?
Happens all the time-- AROUND YOU.
You owe me ten dollars!
Make a wish on THIS shit!!

Panels from page 54. Mostly I use myself as a model with the little webcam built into my laptop.

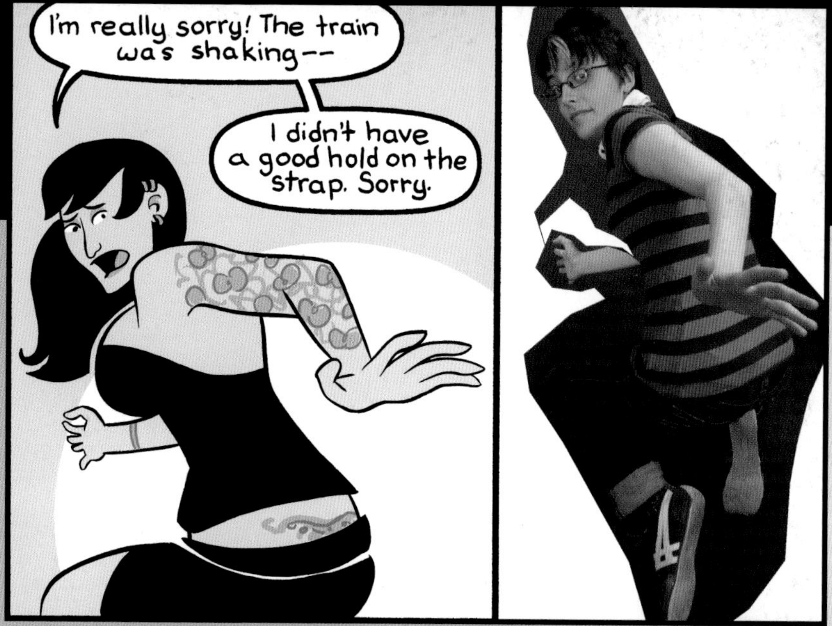

I'm really sorry! The train was shaking--
I didn't have a good hold on the strap. Sorry.

Panel from page 73. Dylan Meconis filling in for Sindee.

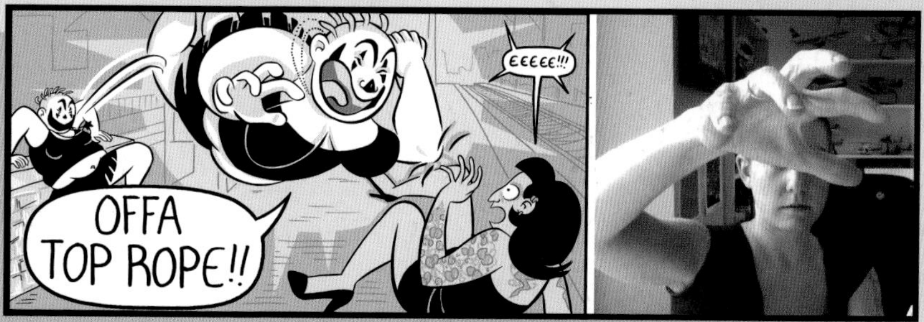

EEEEE!!!
OFFA TOP ROPE!!

Panel from page 75. My hand!

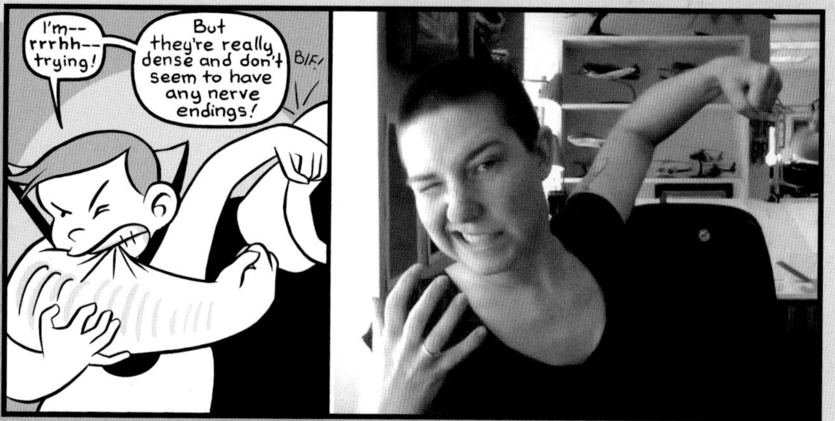

I'm-- rrrhh-- trying!
But they're really dense and don't seem to have any nerve endings!
BIF!

Also from page 75. Me, acting out some righteous arm biting and punching. Also, I shaved my head.

Oh please, not in the face--
--really there's nowhere good to hit on me!
Help! Someone!

Panel from page 79. Me acting out wimpy Chad. "Oh please, not in the face!"

Queenmum Sweetypie.
Mista Bishop.
This guy seems familiar too...
You're just déjà vuin' all over tonight.

Panel from page 97. Steve Lieber kissing the air where Queenmum's hand will be.

Bucko!
RECUMBENT RIDERZ
I'm not hearing things?
Is it you?

Panel from page 106. Me again. With pink hair.

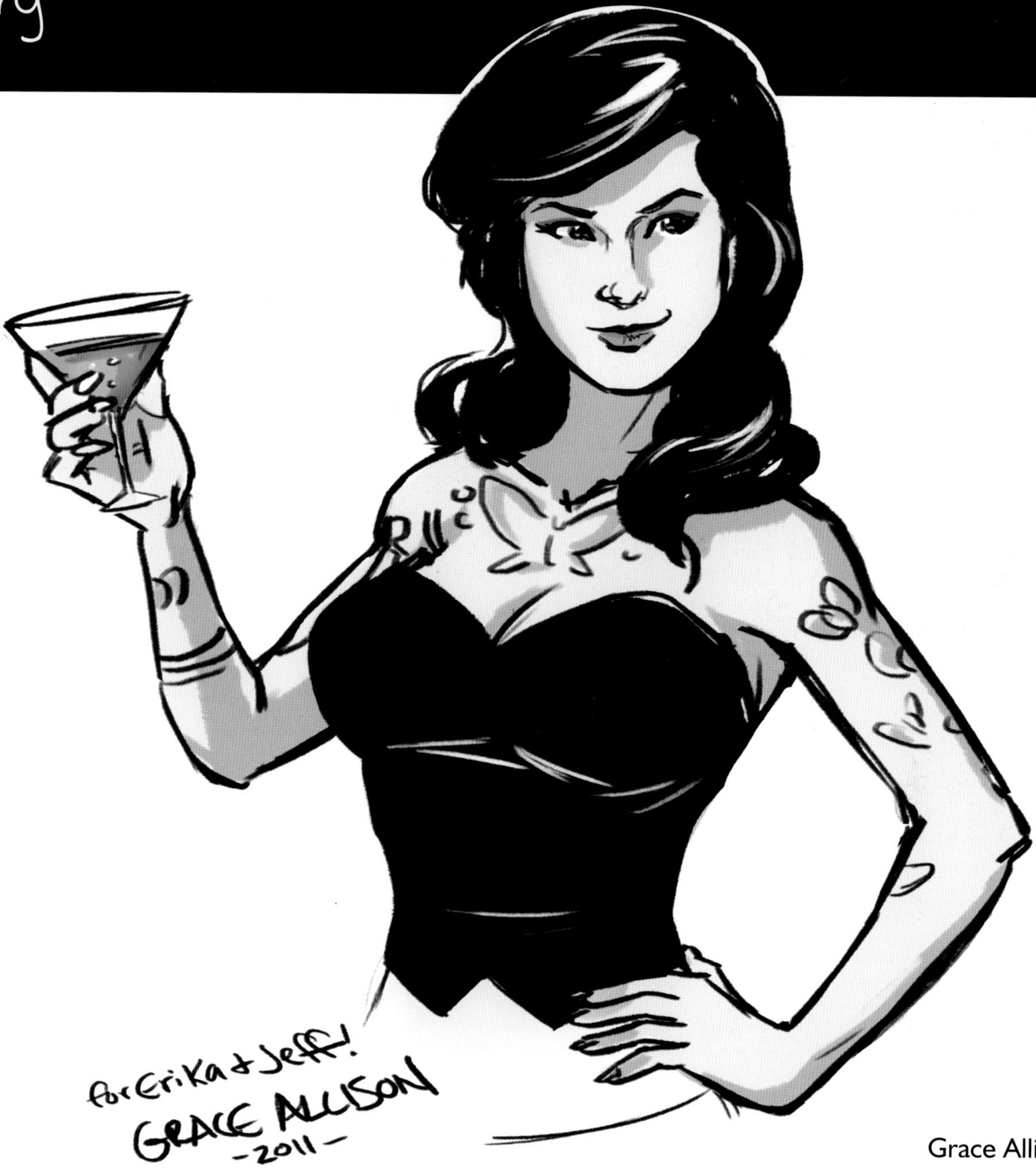
for Erika & Jeff!
GRACE ALLISON
-2011-

Grace Allison

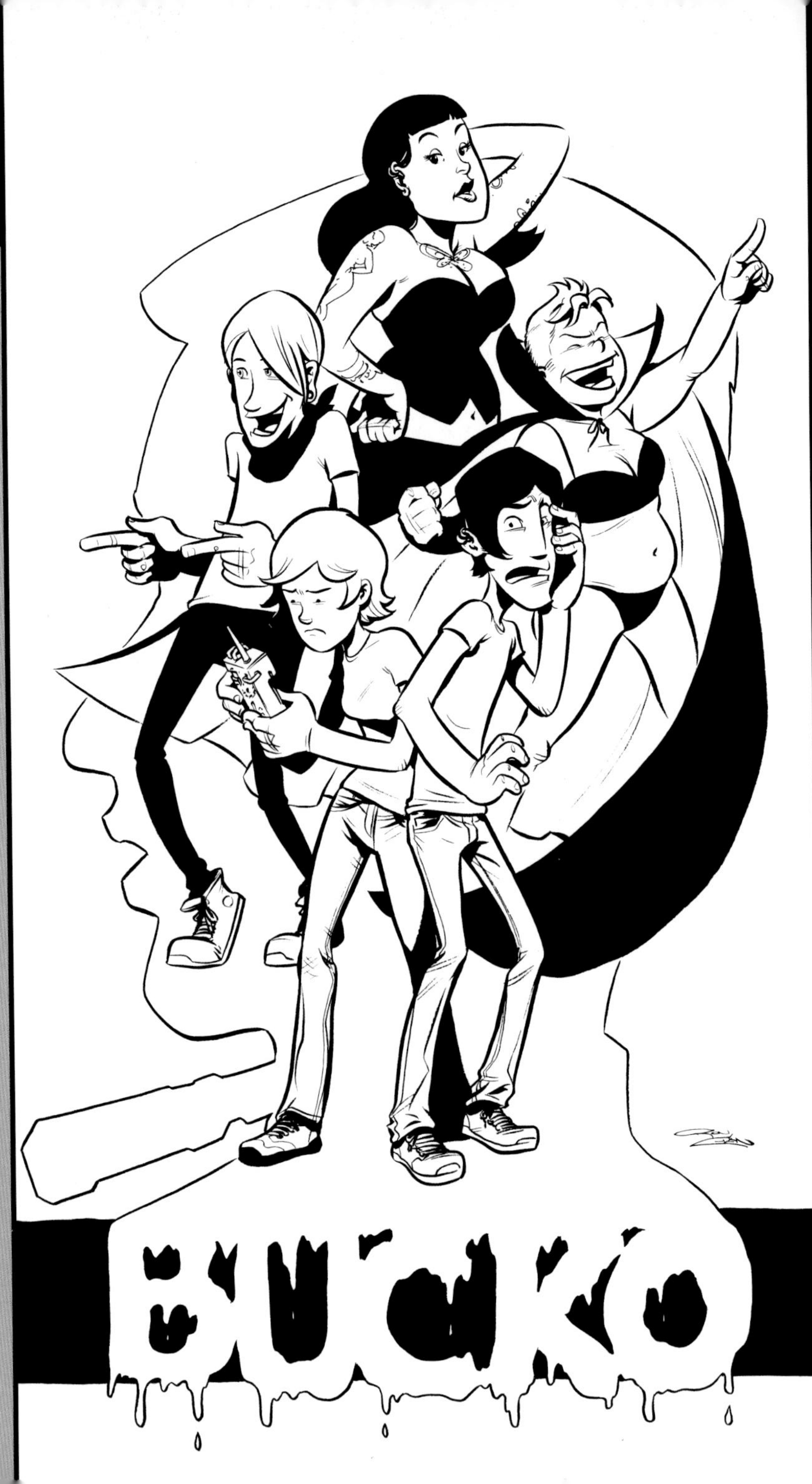
BUCKO

Ron Chan

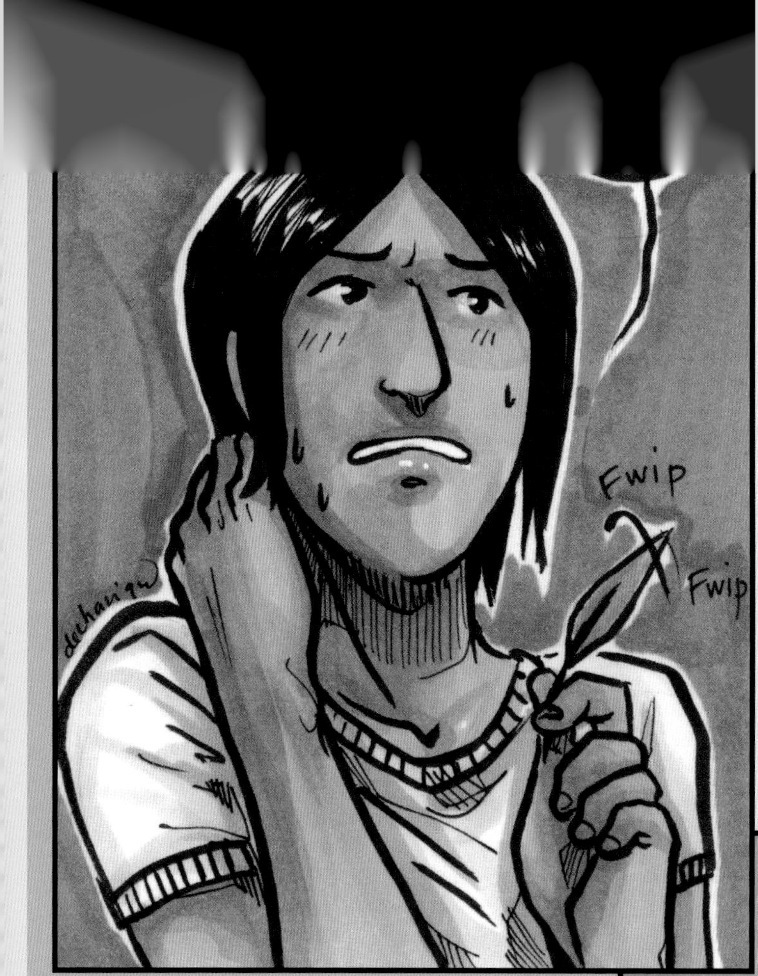
Fwip
Fwip

Deanna Echanique

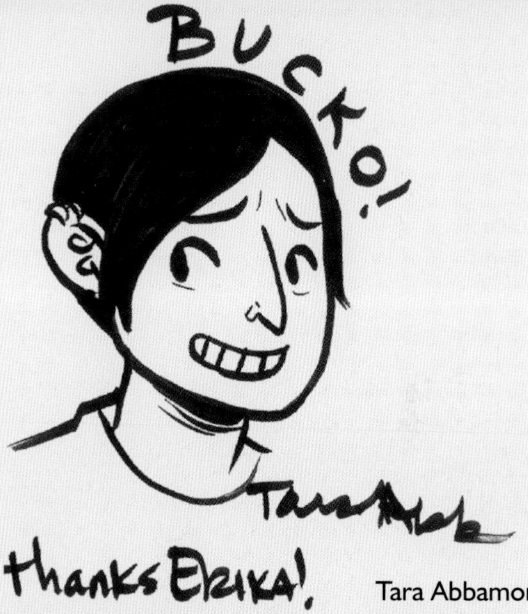
BUCKO!
thanks ERIKA!

Tara Abbamondi

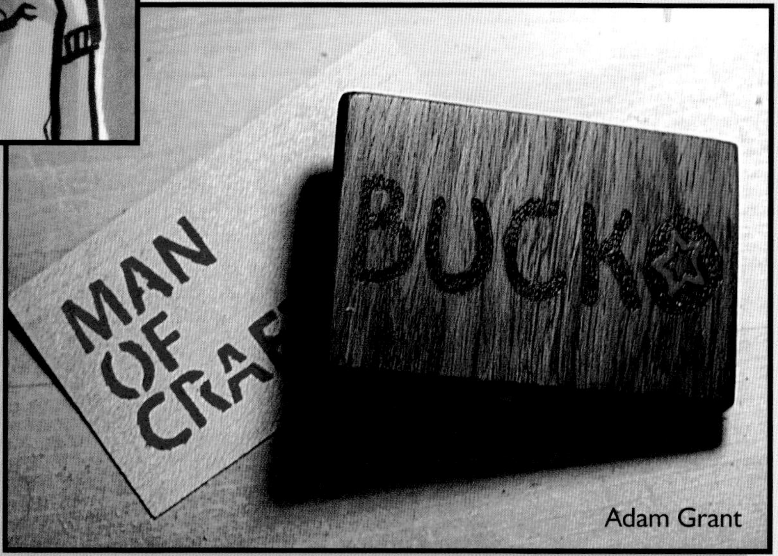
MAN
OF
BUCKO

Adam Grant

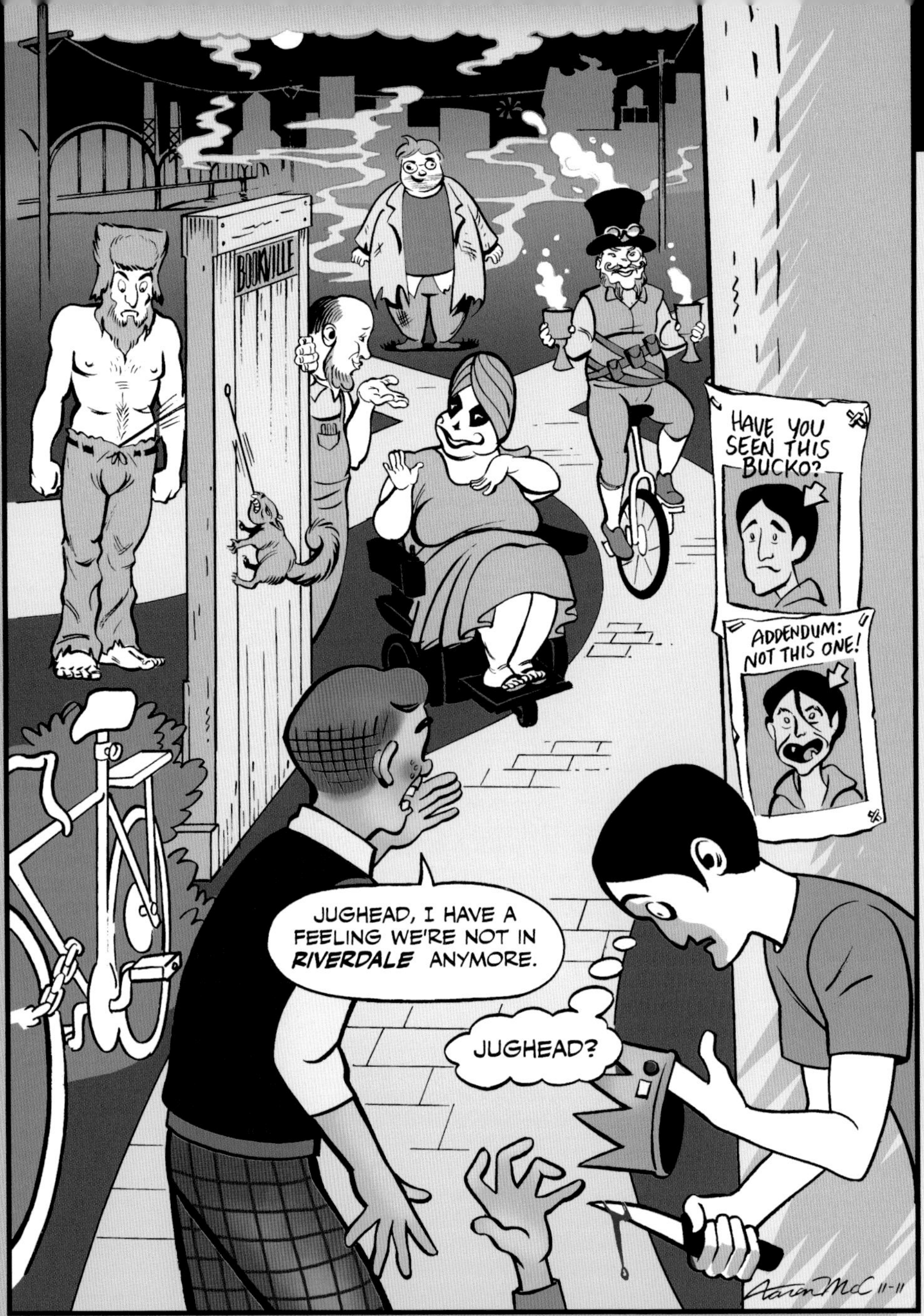
BOOKVILLE
HAVE YOU SEEN THIS BUCKO?
ADDENDUM: NOT THIS ONE!
JUGHEAD, I HAVE A FEELING WE'RE NOT IN *RIVERDALE* ANYMORE.
JUGHEAD?
AaronMcC 11-11

Aaron McConnell

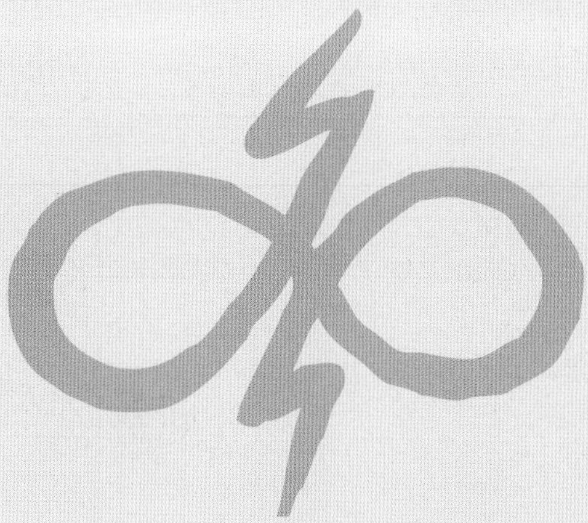

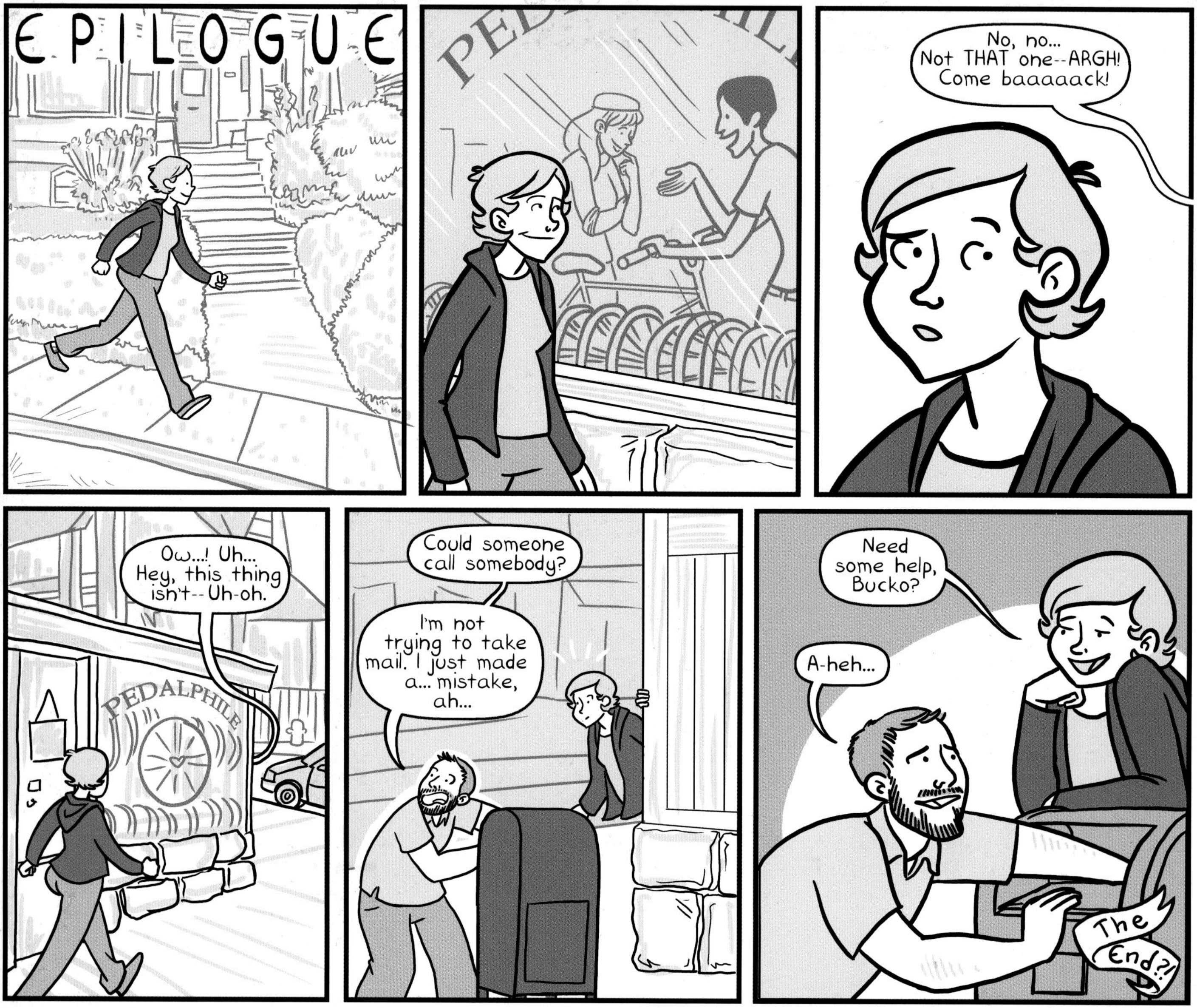

EPILOGUE
PEDALPHILE
No, no... Not THAT one--ARGH! Come baaaaack!
Ow...! Uh... Hey, this thing isn't--Uh-oh.
PEDALPHILE
Could someone call somebody?
I'm not trying to take mail. I just made a... mistake, ah...
Need some help, Bucko?
A-heh...
The End?!

special thanks

ERIKA

Thank you so much to all my studiomates at Periscope Studio, and most especially to Steve Lieber, for guiding me and generously sharing their knowledge with me. Not so much thanks as apologies to Bill Mudron. For everything.

JEFF

Big shout-out to my 'Scopes: Gingerballz, CoCo, Tubesock, Starbuxx, Haitian J, Boilah8t, TanquerDave, Ron Fondle, Karlz Jr., OddSon, Ian, Weng-Weng, FloorChan, Catshot, Sagan, Neuro-Gat, Hammbo, Hung-Bar-Low, Cropdustin', Sonic B, and Spoozin'. And to all y'all interns with the names,

about the authors

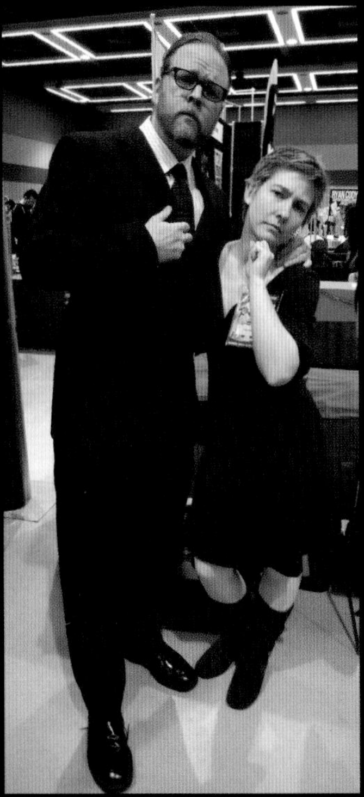

JEFF PARKER began professionally illustrating comics while in college with issues of *Wonder Woman* at DC and *Solitaire* at Malibu, and was a founding member of North Carolina's Artamus Studios. After working as a storyboard artist in animation and live action, Jeff began writing all-ages titles for the Marvel Adventures line, gaining fans amongst young readers and their parents alike. His more recent credits include *Agents of Atlas*, *X-Men: First Class*, *Hulk*, and *Thunderbolts* at Marvel and the creator-owned *The Interman*, *Mysterius the Unfathomable* (with Tom Fowler), and *Underground* (with Steve Lieber). Jeff lives in Portland, Oregon, where he is one of the rare Periscope Studio members who is primarily a writer.

ERIKA MOEN graduated from Pitzer College with a self-designed degree in Illustrated Storytelling and has been creating comics for print and the web for over a decade. Before *Bucko*, Erika was best known for her autobiographical web comic *DAR! A Super Girly Top Secret Comic Diary*, which ran from 2003 through 2009 and is collected into two print volumes. She has also contributed to *Flight*, *True Porn*, and *Best Erotic Comics*. A member of Periscope Studio, Erika lives in Portland, Oregon, with her husband Matthew Nolan.

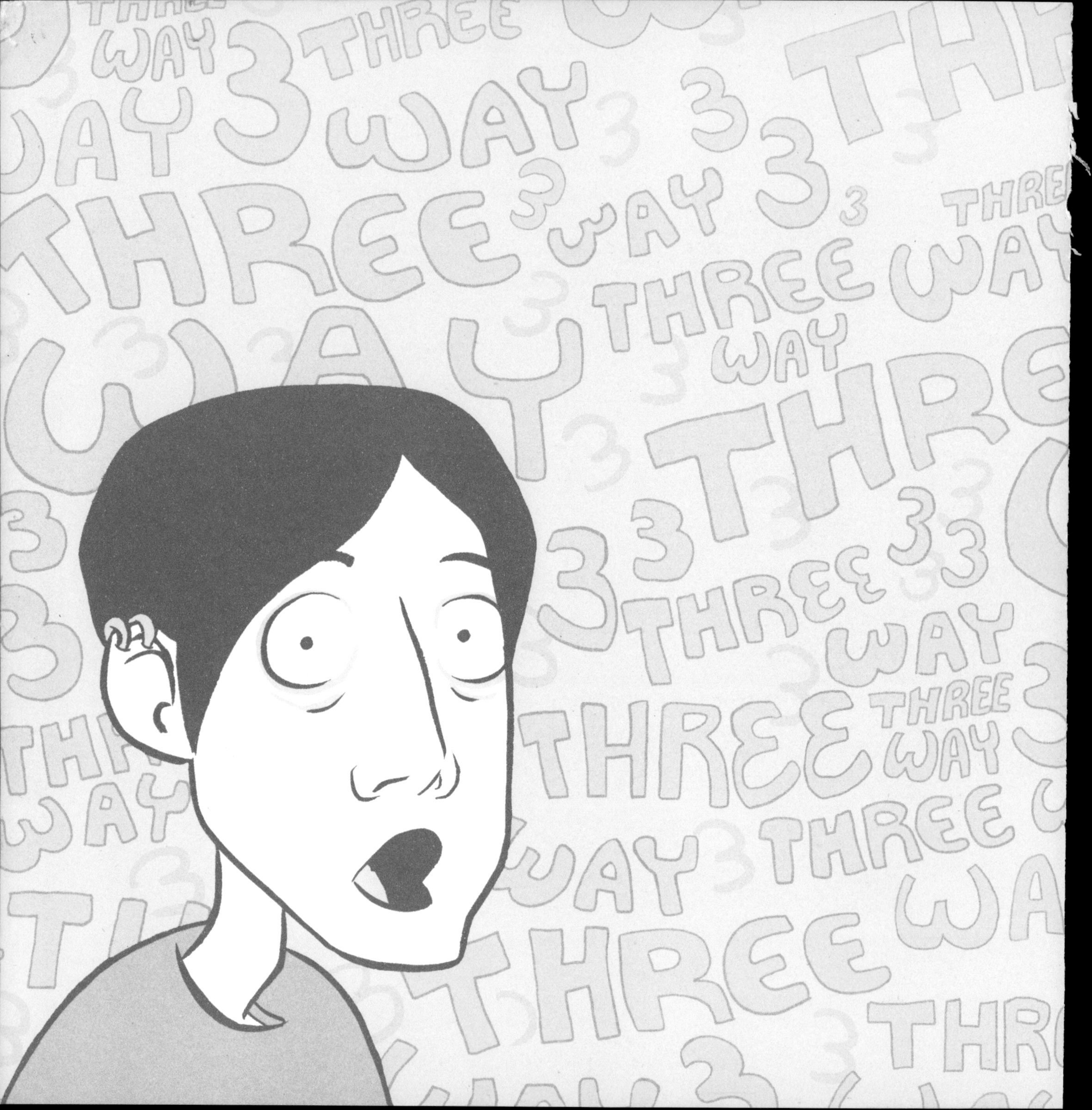
THREE
WAY
3
THREE
WAY